Table of contents

Programming for Analytics

Student Edition

By Kimberly Seefeld, EdD

Published under **DataJoyAI** imprint

Companion resources for this book are available at:

DataJoyAI

https://datajoyai.com

Edition: First Edition
ISBN: 978-1-969233-41-8

Chapter 1

Why Code

1.1 Learning Outcomes

1-1. Explain why programming is valuable for data analysis beyond spreadsheet-based workflows.
1-2. Distinguish programming for data analysis from computer science and software development.
1-3. Describe how programming supports reproducibility, automation, and transparency in data work.
1-4. Recognize how AI tools are changing what it means for analysts to "know how to code."

1.2 Introduction

If you've picked up this book, chances are you're feeling a mix of curiosity and anxiety about programming. Maybe you've heard that "everyone needs to learn to code" but you're not entirely sure why. Perhaps you've been getting by just fine with Excel and are wondering what all the fuss is about. Or maybe you've tried programming before and found it frustrating, intimidating, or just plain confusing.

Let me start with some good news: you don't need to become a computer scientist to use programming effectively in data analysis. You don't need to memorize syntax, build complex algorithms, or understand the inner workings of computers. What you do need is to understand why programming has become such a powerful tool for working with data—and how recent advances in artificial intelligence have fundamentally changed what it means to "know how to code."

This chapter is about removing the fear and mystery around programming by explaining exactly why it matters for data work. We'll explore what changes when you move from spreadsheets to scripts, why reproducibility and automation matter, and how AI tools are revolutionizing the way analysts approach programming. By the end, you'll understand that programming isn't about becoming a technical wizard—it's about thinking more clearly and working more effectively with data.

1.3 From Spreadsheets to Scripts

Most of us start our data analysis journey with spreadsheets. Excel, Google Sheets, or similar tools feel natural and intuitive. You can see your data, click on cells, drag formulas, and create charts with a few mouse clicks. So why would anyone want to give up this visual, immediate approach for typing cryptic commands into a blank screen?

The answer becomes clear when you start working with real data analysis challenges. Let's consider a typical scenario that many students and analysts face.

Imagine you're analyzing survey data from 500 students about their study habits. In Excel, you might:

1. Open the data file
2. Create a new column for calculated values
3. Use formulas to clean up inconsistent entries
4. Create pivot tables to summarize results
5. Generate charts to visualize patterns
6. Copy and paste results into a report

This works fine for a one-time analysis. But what happens when:

- Your advisor asks you to update the analysis with 200 more survey responses?
- You discover an error in your data cleaning and need to redo everything?
- You want to apply the same analysis to survey data from a different semester?
- Someone else needs to verify your results or build on your work?

With the spreadsheet approach, you're back to square one. You'll need to manually repeat every step, hoping you remember exactly what you did and in what order. This is where the fundamental difference between spreadsheets and scripts becomes apparent.

A script is simply a written record of the steps you want the computer to perform. Instead of clicking and dragging, you write instructions like "read this data file," "calculate the average for each group," and "create a bar chart showing the results." The magic isn't in the complexity of these instructions—it's in the fact that they're written down and can be run repeatedly.

Think of it this way: a spreadsheet analysis is like giving someone verbal directions to your house each time they visit. A script is like writing down those directions once so anyone can follow them perfectly, every time. The directions themselves aren't complicated—the value is in having them recorded and repeatable.

This shift from manual steps to written instructions is the core difference between spreadsheet work and programming. You're not learning to think like a computer; you're learning to document your thinking in a way that computers can follow.

1.4 Reproducibility

The word "reproducibility" might sound academic, but it addresses a very practical problem that every data analyst faces: being able to recreate your own work. How many times have you looked at a spreadsheet you created weeks ago and struggled to remember exactly what you did? How often have you needed to explain your analysis to someone else and found yourself saying, "Well, I think what I did was…"?

Reproducibility in data analysis means that you (or someone else) can take your raw data and your analysis instructions and arrive at exactly the same results. This isn't just about being thorough—it's about being able to trust your work and build on it over time.

Let's consider what reproducibility looks like in practice. Suppose you're analyzing data about plant growth under different light conditions for a biology class. In a spreadsheet, your analysis might involve:

- Manually removing outliers that "look wrong"
- Creating calculated columns with formulas
- Generating summary statistics
- Making charts with specific formatting

Six months later, when you want to include this analysis in a larger project, you face a problem. Which data points did you remove and why? What exactly were those formulas? How did you create those charts? Even if you kept the original spreadsheet, the steps you took to create it are invisible.

With a script-based approach, every step is documented. Your code shows exactly which data points were removed and why. The formulas are written out explicitly. The chart creation process is recorded step by step. Most importantly, you can run the entire analysis again with a single command, producing identical results.

This documentation isn't just helpful for your future self—it's essential for collaboration and verification. When you share your analysis with others, they can see not just your results but exactly how you arrived at them. They can check your work, suggest improvements, or apply your methods to their own data.

The reproducibility that programming provides isn't about following rigid academic standards—it's about creating work that you can trust, build upon, and share with confidence.

1.5 Automation: Saving Time on Repetitive Tasks

One of the most immediate benefits of programming becomes apparent when you find yourself doing the same analysis repeatedly. Maybe you need to process monthly sales reports, analyze weekly survey data, or generate regular updates for a research project. The first time you do this analysis, programming might actually take longer than using a spreadsheet. But the second time, third time, and every time after that, the time savings become dramatic.

Automation in data analysis isn't about replacing human judgment—it's about eliminating the tedious, error-prone parts of analysis so you can focus on interpretation and insight. Consider the difference between these two approaches to a recurring analysis task:

Manual approach (each month): 1. Download new data file 2. Open Excel and import the data 3. Clean up formatting issues 4. Apply the same calculations as last month 5. Update charts and tables 6. Copy results into a report template 7. Double-check everything for errors

Automated approach (after initial setup): 1. Run the analysis script 2. Review the generated report

The automated approach doesn't eliminate your role as an analyst—it eliminates the repetitive mechanics so you can spend your time on the parts that actually require human insight: interpreting results, identifying patterns, and making decisions based on the analysis.

This automation becomes even more powerful when you're working with larger datasets or more complex analyses. Tasks that would take hours of manual work can be completed in minutes. More importantly, automated analyses are consistent—they apply exactly the same logic every time, reducing the risk of human error that comes with repetitive manual work.

The key insight here is that automation isn't about being lazy—it's about being strategic with your time and mental energy. By automating the routine parts of analysis, you free yourself to focus on the creative and interpretive aspects that actually add value.

1.6 Transparency

In our current era of data-driven decision making, the ability to show your work has become increasingly important. Whether you're a student submitting an assignment, a researcher publishing findings, or an analyst making business recommendations, people want to understand not just what your results are, but how you arrived at them.

Transparency in data analysis serves multiple purposes. First, it builds trust. When others can see exactly what steps you took, they can evaluate the appropriateness of your methods and the validity of your conclusions. Second, it enables learning and improvement. When your analysis process is visible, others can suggest better approaches or catch potential errors. Third, it facilitates collaboration and knowledge sharing within teams and organizations.

Programming naturally creates this transparency because your analysis process is written down as code. Every decision you made, every calculation you performed, and every assumption you built into your analysis is explicitly documented. This is fundamentally different from spreadsheet-based analysis, where much of your process remains hidden in the sequence of clicks and manual operations you performed.

Consider the difference in transparency between these two approaches to analyzing student performance data:

Feature	Spreadsheet Approach	Programming Approach
Visibility of results	Final results are visible in the spreadsheet.	Final results are produced by running the analysis code.
Documentation of calculations	Formulas can be examined cell by cell.	All calculations are explicitly written in code.
Data cleaning steps	Manual data cleaning steps are not visible or recorded.	Data cleaning decisions are explicitly documented in code.
Chart creation	The chart creation process is not documented.	Chart creation steps are reproducible and recorded.
Assumptions and reasoning	Assumptions and decisions are not formally recorded.	Comments in the code explain reasoning and assumptions.

This transparency isn't just about meeting academic or professional standards about creating work that can be understood, verified, and improved upon. When your analysis process is transparent, you're not just sharing results; you're sharing knowledge and methodology that others can learn from and build upon.

1.7 Programming vs. Computer Science

One of the biggest misconceptions that keeps people away from programming is the belief that you need to understand computer science to write useful code. This confusion is understandable—after all, programming is a fundamental tool in computer science—but it's like thinking you need to understand automotive engineering to drive a car.

Computer science is about understanding how computers work, designing efficient algorithms, and building complex software systems. Programming for data analysis is about using existing tools to solve practical problems with data. The difference is enormous, and understanding this distinction can remove a major barrier to getting started.

Programming Focus: Computer Scientists vs. Data Analysts

Focus Area	Computer Scientists	Data Analysts
Primary concerns	Efficient use of computer memory and processing resources	Extracting insight from data
Algorithm considerations	Mathematical complexity and performance optimization	Applying existing methods and libraries
System scope	Building systems that scale to millions of users	Working with datasets of practical analytical size
Tool creation	Creating new programming languages, frameworks, or tools	Using established tools to analyze data
Typical outputs	Software systems and infrastructure	Calculations, visualizations, and analytical reports

The programming skills needed for data analysis are much more accessible than those required for computer science. You don't need to understand how computers store data in memory—you just need to know how to load your data into a program. You don't need to design efficient algorithms—you can use the ones that others have already created and tested.

Think of it this way: using programming for data analysis is like using a calculator for math. You don't need to understand how the calculator's circuits work to use it effectively for solving problems. Similarly, you don't need to understand how programming languages are implemented to use them effectively for data analysis.

This distinction becomes even clearer when you consider the types of problems that data analysts solve with programming. Most data analysis tasks involve combining existing tools in straightforward ways: read some data, clean it up, perform some calculations, and present the results. The complexity comes from understanding your data and choosing appropriate analytical methods, not from the programming itself.

1.8 How AI Changes What It Means to "Know How to Code"

Perhaps the most exciting development in programming for data analysis is the emergence of artificial intelligence tools that can help write, explain, and debug code. These tools are fundamentally changing what it means to "know how to code" and making programming more accessible than ever before.

Traditional programming education focused heavily on syntax memorization and manual coding skills. Students spent considerable time learning the specific commands and formatting rules of programming languages. While this knowledge was necessary when programmers had to write everything from scratch, AI tools are changing this equation dramatically.

Modern AI assistants can:

- Generate code based on plain English descriptions
- Explain existing code in understandable terms
- Suggest improvements and alternative approaches
- Help debug errors and problems
- Translate code between different programming languages

This doesn't mean that programming knowledge becomes irrelevant—quite the opposite. But it shifts the focus from memorizing syntax to understanding concepts, evaluating solutions, and asking good questions.

Consider how this changes the learning process. Instead of spending weeks memorizing the exact syntax for reading a data file, you can describe what you want to do in plain English and have an AI tool generate the appropriate code. Then, instead of just copying that code, you can ask the AI to explain how it works, why it chose that particular approach, and what alternatives might exist.

This AI-assisted approach to programming offers several advantages for data analysts. It allows for faster learning, enabling you to start solving real problems immediately rather than spending months memorizing syntax fundamentals. It also promotes better understanding, as AI tools can explain code in plain English, helping you grasp not just what the code does, but why it works that way. Additionally, it reduces frustration by assisting with diagnosing and resolving errors, minimizing the time spent stuck on technical issues. Finally, by handling much of the routine coding, AI tools free you to focus more on analyzing your data and developing insights.

However, this AI-assisted approach also requires analysts to develop new skills. You need to be able to clearly describe your analytical goals, evaluate whether AI-generated code is appropriate for the problem at hand, understand the code well enough to modify it for your specific needs, and recognize when AI suggestions might be incorrect or suboptimal. These skills ensure that you remain in control of the analysis and can use AI as an effective tool rather than a black-box solution.

AI doesn't eliminate the need to understand programming, but it changes what aspects of programming are most important to understand. Instead of focusing on memorizing syntax, you can focus on understanding concepts, evaluating approaches, and solving analytical problems.

1.9 Programming as a Tool for Thinking with Data

Throughout this chapter, we've explored various reasons why programming has become important for data analysis: reproducibility, automation, transparency, and the new possibilities created by AI assistance. But there's a deeper reason that ties all of these together: programming changes how you think about data and analysis.

When you work with data in a spreadsheet, you're primarily thinking about individual operations: "I need to calculate this average," "I should create this chart," "I want to filter these rows." Programming encourages you to think more systematically about the entire analytical process: "What are all the steps needed to go from raw data to final results?" "How can I organize this analysis so it's clear and logical?" "What assumptions am I making, and how can I document them?"

This shift in thinking has practical benefits beyond just the technical advantages we've discussed. Programming encourages you to:

Break complex problems into smaller steps: Instead of trying to do everything at once, you learn to decompose analytical tasks into manageable pieces.

Think about data structure and organization: You become more aware of how your data is organized and what that means for your analysis options.

Consider alternative approaches: Because code can be easily modified and re-run, you're more likely to experiment with different analytical methods.

Document your reasoning: The process of writing code naturally encourages you to think explicitly about your analytical choices and assumptions.

Plan for reuse and extension: Knowing that you might need to repeat or modify your analysis encourages you to organize your work more thoughtfully.

These thinking skills are valuable regardless of whether you continue using programming tools throughout your career. The systematic, documented approach to problem-solving that programming encourages will make you a better analyst even if you eventually return to other tools.

1.10 Conclusion

As we conclude this first chapter, it's worth reflecting on what we've covered and what lies ahead. We've seen that programming for data analysis isn't about becoming a computer scientist or memorizing complex syntax. Instead, it's about adopting a more systematic, reproducible, and transparent approach to working with data.

The benefits we've discussed—reproducibility, automation, transparency, and AI assistance—aren't abstract ideals. They're practical advantages that will make your work more efficient, more reliable, and more valuable to others. Whether you're a student working on research projects, an analyst in a business setting, or someone who just wants to understand data better, these benefits will serve you well.

The emergence of AI tools makes this an particularly exciting time to learn programming for data analysis. You can start solving real problems immediately, without getting bogged down in syntax details. You can learn by doing, with AI assistants helping to explain concepts and debug problems along the way.

But perhaps most importantly, learning to program will change how you think about data and analysis. You'll develop a more systematic approach to problem-solving, a greater awareness of your analytical choices, and the ability to create work that others can understand, verify, and build upon.

In the chapters that follow, we'll explore the practical aspects of this journey. We'll look at the tools analysts use, how code is structured, and how to work effectively with data. We'll cover both R and Python, showing how the concepts you learn transfer between languages. And throughout, we'll emphasize the AI-assisted approach that makes modern programming more accessible and powerful than ever before.

The goal isn't to turn you into a programmer—it's to give you the tools and mindset needed to work more effectively with data in an increasingly data-driven world. Programming is simply a means to that end: a powerful tool for thinking with data, not an end in itself.

As you begin this journey, remember that every expert was once a beginner. The intimidating code you might see in advanced examples started with simple concepts and basic operations. With patience, practice, and the help of modern AI tools, you'll find that programming for data analysis is not only achievable but genuinely enjoyable.

The data analysis landscape is changing rapidly, and those who can combine analytical thinking with programming skills will be well-positioned to take advantage of new opportunities and solve increasingly complex problems.

1.11 Review Questions

1. Why does programming become more valuable than spreadsheets as data analysis tasks grow in size, complexity, or repetition?
2. What is the key difference between a spreadsheet-based workflow and a script-based workflow?
3. How does programming support **reproducibility**, and why is reproducibility important in data analysis?
4. In what ways does automation change how analysts spend their time and effort?
5. Why is transparency easier to achieve with code than with spreadsheets?
6. How does programming for data analysis differ from computer science or software development?
7. Why is it a misconception that analysts need to "think like computer scientists" to use programming effectively?
8. How are AI tools changing what it means for analysts to "know how to code"?
9. What new skills become more important for analysts in an AI-assisted programming environment?
10. How does learning to program change the way analysts think about data, problems, and analytical workflows?

1.12 Ch 1 Lab Introduction

Before diving into programming concepts, you need a place to write and run your code. An Integrated Development Environment (IDE) or code editor is your primary tool for programming—think of it as your digital workspace where you'll spend most of your time learning and practicing.

This chapter introduces the most practical options for getting started with programming, particularly for data analysis using R and Python. Rather than overwhelming you with dozens of choices, we focus on proven solutions that work well for beginners and remain useful as you advance.

Why Your Choice Matters

Your development environment affects how quickly you can start coding, how easily you can debug problems, and how smoothly you can transition between different programming languages. A good environment should:

- Get you coding quickly without complex setup procedures
- Provide helpful features like syntax highlighting and error detection

- Support both R and Python seamlessly
- Work reliably across different operating systems
- Scale with your growing skills and project complexity

1.12.1 2. Cloud-Based Development Environments

Cloud-based environments run in your web browser and require no local installation. They're ideal for beginners because you can start coding immediately, and they work identically across different computers and operating systems.

Posit Cloud (Recommended for Beginners)

Posit Cloud provides a complete data science environment in your browser, with both R and Python pre-installed and ready to use. It's specifically designed for data analysis and statistical computing, making it an excellent match for this textbook's focus.

Key advantages:

- No installation required—works immediately in any modern web browser
- R and Python environments are pre-configured and ready to use
- Includes RStudio interface for R and Jupyter notebooks for Python
- Free tier provides sufficient resources for learning and coursework
- Automatic saving and project management

Getting started: Visit posit.cloud, create a free account, and start a new project. You'll have access to both R and Python environments within minutes.

Google Colab

Google Colab excels for Python-based data analysis and machine learning. It provides free access to powerful computing resources, including GPUs for advanced projects.

Best for: Python programming, data visualization, machine learning projects, and collaborative work. Limited R support makes it less ideal if you plan to use both languages equally.

GitHub Codespaces

GitHub Codespaces provides a full Visual Studio Code environment in the browser, with excellent support for both R and Python. It's particularly valuable if you're already using GitHub for version control.

Best for: Students comfortable with Git/GitHub, those wanting a professional development environment, and projects requiring custom package installations.

1.12.2 3. Desktop IDEs and Editors

Desktop environments offer more control and often better performance than cloud solutions. They're worth considering if you prefer working offline or need specific customizations.

Visual Studio Code (VS Code)

VS Code has become the most popular code editor among data scientists and programmers. It supports both R and Python excellently through extensions and provides a consistent experience across Windows, Mac, and Linux.

Essential extensions for data analysis:

- Python extension (by Microsoft) - provides IntelliSense, debugging, and Jupyter notebook support
- R extension - adds R language support and integration with R terminals
- Jupyter extension - enables notebook editing directly in VS Code

Setup process: Download VS Code from code.visualstudio.com, install the software, then add the Python and R extensions from the Extensions marketplace.

RStudio Desktop

RStudio remains the gold standard for R programming. While primarily designed for R, recent versions include basic Python support, making it viable for mixed-language projects.

Strengths: Exceptional R support, integrated help system, excellent data viewing capabilities, and built-in package management. The interface is specifically designed for data analysis workflows.

Considerations: Python support is limited compared to dedicated Python IDEs. Best choice if you'll primarily use R with occasional Python work.

PyCharm Community Edition

PyCharm offers professional-grade Python development tools in a free community edition. It excels for larger Python projects and provides excellent debugging capabilities.

Best for: Python-focused development, complex projects requiring advanced debugging, and students planning to pursue software development alongside data analysis.

1.12.3 4. Language-Specific Environments

Understanding the native environments for R and Python helps you make informed choices and troubleshoot issues when they arise.

R Environment

R includes a basic console interface that works on all platforms. While functional, most users prefer RStudio or VS Code for their enhanced features. However, understanding the base R environment helps you:

- Troubleshoot installation issues
- Understand how RStudio and other IDEs interact with R
- Work in environments where only base R is available

Python Environment

Python can be run from the command line, through IDLE (Python's built-in IDE), or via Jupyter notebooks. For data analysis, Jupyter notebooks have become the standard because they allow you to mix code, visualizations, and explanatory text in a single document.

Jupyter Notebooks: These browser-based documents let you write code in cells, run them individually, and see results immediately. They're excellent for exploratory data analysis and creating reproducible research.

Package Management

Both R and Python rely heavily on additional packages (libraries) that extend their capabilities. Understanding package management is crucial:

R packages: Installed using install.packages("package_name") and loaded with library(package_name). CRAN (Comprehensive R Archive Network) hosts most R packages.

Python packages: Typically installed using pip install package_name and imported with import package_name. PyPI (Python Package Index) is the main repository.

1.12.4 5. Getting Started Recommendations

Your best choice depends on your specific situation, technical comfort level, and learning goals. Here are our recommendations for different scenarios:

Scenario	Recommended Option	Why This Choice
Complete beginner who wants to start immediately	Posit Cloud	No installation required, works in a web browser, and is designed for learning and data analysis.
Primarily interested in Python and machine learning	Google Colab	Supports Python natively, provides free access to computational resources, and is widely used for machine learning.

Scenario	Recommended Option	Why This Choice
Want a professional development environment	VS Code	Widely used in industry, supports both R and Python, and offers extensive customization.
Focused on statistical analysis and R	RStudio Desktop	Designed specifically for R and provides strong support for statistical analysis, visualization, and reproducible research.

Our Strong Recommendation for This Course

For students using this textbook, we recommend starting with **Posit Cloud**. Here's why:

1. **Immediate access:** You can start coding within minutes of reading this chapter
2. **Consistent experience:** Everyone in your class will have the same environment, reducing technical support issues
3. **Both languages ready:** R and Python are pre-installed and configured correctly
4. **No installation headaches:** Avoid the common beginner frustration of environment setup
5. **Easy transition:** You can always move to a desktop environment later as your needs grow

1.12.5 6. Troubleshooting Common Issues

Even with the best planning, you may encounter technical issues. Here are solutions to the most common problems beginners face:

Cloud Environment Issues

Problem: Posit Cloud project won't load or runs very slowly.

Solutions:

- Check your internet connection—cloud environments require stable connectivity
- Try a different web browser (Chrome and Firefox work best)
- Clear your browser cache and cookies
- Free accounts have usage limits—you may need to wait or upgrade

Package Installation Problems

Problem: Error messages when trying to install R or Python packages.

Solutions:

- Check package name spelling—case matters in many systems
- For R: Use install.packages("package_name") with quotes around the package name
- For Python: Ensure you're using pip install package_name in a terminal, not in the Python interpreter
- Some packages require system dependencies—cloud environments usually handle this automatically

Code Not Running

Problem: Code examples from the textbook don't work in your environment.

Solutions:

- Verify you're running the code in the correct language (R vs. Python)
- Check that required packages are loaded (library() for R, import for Python)
- Copy and paste code exactly—small typos can cause big problems
- Run code in the order presented—later examples often depend on earlier ones

Getting Help

When you encounter problems not covered here:

6. **Read error messages carefully**—they often contain specific information about what went wrong
7. **Search for the exact error message** online—someone else has likely encountered the same issue
8. **Ask for help with context**—include what you were trying to do, what you expected to happen, and what actually happened
9. **Use AI assistants** like those built into modern IDEs—they can often explain error messages and suggest solutions

Moving Forward

Remember that choosing a development environment is not a permanent decision. Many professional programmers use different tools for different projects. Start with something that gets you coding quickly, then explore other options as your skills and needs evolve.

The most important thing is to start programming. The environment is just a tool—your understanding of programming concepts, problem-solving skills, and ability to work with data are what truly matter. Choose an environment that removes barriers to learning, and focus your energy on mastering the fundamental concepts covered in the following chapters.

Chapter 2

R and Python in Data Analytics

2.1 Learning Outcomes

2-1: Describe the primary purposes and typical applications of R and Python in data analysis.

2-2: Explain the strengths of R and Python and the contexts where each is commonly used.

2-3: Discuss how AI-assisted tools change the process of learning and using programming languages.

2-4: Explain how analytical thinking and problem-solving skills transfer between programming languages.

2.2 Introduction

If you've spent any time looking into programming for data analysis, you've probably encountered what feels like a fundamental choice: should you learn R or Python? This question seems to generate endless debates online, with passionate advocates on both sides making compelling arguments for their preferred language. Students often feel paralyzed by this decision, worried that choosing the "wrong" language will somehow derail their learning or limit their career prospects.

Let me start with the most important point of this chapter: this anxiety is largely misplaced. The choice between R and Python is far less consequential than it might seem, especially in an era where AI tools can help you work effectively in both languages. The analytical thinking skills you develop, the understanding of data concepts you build, and the problem-solving approaches you learn are fundamentally the same regardless of which language you use to express them.

This chapter is about setting realistic expectations and reducing the confusion that surrounds programming languages in data analytics. We'll explore what R and Python are actually used for in practice, understand their respective strengths, and see why this course teaches R first. Most importantly, we'll discover how AI assistance has fundamentally changed what it means to learn programming languages, making the traditional barriers between languages much less significant than they once were.

2.3 What R and Python Are Used For in Practice

Before we dive into comparisons and debates, it's worth understanding what these languages actually do in the real world of data analysis. Both R and Python are tools for working with data, but they emerged from different communities and evolved to serve somewhat different needs.

R was created by statisticians, for statisticians. It grew out of the academic statistics community in the 1990s as a free alternative to expensive statistical software packages. From the beginning, R was designed with data analysis as its primary purpose. Every aspect of the language reflects this focus: how it handles data, how it approaches statistical calculations, and how it creates visualizations.

Python, on the other hand, is a general-purpose programming language that was designed to be readable and versatile. It wasn't created specifically for data analysis, but over time, the Python community built powerful libraries and tools that made it excellent for working with data. Python's strength lies in its flexibility—it can handle data analysis, but it can also build websites, automate tasks, create games, and power artificial intelligence systems.

In practice, this means that R and Python often show up in different contexts, though with significant overlap:

R	Python
Academic research and statistical analysis	Data science in technology companies
Exploratory data analysis and visualization	Machine learning and artificial intelligence
Statistical modeling and hypothesis testing	Data engineering and automation
Biostatistics and clinical research	Web scraping and data collection
Survey analysis and social science research	Integration with larger software systems
Financial modeling and risk analysis	General-purpose programming that includes data analysis

Notice that there's substantial overlap in these lists. Both languages can handle statistical analysis, create visualizations, work with large datasets, and perform machine learning. The differences are often more about community and context than fundamental capabilities.

Here's what this means for you: the choice between R and Python is less about what you can accomplish and more about which community and ecosystem feel more natural for your work. If you're primarily interested in statistical analysis and research, R's design and community might feel more intuitive. If you're interested in broader data science applications or want to combine data analysis with other programming tasks, Python's versatility might be appealing.

But here's the crucial insight: with modern AI assistance, you don't need to make this choice as definitively as previous generations of analysts did. AI tools can help you work effectively in both languages, translate between them, and focus on the analytical concepts rather than the syntactic details.

2.4 Strengths of R for Data Analysis

R's design as a language specifically for statistics and data analysis gives it several distinctive advantages. Understanding these strengths helps explain why R remains popular in academic and research settings, and why this course begins with R.

Statistical Thinking Built In

R was designed by people who think about data the way data analysts think about data. This shows up in countless small ways that make data analysis feel natural. For example, R treats missing values (those inevitable gaps in real-world data) as a fundamental part of the language. You don't need to learn special techniques to handle missing data—R assumes you'll encounter it and provides built-in ways to work with it appropriately.

Similarly, R's approach to data types reflects how analysts actually categorize information. The distinction between categorical data (like survey responses or experimental conditions) and numerical data (like measurements or counts) is built into how R stores and manipulates information. This means that when you perform statistical operations, R often "knows" the appropriate method to use based on your data types.

Visualization as a First-Class Citizen

One of R's greatest strengths is its approach to data visualization. Creating charts and graphs isn't an afterthought in R—it's a core part of how the language works. The built-in plotting capabilities are extensive, and packages like ggplot2 have revolutionized how people think about creating visualizations.

What makes R's visualization capabilities special isn't just that they're powerful (though they are), but that they're designed around the way analysts actually explore data. You can quickly create a scatter plot to examine relationships, generate histograms to understand distributions, or build complex multi-panel displays to compare groups. The process feels natural because it mirrors the exploratory process that good data analysis requires.

Rich Statistical Ecosystem

Because R emerged from the statistics community, it has an incredibly rich ecosystem of statistical methods and techniques. If there's a statistical procedure you need—from basic t-tests to advanced machine learning algorithms—there's likely an R package that implements it, often written by the researchers who developed the method.

This ecosystem advantage is particularly important for academic work and research. New statistical methods often appear in R packages before they're available in other languages or software. If you're working in a field that uses specialized statistical techniques, R is often where you'll find the most current and comprehensive implementations.

Data Frame Thinking

R's approach to organizing data around "data frames" (essentially tables with rows and columns) aligns perfectly with how most analysts think about their data. Whether you're working with survey responses, experimental results, or observational data, you're usually thinking in terms of cases (rows) and variables (columns). R's data frame structure makes this conceptual model explicit and provides tools that work naturally with this organization.

Reproducible Research Integration

R has excellent tools for creating reproducible research documents that combine code, results, and narrative text. The R Markdown system allows you to write reports where the analysis code is embedded directly in the document, ensuring that your results are always up-to-date with your data and methods. This integration between analysis and reporting is particularly valuable in academic and research contexts.

These strengths don't make R "better" than Python in any absolute sense, but they do explain why R feels natural and intuitive for many data analysis tasks, especially those that involve statistical thinking and academic research.

2.5 Strengths of Python for General-Purpose Analytics

While R was designed specifically for statistics, Python's strength lies in its versatility and its integration with the broader world of programming and technology. These characteristics give Python several advantages, particularly for data science work that extends beyond traditional statistical analysis.

Integration and Automation

Python excels when your data analysis needs to connect with other systems or processes. If you need to automatically download data from websites, connect to databases, send results via email, or integrate your analysis with web applications, Python's general-purpose nature makes these tasks straightforward. While R can do these things, Python's design makes them feel more natural and well-supported.

This integration strength becomes particularly important in business and technology contexts, where data analysis is often part of larger automated systems. Python's ability to serve as both the analysis tool and the automation platform makes it attractive for organizations that want to build data pipelines and automated reporting systems.

Machine Learning and AI Ecosystem

Python has become the dominant language for machine learning and artificial intelligence work. Libraries like scikit-learn, TensorFlow, and PyTorch have made Python the go-to choice for everything from basic predictive modeling to cutting-edge deep learning research. If your data analysis work involves machine learning—and increasingly, it does—Python's ecosystem provides unparalleled resources and community support.

This machine learning strength isn't just about having access to algorithms; it's about being part of a community that's actively developing and sharing new approaches. The rapid pace of innovation in machine learning means that new techniques and improvements often appear in Python libraries first.

Data Engineering Capabilities

Python excels at the "data engineering" aspects of analysis—the often unglamorous but crucial work of collecting, cleaning, and preparing data for analysis. Python's libraries for working with different data formats, connecting to various data sources, and processing large datasets are mature and well-developed.

This strength becomes important when you're working with messy, real-world data that doesn't come pre-packaged in a nice, clean format. Python's tools for web scraping,

API interaction, and data transformation can handle the complex data preparation tasks that often consume the majority of time in real data projects.

Scalability and Performance

While both R and Python can handle large datasets, Python's general-purpose design gives it advantages when you need to scale your analysis or optimize performance. Python's integration with distributed computing frameworks and its ability to interface with high-performance computing resources make it attractive for organizations dealing with very large datasets or computationally intensive analyses.

Industry Adoption

Python's versatility has led to widespread adoption in technology companies and data-driven organizations. This means that Python skills often translate more directly to industry job opportunities, particularly in data science roles at technology companies. The language's use extends beyond data analysis to web development, automation, and system administration, making Python programmers valuable in many different contexts.

Learning Pathway to Software Development

If you think you might want to expand beyond data analysis into broader programming or software development, Python provides a more natural pathway. The skills you develop doing data analysis in Python transfer more directly to other programming domains than R skills typically do.

Again, these strengths don't make Python inherently superior to R, but they do explain why Python has become popular in certain contexts, particularly in industry data science roles and in work that requires integration with larger technical systems.

2.6 Why This Course Teaches R First

Given the strengths of both languages, you might wonder why this course begins with R rather than Python. This decision reflects both pedagogical considerations and practical realities about how people learn programming for data analysis.

Conceptual Clarity

R's design around statistical concepts makes it easier to understand what you're actually doing when you analyze data. Because R was built specifically for data analysis, the connection between your analytical intentions and the code you write tends to be more direct and transparent. When you calculate a mean in R, create a histogram, or fit a regression model, the code closely reflects the conceptual operation you're performing.

This conceptual clarity is particularly valuable when you're learning both programming and data analysis simultaneously. With R, you can focus on understanding analytical concepts without getting distracted by the general-purpose programming features that Python includes but that aren't directly relevant to data analysis.

Immediate Gratification

R is designed to give you quick, meaningful results with minimal setup. You can load a dataset, create visualizations, and perform statistical analyses with just a few lines of code. This immediate feedback is crucial for maintaining motivation and building confidence when you're starting to learn programming.

Python can certainly do all of these things, but it often requires more initial setup and boilerplate code. While this additional structure becomes valuable as you work on larger projects, it can be discouraging when you're just trying to create your first scatter plot or calculate some basic statistics.

Statistical Intuition

Learning R first helps develop statistical intuition because the language embeds statistical thinking in its design. Concepts like data types, missing values, and statistical distributions are built into how R works, which means you encounter and internalize these ideas naturally as you learn the language.

This statistical foundation becomes valuable regardless of which language you use later. The conceptual understanding you develop working with R transfers directly to Python or any other tool you might use for data analysis.

Academic Context

Since this course is taught in an academic setting, R's strengths in research and statistical analysis align well with the types of projects and analyses you're likely to encounter in your coursework. R's integration with reproducible research tools and its extensive statistical capabilities make it particularly well-suited for academic work.

AI-Assisted Learning Advantage

Here's where the modern context becomes crucial: AI tools are particularly effective at helping you learn R because the language's statistical focus makes it easier for AI to understand your analytical intentions. When you describe what you want to do with your data, AI assistants can more easily translate your goals into appropriate R code because R's design aligns closely with analytical thinking.

Moreover, once you understand the concepts through R, AI tools can help you translate those same concepts into Python syntax when needed. This means that starting with R doesn't limit your future options—it provides a solid conceptual foundation that AI can help you express in any language.

The Transition Strategy

Learning R first, with AI assistance, actually makes learning Python easier later. You'll understand the analytical concepts, and AI tools can help you express those same concepts in Python syntax. This approach lets you focus on learning data analysis thinking first, then expand to additional languages as needed.

This is fundamentally different from the traditional approach, where choosing a language felt like a major commitment. With AI assistance, your first language becomes a foundation for understanding concepts, not a limitation on your future options.

2.7 How Skills Transfer Between Languages

One of the most liberating realizations for new programmers is understanding how much transfers between programming languages. While the syntax—the specific commands and formatting rules—differs between R and Python, the underlying concepts and thinking patterns are remarkably similar. This transferability is even more pronounced in the age of AI assistance.

Conceptual Foundations Are Universal

The fundamental concepts of data analysis remain the same regardless of the language you use to implement them. Understanding what a mean represents, how to interpret a correlation, or when to use a particular statistical test doesn't change when you switch from R to Python. These analytical concepts form the core of your expertise, and they transfer completely between languages.

Similarly, the programming concepts you learn—variables, functions, loops, conditional logic—work the same way in both languages, even though they might look different syntactically. Once you understand that a variable is a way to store and reference a value, you can apply that concept in any programming language.

Data Manipulation Patterns

Both R and Python organize data analysis around similar patterns: read data, clean and transform it, analyze it, and present results. While the specific commands differ, the logical flow and the types of operations you perform are nearly identical. If you know how to filter rows, create new columns, and summarize data in R, you already understand the conceptual framework for doing the same things in Python.

Problem-Solving Approaches

Perhaps most importantly, the problem-solving approaches you develop while learning one language transfer directly to others. Learning to break complex analytical tasks into smaller steps, debugging code when things go wrong, and thinking systematically about data problems are skills that transcend any particular language.

AI as a Translation Layer

This is where AI assistance becomes transformative. Modern AI tools can serve as real-time translators between programming languages. If you know how to describe what you want to do analytically, AI can help you express that intention in R, Python, or any other language.

For example, if you understand the concept of creating a scatter plot with a trend line, you can describe this goal to an AI assistant and get appropriate code in either language. The AI handles the syntactic translation while you focus on the analytical concepts.

Practical Translation Examples

Let's consider how similar analytical operations look in both languages. While the syntax differs, the underlying logic is identical:

Task	R Approach	Python Approach	Transferable Concept
Reading a data file	read.csv() function and data frame structure	pandas library with pd.read_csv() and DataFrame objects	Loading tabular data into a structured format for analysis
Creating visualizations	Base plotting or ggplot2 grammar of graphics	matplotlib or seaborn libraries	Mapping data variables to visual elements like position, color, and size
Statistical analysis	Built-in statistical functions and specialized packages	scipy.stats and scikit-learn libraries	Applying appropriate statistical methods to answer research questions

The Learning Acceleration Effect

Here's what many people don't realize: learning a second programming language is dramatically easier than learning your first. Once you understand programming concepts through one language, picking up another becomes primarily a matter of learning new syntax rather than new ideas.

With AI assistance, this acceleration becomes even more pronounced. You can focus on understanding the concepts deeply in your first language, then use AI to help express those same concepts in additional languages as needed. This approach is much more efficient than trying to learn multiple languages simultaneously.

2.8 When Language Choice Actually Matters

Understanding when language choice is important—and when it's not—can help you make practical decisions and avoid unnecessary anxiety about this topic. The reality is that for most data analysis tasks, the choice between R and Python matters much less than you might expect.

When Language Choice Doesn't Matter Much

For the vast majority of data analysis work, both R and Python are perfectly capable tools. This includes:

Basic Statistical Analysis: Calculating means, performing t-tests, fitting regression models, and other fundamental statistical operations work equally well in both languages. The concepts are identical, and both languages have mature, well-tested implementations.

Data Visualization: Both languages can create publication-quality charts, graphs, and complex visualizations. While the syntax differs, the capabilities are comparable, and both can produce professional results.

Data Cleaning and Manipulation: Filtering data, creating new variables, handling missing values, and reshaping datasets are core operations that both languages handle effectively. The approaches might look different, but the results are equivalent.

Exploratory Data Analysis: The iterative process of examining data, identifying patterns, and generating insights works equally well in both languages. Both provide the interactive capabilities and visualization tools needed for effective exploration.

Learning and Education: For understanding statistical concepts, developing analytical thinking, and building programming skills, both languages are excellent choices. The educational value comes from the thinking process, not the specific syntax.

When Language Choice Might Matter

There are some contexts where one language might have practical advantages:

Specialized Statistical Methods: If your work requires cutting-edge statistical techniques or methods from specific research communities, R often has implementations available sooner. The academic statistics community tends to publish new methods as R packages first.

Machine Learning and AI: For advanced machine learning work, particularly deep learning and neural networks, Python's ecosystem is more mature and comprehensive. If your primary focus is machine learning rather than traditional statistics, Python might offer more resources.

Integration Requirements: If your analysis needs to integrate with existing systems, web applications, or automated processes, Python's general-purpose nature might make integration easier. Conversely, if you're working in an environment where R is already established, staying with R might be more practical.

Team and Organizational Context: If your colleagues, collaborators, or organization have established practices around one language, there are practical advantages to using the same tools for collaboration and knowledge sharing.

Career Considerations: Different industries and job markets have different language preferences. Academic and research positions often favor R, while technology companies often prefer Python. However, these preferences are trends rather than absolute requirements.

The AI Game-Changer

Here's where AI assistance fundamentally changes the calculation: with AI tools, you can work effectively in both languages without needing to master both syntaxes. This means that many of the traditional reasons for choosing one language over another become less important.

If you encounter a situation where Python would be advantageous, AI can help you translate your R knowledge into Python code. If you need to use a specialized R package, AI can help you understand and implement it even if you're more comfortable with Python. The barriers between languages become much more permeable.

2.9 Modern Reality: AI Changes Everything

Throughout this chapter, we've touched on how AI assistance changes the traditional considerations around programming languages. It's worth making this point explicitly: AI tools are fundamentally altering what it means to learn and use programming languages for data analysis.

From Syntax Memorization to Concept Understanding

Traditional programming education required extensive syntax memorization. You needed to remember the exact commands, formatting rules, and function names for your chosen language. This created high barriers to entry and made switching between languages difficult.

AI assistance shifts the focus from memorizing syntax to understanding concepts. You can describe what you want to do in plain English, and AI tools can generate the appropriate code in your chosen language. This means you can focus your mental energy on understanding analytical concepts rather than remembering programming syntax.

Real-Time Language Translation

AI tools can serve as real-time translators between programming languages. If you know how to do something in R but need to do it in Python, you can ask an AI assistant to translate the approach. This makes the barriers between languages much more permeable than they've ever been.

Learning Acceleration

With AI assistance, you can start solving real analytical problems immediately, rather than spending weeks or months learning syntax fundamentals. The AI handles the syntactic details while you focus on the analytical thinking. This acceleration is particularly valuable for students who want to apply programming to their coursework and research projects right away.

Error Diagnosis and Debugging

One of the most frustrating aspects of learning programming has always been debugging—figuring out why your code doesn't work. AI tools excel at diagnosing common errors and suggesting fixes, dramatically reducing the time you spend stuck on technical problems.

Explanation and Education

Perhaps most importantly, AI tools can explain code in plain English, helping you understand not just what the code does, but why it works that way. This educational capability means you can learn by doing, with AI serving as a patient tutor that can explain concepts at whatever level of detail you need.

The New Learning Model

This AI-assisted approach suggests a new model for learning programming languages:

1. **Start with concepts:** Focus on understanding analytical and statistical concepts first
2. **Use AI for implementation:** Let AI help translate your conceptual understanding into working code
3. **Learn through explanation:** Ask AI to explain how the code works and why it's structured that way
4. **Iterate and experiment:** Use AI to help you try different approaches and understand the trade-offs
5. **Expand gradually:** As you become comfortable with concepts in one language, use AI to help you express the same ideas in other languages

2.10 Languages Differ in Syntax, Not in Analytical Thinking

The most important skills—understanding data, thinking analytically, and solving problems—transfer across R, Python, and other tools. Syntax is just the surface layer; AI can handle it, letting you focus on concepts. Analytical thinking includes knowing which methods to use, interpreting results, spotting patterns, and thinking systematically. Problem-solving skills like breaking tasks into steps, debugging, organizing work, and testing assumptions also transfer between languages. Core programming concepts—variables, functions, loops, and logic—are universal, as are data analysis concepts like distributions, relationships, and visualization.

2.11 Conclusion

R and Python are just tools. The real skill is understanding data, thinking analytically, and solving problems. With AI assistance, the barriers between languages are mostly gone—you can focus on concepts, not syntax. Start with R to build a strong foundation in statistical thinking, and know that everything you learn there transfers to Python or any other language. Your goal isn't to memorize commands; it's to develop the thinking and problem-solving skills that make data analysis work.

2.12 Review Questions

1. What were the original purposes of R and Python, and how did those origins shape how each language is used today in data analytics?
2. In what types of data analysis contexts does R tend to be a more natural fit, and why?
3. In what types of projects or organizational settings does Python often have an advantage, and why?
4. Why does the chapter argue that the choice between R and Python is less important than many students assume?
5. How does AI assistance change the way students learn and use programming languages for data analysis?
6. What analytical skills and concepts transfer directly between R and Python, regardless of syntax differences?
7. Why does this course choose to teach R first instead of Python?
8. How does learning one programming language make learning a second language easier?
9. In what situations might the choice between R and Python actually matter?

10. According to the chapter, what should students focus on developing instead of memorizing programming syntax?

Chapter 3

Programming Environments

3.1 Learning Outcomes

3-1: Explain the purpose and benefits of programming environments for data analysis.

3-2: Compare IDEs, notebooks, and reports, and describe when each is most appropriate.

3-3: Organize projects and use relative file paths to ensure reproducible and portable analyses.

3-4: Recognize how AI assistance can enhance workflow, learning, and problem-solving in programming environments.

3.2 Introduction

If you've ever watched someone work with data using programming, you might have been struck by how different their screen looks from what you're used to. Instead of a single application like Excel or Word, they seem to have multiple windows open, with code in one place, results in another, and files scattered across various panels. It can look chaotic and intimidating, especially when you're accustomed to the clean, unified interface of a spreadsheet.

Let me reassure you: this apparent complexity is actually designed to make your work easier, not harder. The programming environments that data analysts use are carefully designed tools that help organize, streamline, and improve the analytical process. They might look unfamiliar at first, but they're built around the same organizational principles you already use in other aspects of your work and life.

This chapter is about making these tools feel familiar and non-threatening. We'll explore what programming environments are and why analysts choose to use them, look at different ways to organize your analytical work, and understand how good organization forms the foundation for reliable, reproducible analysis.

The key insight of this chapter is that good analysis starts with an organized workspace. Just as you wouldn't try to write a research paper with documents scattered randomly across your computer, you shouldn't try to do data analysis without thoughtful organization of your code, data, and results.

3.3 What an IDE Is and Why Analysts Use Them

The term "IDE" stands for "Integrated Development Environment," which sounds intimidating but describes something quite practical. An IDE is simply a software application that brings together all the tools you need for programming in one place. Think of it as the difference between having a well-organized workshop with all your tools within reach versus having to hunt through different rooms to find what you need for each task.

When working with data using programming, you need several key capabilities:

- Code editor: A place to write and edit your code.
- Execution environment: A way to run your code and see results.
- Data access: Easy access to your data files and other project materials.
- Visualization tools: Tools for creating charts, graphs, and viewing output.
- Support resources: Help documentation and informative error messages.
- Project organization: File management and structured organization of your projects.

You could use separate applications for each of these tasks—write code in a basic text editor, run it from a command line, view results in another window, and manage files through your operating system. Some people do work this way, but it's inefficient and error-prone. An IDE brings all these capabilities together in a single, coordinated interface.

Why This Matters for Data Analysis

Data analysis is inherently iterative. You write some code, run it to see what happens, modify it based on the results, run it again, create a visualization, adjust the analysis, and so on. This back-and-forth process works much better when all your tools are integrated and can communicate with each other.

For example, when you're working in a good IDE, you can run a single line of code to test an idea without executing your entire analysis. Variables and data created in one part of your code remain available for use elsewhere, allowing seamless continuity in your workflow. You can easily switch between writing code and examining your data, while error messages appear in context, making it simpler to understand and fix problems. Additionally, your plots and visualizations appear immediately alongside your code, providing instant feedback and helping you explore your data more effectively.

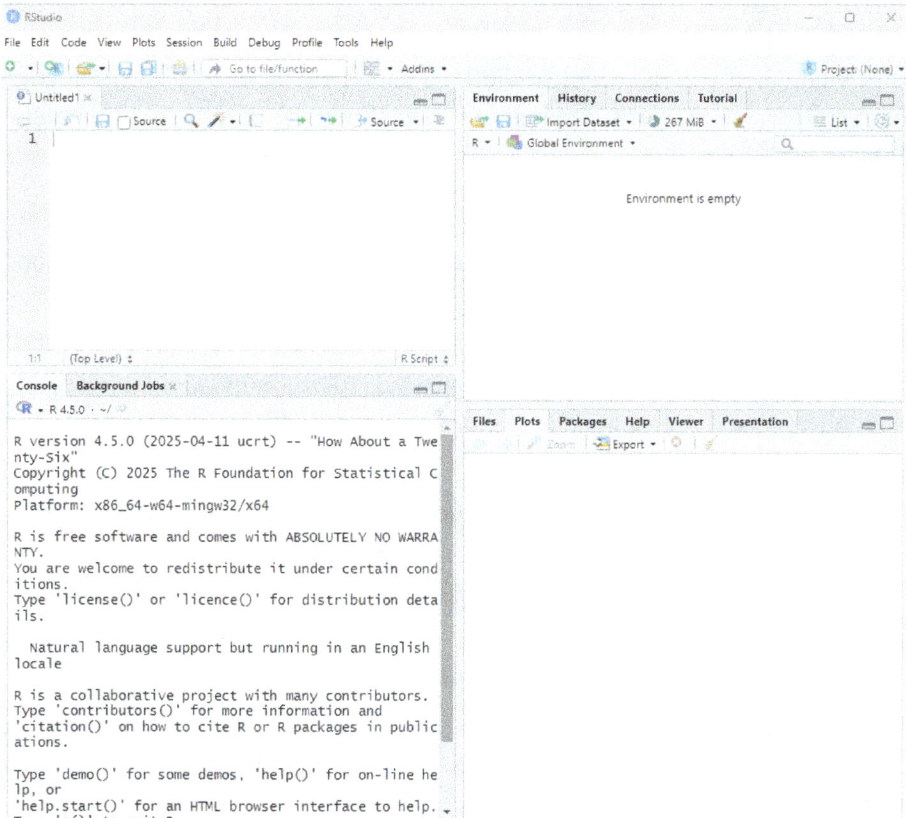

When you first open an IDE like Posit (RStudio), take a moment to identify four key areas. The **Source panel** (usually top-left) is where you write your code. The **Console panel** (usually bottom-left) is where your code runs and displays results. The **Environment panel** (usually top-right) shows your data and variables. Finally, the **Files/Plots panel** (usually bottom-right) is used for navigating files and viewing output.

Don't worry about understanding everything at once—just notice how each area serves a different purpose in your workflow.

3.4 Scripts vs Notebooks vs Reports

One of the first decisions you'll face when starting a data analysis project is how to organize your work. Should you write a script, create a notebook, or build a report? Each approach has its strengths and is suited to different types of analytical work.

Scripts

A script is the most straightforward way to organize programming code. It's simply a text file containing a sequence of instructions that the computer executes from top to bottom. Think of a script like a recipe. It lists the ingredients (your data and variables) and then provides step-by-step instructions for transforming those ingredients into a result.

Scripts work well when you have a clear, defined analytical task, want to automate a process that you'll repeat regularly, are building something that others will use without modification, or need maximum efficiency with minimal overhead.

Notebooks

Notebooks represent a different philosophy. Instead of a linear sequence of instructions, notebooks are organized into "cells" that can contain code, text, or visualizations. You can run these cells individually, in any order, and see the results immediately.

Think of a notebook like a laboratory notebook that scientists use to record their experiments. It combines observations, hypotheses, procedures, results, and interpretations in a single document.

Notebooks excel when you're exploring data and don't know exactly what you'll find, want to combine code, results, and explanations in a single document, are developing and testing ideas before committing to a final approach, or need to communicate your process and findings to others.

Reports: Communication and Documentation

Reports combine the computational power of scripts with the communication capabilities of traditional documents. Reports can include code, results, visualizations, and narrative text, all integrated into a polished final product.

Think of a report like a research paper that can automatically update its results when the underlying data changes. The analysis code is embedded in the document, but the final output looks like a professional report or academic paper.

Choosing the Right Approach

Many analysts use all three approaches for different aspects of their work: scripts for data cleaning, automated processes, and production analyses; notebooks for exploration, experimentation, and collaborative work; and reports for final documentation, communication, and formal presentations.

3.5 Posit (RStudio)

Posit (formerly RStudio) is the most popular IDE for R programming, but it also supports Python. Understanding how it works gives insight into how data analysts organize projects, and the same organizational principles apply no matter which language or tool you use.

The Four-Panel Philosophy

When you open Posit, the workspace is organized into four main areas: the Source panel (top left) for writing and editing code, the Console panel (bottom left) for running code and seeing results, the Environment panel (top right) showing your current data and variables, and the Files/Plots/Help panel (bottom right) for navigating files, viewing visualizations, and accessing documentation. This layout supports the natural workflow of data analysis: write, run, monitor, and reference.

Project-Based Organization

One of Posit's most useful features is its project system, which helps you keep all files for a particular analysis organized in a single folder instead of scattered across your computer. A typical project contains subfolders like data/ for raw and processed datasets, scripts/ for R code, output/ for plots, tables, and results, and docs/ for documentation and reports. Setting up a project is straightforward: click File → New Project, select New Directory → New Project, name your project, and choose a location. Posit automatically creates the folder and sets it as your working directory. You can then add subfolders for data, scripts, and output. This simple structure supports organized, efficient analysis, and you'll practice using it in later labs.

Jupyter and Colab

While Posit represents a traditional IDE approach, Jupyter notebooks follow a different philosophy focused on interactive computing. Notebooks treat data analysis as an exploratory process, allowing you to work in small chunks of code and immediately see the results rather than writing a complete program all at once. Each notebook contains "cells" that can include executable code, formatted text for explanations or documentation, and the results of your analysis, such as tables or visualizations.

Google Colab takes this concept into the cloud. With Colab, you can perform data analysis entirely through a web browser without installing any software. It provides immediate access to computing resources, integrates with Google Drive for easy file management, and allows straightforward sharing and collaboration with others.

In practice, traditional IDEs like Posit are most useful when you are developing production systems, building automated processes, or managing large, complex projects where a structured workflow is important. Notebooks, on the other hand, are better suited for exploring data, experimenting with new techniques, and combining code with explanations in a way that clearly communicates your process and findings. Both approaches reflect different ways analysts organize their work, and understanding them helps you choose the right tool for the task at hand.

3.6 Files, Folders, and Working Directories

A fundamental part of programming for data analysis is understanding how your code locates and accesses the files it needs. Every time you start a programming environment, it operates from a specific location on your computer called the **working directory**. When you instruct your code to read a file such as "data.csv," the environment looks for that file within the working directory. This is similar to navigating your computer manually: when you open a folder and double-click a file, your current location is effectively the working directory.

File paths tell your code where to find a file. An **absolute path** specifies the complete location from the root of your computer's file system, such as C:\Users\YourName\Documents\Project\data.csv on Windows or /Users/YourName/Documents/Project/data.csv on Mac or Linux. A **relative path**, in contrast, specifies a file's location relative to the working directory. For example, if your working directory is the "Project" folder, the file data.csv can be referenced simply as data.csv, or as data/survey_responses.csv if it is stored in a subfolder. Using relative paths is generally preferable because it makes your code portable. As long as the relative relationships between files are maintained, the code will work on any machine.

To practice, you can create a simple project folder on your desktop called "MyAnalysis" and add a subfolder named "data." Place a CSV file in the subfolder, set your IDE's working directory to the main project folder, and try referencing your data file as data/filename.csv. A common source of frustration for beginners is encountering "file not found" errors despite the file existing. This usually happens because the working directory is set incorrectly or the file path does not match the folder structure. Another issue arises when code works on your computer but fails for collaborators; organizing all files within a single project folder and using relative paths can prevent such problems.

3.7 Why Environment Setup Matters for Reproducibility

How you set up and organize your programming environment has a direct impact on the reproducibility of your work. Reproducibility means that someone else—or even your future self—can use the same environment, code, and data to produce exactly the same results. Without careful setup, this can easily break. Software updates may change how functions behave, code may rely on packages that others do not have installed, file paths that work on your computer may fail elsewhere, and analyses can depend on undocumented settings or hidden data.

To ensure reproducible work, it is important to follow best practices. Using a project-based organization helps by keeping all files related to a single analysis within a coherent folder hierarchy. Documenting your environment, including which versions of software and packages you are using, allows others to replicate your setup. Organizing files so that your code uses relative paths rather than absolute locations ensures that your project can run on different computers without modification. Finally, testing your code in a clean environment—starting from scratch with only the documented files—helps identify hidden dependencies or assumptions.

For example, when creating a reproducible project, you might start by establishing a clear folder structure and including a README file that explains the project's purpose. You would document the software and package versions, ensure all file paths are relative, and then test the workflow by having a colleague run the analysis from start to finish.

Following these practices makes your analyses more reliable, easier to share, and more professional, which is critical in both academic and professional data work.

AI assistance is transforming programming environments, making them more accessible, efficient, and powerful than ever. Modern environments increasingly integrate AI directly into the workspace, providing help in several key areas. For example, AI can generate code from plain English descriptions, diagnose errors and suggest fixes, troubleshoot file paths and package issues, and even recommend project structures and file organization strategies. Beyond these practical supports, AI accelerates learning by explaining code and concepts in clear, understandable language, making complex environments less intimidating for beginners.

This integration enables a new model for learning programming. Rather than focusing on memorizing syntax, you can concentrate on understanding the underlying concepts. AI provides immediate guidance when you encounter technical difficulties, allows you to learn by doing with explanations along the way, and encourages experimentation by helping you correct mistakes quickly. While AI does not replace the need to grasp fundamental concepts, it significantly amplifies your ability to apply them effectively and confidently.

3.8 Good Analysis Starts with an Organized Workspace

Throughout this chapter, we've examined different aspects of programming environments, but they all reinforce a single principle: effective data analysis begins with an organized workspace. Just as a chef wouldn't attempt a complex recipe in a cluttered kitchen, analysts cannot perform sophisticated work in a disorganized digital environment. Your workspace—the combination of tools, files, and organizational systems you use—forms the foundation for everything you do.

An organized workspace provides clarity and efficiency. It allows you to focus on analytical thinking rather than hunting for files, reduces the likelihood of errors, and makes collaboration with others much smoother. Well-structured projects are also easier to revisit months later, and the habits you establish scale to more complex analyses as your skills grow.

Developing good organizational practices early is essential. Simple habits—like setting up clear folder structures, using consistent patterns across projects, documenting your setup, and occasionally testing your code in a clean environment—lay the groundwork for a lifetime of productive work. While these steps may take a few extra minutes initially, they save hours of confusion later and make you a more effective collaborator and analyst.

3.9 Conclusion

Effective data analysis depends not just on technical skill, but on how well you organize your workspace. Programming environments—whether traditional IDEs like Posit, interactive notebooks like Jupyter, or cloud-based platforms like Colab—are designed to support exploration, experimentation, and reproducibility. By understanding how these tools structure code, data, and results, you can work more efficiently, reduce errors, and make your analyses easier to share and reproduce. Developing good organizational habits early, using project-based structures, relative file paths, and documenting your environment, provides a foundation that supports both learning and professional practice. AI integration further amplifies your capabilities by assisting with coding, troubleshooting, and workflow organization, making these environments more accessible and enabling a focus on understanding concepts rather than memorizing syntax.

3.10 Review Questions

1. What is a programming environment, and why do data analysts rely on environments rather than single tools like spreadsheets?
2. What is an IDE, and what key tasks does it bring together in one workspace?
3. How do scripts, notebooks, and reports differ in purpose, and when is each most appropriate to use?
4. Why is data analysis described as an iterative process, and how do programming environments support this workflow?
5. How does project-based organization improve efficiency and reduce errors in data analysis?
6. What is a working directory, and why do analysts prefer relative file paths over absolute file paths?
7. How does good file and folder organization contribute to reproducibility?

8. Why might an analysis work on one computer but fail on another, and how can this be prevented?
9. How do IDEs like Posit differ from notebook environments like Jupyter or Colab in how they support analytical work?
10. In what ways can AI assistance enhance learning, workflow, and problem-solving within programming environments?

Chapter 4

How Code Is Structured

4.1 Learning Outcomes

4-1: Explain what a computer program is and describe how programs function as ordered sequences of instructions.

4-2: Describe how statements and expressions work together in code and explain why execution order is critical to correct program behavior.

4-3: Explain the role of variables as labeled values and describe how variable values can change as a program runs.

4-4: Identify major conceptual data types (numbers, text, logical values, and collections) and explain why data types matter for analysis and computation.

4-5: Describe what happens when code executes, explain why small errors can cause program failures, and recognize how modern tools and AI assistance support debugging and learning.

4.2 Introduction

If you've ever looked at a piece of programming code, you might have felt overwhelmed by what seems like a jumbled collection of symbols, words, and punctuation marks. It can look like a foreign language—which, in a sense, it is. But here's the reassuring truth: code follows logical, predictable patterns that are much simpler than they first appear.

This chapter is about developing the right mental models for understanding how code works. We're not going to focus on memorizing syntax or learning specific commands. Instead, we'll build an intuitive understanding of what code actually is, how it's organized, and why it behaves the way it does. Think of this as learning the grammar and structure of a language before worrying about vocabulary.

The key insight of this chapter is deceptively simple but profoundly important: code is read top-to-bottom, one instruction at a time. Once you truly understand this principle and its implications, much of the mystery around programming will disappear. You'll start to see code not as an incomprehensible tangle, but as a logical sequence of instructions that you can follow, understand, and eventually write yourself.

4.3 What a Program Actually Is

Let's start with the most fundamental question: what is a program? At its core, a program is simply a list of instructions that tells a computer what to do. Think of it like a recipe, a set of driving directions, or assembly instructions for furniture. Each of these is a sequence of steps designed to achieve a specific goal.

A Recipe Analogy

Consider this simple recipe:

1. Preheat oven to 350°F
2. Mix flour, sugar, and eggs in a bowl
3. Pour mixture into a baking pan
4. Bake for 30 minutes
5. Remove from oven and let cool

This recipe has several important characteristics that programs share. It must be completed in a specific sequential order, meaning each step needs to happen in the correct sequence for the result to work. The instructions are clear, with each step telling you exactly what to do. The recipe also operates on certain assumptions, such as already understanding what it means to "mix" or "pour." Finally, it is goal-oriented, because every step works together toward producing the outcome finished cake.

A computer program works the same way. It's a sequence of instructions that the computer follows, step by step, to accomplish a task.

A Data Analysis Example

Here's what a simple data analysis "recipe" might look like in plain English:

1. Load the survey data from a file
2. Remove any incomplete responses
3. Calculate the average age of respondents
4. Create a histogram showing the age distribution
5. Save the results to a new file

This is essentially what a data analysis program does—it just expresses these instructions in a language the computer can understand.

Programs vs. Applications

It's worth distinguishing between programs (the instructions) and applications (the software you interact with). When you use Excel or Word, you're using an application that someone else programmed. When you write code for data analysis, you're creating your own small program that tells the computer exactly what you want it to do with your data.

4.4 Statements, Expressions, and Execution Order

Now that we understand what a program is conceptually, let's look at how it's actually structured. Programs are built from two main types of components: statements and expressions.

Statements: Commands That Do Things

A statement is a complete instruction that tells the computer to perform an action, much like individual steps in a recipe. Each statement represents a full thought that accomplishes a specific task, such as loading data from a file, calculating a mathematical result, creating a visualization, saving results, or displaying information on the screen. In most programming languages, statements typically appear on separate lines so it is easy to see the sequence of instructions the program will follow.

Expressions: Calculations and Values

An expression is a piece of code that produces a value, similar to the ingredients and measurements in a recipe that supply the raw materials needed to complete each step. Expressions can take many forms, such as mathematical calculations like 2 + 3, text values like "Hello, world!", data lookups that retrieve specific information from a dataset, or function calls that return useful results. These values are then used by statements to perform larger actions within a program.

How They Work Together

Statements often contain expressions. For example, a statement might say "calculate the average of these numbers and store the result," where "calculate the average of these numbers" is an expression that produces a value, and the entire statement stores that value for later use.

Execution Order: The Golden Rule

Execution Order: The Golden Rule in programming is that the computer reads and executes statements in order, from top to bottom, one at a time. Although this may seem simple, it has powerful consequences for how programs behave. The order of instructions matters, meaning that placing steps in the wrong sequence can lead to unexpected or incorrect results. Prerequisites must always come first, because you cannot use something before it has been created or defined. Each step builds on the ones that came before it, allowing later instructions to rely on previously produced results. Finally, the computer never "looks ahead"; it only understands what has already been executed up to that point, so every instruction depends entirely on the program's current state.

A Concrete Example

Imagine these instructions for analyzing survey data:

```
Step 1: Load survey data from file
Step 2: Calculate average age
Step 3: Remove incomplete responses
Step 4: Create age histogram
```

This sequence has a problem—Step 2 tries to calculate the average age before Step 3 removes incomplete responses. This might give you an inaccurate average. The computer will dutifully follow these instructions in order, even though the logic is flawed.

The correct order would be:

```
Step 1: Load survey data from file
Step 2: Remove incomplete responses
Step 3: Calculate average age
Step 4: Create age histogram
```

4.5 Variables as Labeled Values

One of the most important concepts in programming is the idea of variables. Despite the intimidating name, variables are actually quite simple: they're just labels that you attach to values so you can refer to them later.

The Label Analogy

Think of variables like labels on storage containers. If you have a box of holiday decorations, you might put a label on it that says "Christmas Decorations" so you can find it later. The label isn't the decorations themselves but just a way to identify and locate them.

Variables work the same way. When you have a piece of information—like the average age of survey respondents—you can attach a label to it (like `average_age`) so you can refer to it later in your program.

Why Variables Matter

Variables play several essential roles in programming. They provide storage by allowing you to save the results of calculations so you can use them later, and they improve clarity by giving meaningful names to values, making code easier to read and understand. Variables also support reusability, since once a value is stored, it can be used multiple times without needing to be recalculated. Finally, they offer flexibility because the value a variable refers to can be changed as the program runs, allowing programs to adapt and respond to new information or actions.

A Practical Example

Instead of writing:

```
Calculate the average of survey responses
Create a histogram using the average of survey responses
Display "The average age is" followed by the average of survey responses
```

You can write:

```
Calculate the average of survey responses and call it "average_age"
Create a histogram using average_age
Display "The average age is" followed by average_age
```

This is clearer, more efficient, and less error-prone.

Variables Change Over Time

Here's something that confuses many beginners: variables can change what they refer to as a program runs. The label stays the same, but what it points to can change.

For example:

```
Step 1: Let "total" refer to 0
Step 2: Add 5 to total (now total refers to 5)
Step 3: Add 3 to total (now total refers to 8)
Step 4: Display total (shows 8)
```

The variable name `total` stays the same throughout, but its value changes as the program executes.

Common Variable Naming Patterns

Common variable naming patterns focus on making code clear, readable, and easy to understand. Good variable names are descriptive, such as using student_count instead of a vague name like x, so the purpose of the variable is immediately clear. They should also be consistent, meaning that if you choose a style like student_count, you should continue with similar forms such as teacher_count instead of switching to something like num_teachers. Finally, variable names should be readable, so options like average_age are better than shortened or hard-to-interpret versions like avgAge or avg_a.

4.6 Data Types at a Conceptual Level

Just as the physical world contains different kinds of things—numbers, text, images, and sounds—the programming world organizes information into different data types. Understanding data types helps you think clearly about what kind of information you are working with and what kinds of operations make sense to perform on it.

Numbers: The Foundation of Analysis

Numbers are the most familiar data type, but they exist in more than one form. Whole numbers, or integers (such as 1, 2, 100, or −5), are typically used for counting things like numbers of students or survey responses, and they support common mathematical operations such as addition, subtraction, multiplication, and division. Decimal or floating-point numbers (such as 3.14, 2.5, or −0.75) are often used for measurements like height, weight, temperature, or percentages, and they also support mathematical operations while allowing greater precision.

Text: More Than Just Words

Text data, often called "strings," includes any sequence of characters. This might include names such as "John Smith" or "University of California," categories such as "Male," "Female," or "Prefer not to say," and identifiers such as "Student_ID_12345" or "Course_STAT101." Text supports different operations from numbers. You can combine pieces of text, search within text, or change its formatting, but you cannot "add" text in a mathematical sense.

True/False: Logical Data

Boolean data represents yes/no, true/false, or on/off values and is essential for decision-making in programs and analyses. Examples include whether a student graduated, whether a GPA is above a certain value, or whether to include a particular response in an analysis. Boolean values are fundamental to filtering, comparisons, and conditional logic.

Collections: Groups of Related Data

Most real-world data analysis involves working with groups of related information rather than individual values. Lists are ordered sequences of items, such as a list of student ages or a list of course names. Tables, on the other hand, organize data into rows and columns like a spreadsheet, where each row represents one case (such as a student) and each column represents one variable (such as age, major, or GPA).

Why Data Types Matter

Understanding data types is essential because it helps you choose appropriate operations, avoid errors, and think more clearly about your data. You can calculate the average of numbers but not of names, and attempting mathematical operations on text will lead to problems. Knowing what type of data you have guides your analysis choices and helps ensure accuracy.

Data Type Flexibility

It is also important to remember that the same information can sometimes be represented in different ways. Age might appear as a number (22) or as text ("twenty-two"). Survey responses might be stored as descriptive text ("Strongly Agree") or as numerical ratings on a scale. Dates might appear as text ("January 15, 2024") or as special date values. The key is choosing the representation that makes analysis clearer, easier, and more accurate.

4.7 What Happens When Code Runs

Understanding what happens when you execute a program helps demystify the entire programming process. When you "run" code, you are basically instructing the computer to follow your set of instructions step by step, just like following a recipe, until it either completes the task or encounters a problem that stops it.

The Execution Process

When a program runs, the computer begins by reading the first instruction in the code. It then interprets or "understands" what that instruction means and determines what action is required. Next, the computer executes the instruction and performs the requested task. After completing that step, it moves on to the next instruction and repeats the same cycle of reading, understanding, and executing. This continues in order until one of three things happens: the program successfully reaches the end of all instructions, it encounters an error that it cannot handle, or it is intentionally told to stop.

A Step-by-Step Example

Let's trace through a simple data analysis program:

```
Instruction 1: Load data from "survey.csv"
Instruction 2: Store the data in a variable called "survey_data"
Instruction 3: Calculate the average age from survey_data
Instruction 4: Store the result in a variable called "avg_age"
Instruction 5: Display "Average age is:" followed by avg_age
```

When you run this program:

1. Computer loads the CSV file
2. Computer creates a variable called "survey_data" and stores the file contents
3. Computer calculates the average age from the data
4. Computer creates a variable called "avg_age" and stores the calculated average
5. Computer displays the result on screen

The Computer's Perspective

From the computer's perspective, each instruction is completely independent. It doesn't understand that you're analyzing survey data or trying to find an average age. It simply follows each instruction literally and mechanically. This is why precision matters so much in programming. The computer will do exactly what you tell it to do, even if that's not what you meant to tell it to do.

Memory and State

As a program runs, the computer keeps track of several key elements: the variables that exist and what they refer to, the actual data being processed, and its current position in the sequence of instructions. This collection of information is known as the program's "state." The state constantly changes as each instruction is executed, accumulating the information necessary for the program to carry out subsequent steps correctly.

Interactive vs. Batch Execution

There are two main ways programs can run. In batch execution, the entire program runs from start to finish without interruption, much like following a complete recipe from beginning to end. In interactive execution, you can run individual instructions or small groups of instructions, examine the results, and then continue, similar to cooking where you taste and adjust as you go. Most data analysis environments support interactive execution, which makes learning, experimentation, and debugging much easier.

4.8 Why Small Mistakes Can Break Everything

One of the most frustrating aspects of learning programming is that even a tiny error can cause an entire program to fail. Understanding why this happens—and how to think about it—can reduce frustration and improve your debugging skills.

The Precision Requirement

Computers are extremely literal. They follow instructions exactly as written, with no ability to guess what you "probably meant." This precision is both a strength and a weakness. It is a strength because when your instructions are correct, the computer will execute them perfectly and consistently every time. It is a weakness because even small errors prevent the computer from compensating or making reasonable assumptions.

Common Types of Small Mistakes

Small mistakes often include spelling errors, such as creating a variable called student_age but later referring to student_ages; the computer treats these as entirely different items. Order problems can occur if you try to use a variable before creating it or perform operations in the wrong sequence. Type mismatches happen when you attempt mathematical operations on text or text operations on numbers. Punctuation errors, like missing commas or parentheses, can also break code. Additionally, many programming languages are case-sensitive, so StudentAge and studentage are considered different variables.

Why Small Errors Have Big Effects

Think of a program like a chain of dependencies. Each instruction often depends on the results of previous instructions. If one link in the chain breaks, everything that depends on it also breaks.

For example:

```
Step 1: Load survey data → Creates "survey_data"
Step 2: Clean the data → Uses "survey_data", creates "clean_data"
Step 3: Calculate statistics → Uses "clean_data", creates "results"
Step 4: Create visualization → Uses "results"
Step 5: Save report → Uses visualization
```

If Step 1 fails (maybe the file doesn't exist), then Steps 2-5 can't work because they depend on data that was never loaded.

The Error Cascade Effect

Sometimes a single small error can cause multiple error messages, making the problem seem worse than it is. For example, if you misspell a variable name early in your program, every subsequent use of that variable will generate an error message.

Developing Error Tolerance

Dealing with the precision required in programming is easier when you adopt strategies to handle mistakes effectively. First, expect errors are a normal part of programming and not a sign of personal failure. Read error messages carefully, as they often indicate exactly what went wrong and where. When debugging, check one thing at a time by making small, isolated changes and testing them, rather than changing multiple things at once. Using descriptive variable names also helps, making it easier to spot spelling mistakes or inconsistencies. Finally, test your program frequently by running small sections of code to catch errors early before they compound.

The Positive Side of Precision

While a computer's literal-mindedness can be frustrating, it is also what makes programming so powerful. Once you learn to communicate precisely with the computer, you gain the ability to automate complex tasks with perfect consistency, process large amounts of data without human error, create analyses that others can reproduce exactly, and build on your work with confidence. This precision transforms programming into a reliable and scalable tool for solving a wide range of problems.

Modern Help: AI and Error Detection

Modern programming environments and AI tools have made detecting and correcting errors much easier. Features like syntax highlighting use colors and formatting to make mistakes more visible, while auto-completion provides suggestions that help prevent spelling errors. Error detection tools can identify problems before you even run your code, and AI assistance can explain error messages and offer guidance on how to fix them. These tools reduce frustration and make learning and programming more efficient.

4.9 Code Is Read Top-to-Bottom, One Instruction at a Time

As we conclude this chapter, it is important to return to the fundamental principle underlying everything we have discussed: code is read top-to-bottom, one instruction at a time. Although simple, this rule has profound implications for how you should approach programming.

Why This Principle Matters

Understanding that code executes sequentially makes program behavior predictable, allowing you to trace through code and know exactly what will happen. It also aids debugging, as you can work through the program step by step to locate errors. Execution order informs good program design, helping you organize code logically and avoid dependency problems. Additionally, it enhances communication: when reading someone else's code, following it from top to bottom lets you understand their logic clearly.

Mental Model Development

Think of a program as a story that unfolds sequentially, where each line is a sentence building on what came before. Just as you would not expect to understand a story by reading random sentences out of order, you cannot understand a program without following its sequential logic.

Exceptions and Advanced Concepts

While the top-to-bottom rule is fundamental, some advanced programming concepts modify it. Functions are reusable blocks of code that can be called from multiple places, loops repeat instructions multiple times, and conditionals execute instructions only under certain conditions. Even with these structures, the basic principle remains that instructions are executed in a defined order, with these concepts adding controlled structure to the sequence.

Building Your Programming Intuition

As you continue learning programming, keep this principle in mind. When reading code, start at the top and work downward. When writing code, consider the logical sequence of operations. When debugging, trace the execution step by step. And when planning a program, outline the sequence of operations first to ensure clarity, correctness, and efficiency.

4.10 Conclusion

Understanding how code is structured provides the foundation for everything else you'll learn about programming. The mental models we've developed in this chapter—programs as sequences of instructions, variables as labeled values, data types as categories of information, and execution as a step-by-step process—will serve you throughout your programming journey.

In the next chapter, we'll build on these concepts by exploring data as the central object of analysis. We'll see how the structural principles we've learned apply specifically to working with datasets, and how understanding data organization makes analysis more effective and reliable.

Remember that the goal isn't to memorize syntax or specific commands—it's to develop clear mental models of how programming works. These conceptual foundations will make learning specific languages and techniques much easier and more intuitive.

The precision and sequential nature of programming might seem restrictive at first, but they're actually what make programming so powerful. Once you learn to think in terms of clear, sequential instructions, you'll be able to automate complex analyses, ensure reproducible results, and tackle data problems that would be impossible to solve manually.

As you move forward, keep coming back to these fundamental principles. When you encounter new concepts or face challenging problems, ask yourself: What sequence of instructions would solve this? What information do I need at each step? How can I organize this logically? These questions will guide you toward clear, effective solutions.

4.11 Review Questions

1. How does the chapter define a program, and why is the recipe analogy useful for understanding how code works?
2. What does it mean that code is executed "top to bottom, one instruction at a time," and why is this rule so important?
3. What is the difference between a **statement** and an **expression**, and how do they work together in a program?
4. Why does execution order matter in data analysis programs, and what kinds of problems can occur if steps are out of order?
5. What is a variable, and how does the "label" analogy help explain its role in a program?
6. Why can the value of a variable change over time, even though the variable name stays the same?
7. What are data types, and why is it important to understand the difference between numbers, text, logical values, and collections?
8. What happens inside the computer when code runs, step by step?
9. Why can small mistakes—such as spelling errors or type mismatches—cause a program to fail completely?

10. How do modern tools, including IDE features and AI assistance, help programmers detect, understand, and fix errors?

4.12 Ch 4 Lab Understanding How Programs Work

Programming is not about memorizing commands. It's about understanding how a computer reads and executes instructions. Unlike humans, computers do not infer, guess, or fill in missing steps. They follow instructions exactly, literally, and in order. This chapter introduces the foundational ideas that every new programmer must understand:

- Programs run top to bottom
- Variables store information the program can use later
- Execution order matters — a lot
- Data comes in different types, and each type behaves differently

These ideas form the backbone of every program you will ever write.

4.12.1 Demonstration

A useful way to understand program structure is to compare it to a recipe. A recipe works because the steps are written in a logical order. You gather ingredients before mixing them. You heat the pan before cooking. If you reverse the steps, the recipe fails — not because you're a bad cook, but because the order is wrong.

Programs work the same way.

One of the most important ideas in programming is that a computer executes instructions in order, from the first line of a script to the last. It does not skip ahead, fill in missing steps, or guess what you meant. To see why this matters, it helps to compare a program to something familiar: a recipe.

A recipe works because the steps are arranged in a logical sequence. You gather ingredients before mixing them. You mix before cooking. You cook before serving. If you reverse the steps, the recipe fails—not because you don't understand pancakes, but because the order is wrong.

Let's look at a simple R script that behaves like a pancake recipe. As you read it, imagine the computer following the instructions exactly as written, one line at a time.

Step 1: Gathering Ingredients

```
flour_cups <- 2

milk_cups <- 1.5

eggs <- 2
```

```
sugar_spoons <- 3
```

Just as a cook begins by assembling ingredients, a program begins by creating the data it will need later. Each line assigns a value to a variable. These variables act like labeled containers: flour_cups holds the number 2, milk_cups holds 1.5, and so on. At this point, the program has simply stored information—it hasn't done anything with it yet.

Step 2: Checking What We Have

```
print(paste("Flour:", flour_cups, "cups"))
```

```
[1] "Flour: 2 cups"
```

```
print(paste("Milk:", milk_cups, "cups"))
```

```
[1] "Milk: 1.5 cups"
```

```
print(paste("Eggs:", eggs))
```

```
[1] "Eggs: 2"
```

```
print(paste("Sugar:", sugar_spoons, "spoons"))
```

```
[1] "Sugar: 3 spoons"
```

Now that the ingredients exist, the program can display them. Notice that this step depends entirely on Step 1. If the variables had not been created earlier, these print statements would fail. This is the essence of sequential execution: later steps rely on earlier ones.

Step 3: Mixing Ingredients

```
total_wet <- milk_cups + eggs

total_dry <- flour_cups + sugar_spoons
```

Here the program begins to combine information. Just as a cook mixes wet and dry ingredients separately, the program calculates totals by adding the values stored in the earlier variables. Again, the order matters: the program cannot compute total_wet until milk_cups and eggs exist.

Step 4: Estimating Servings

```
servings <- total_wet + total_dry

print(paste("This recipe serves approximately", servings))
```

```
[1] "This recipe serves approximately 8.5"
```

Finally, the program uses the results of the previous step to estimate how many servings the recipe might produce. This is the culmination of the sequence: each step builds on the last, and the final output is only possible because the earlier steps were completed in the correct order.

A computer executes instructions from top to bottom, and it cannot use information that has not yet been created.

If you try to print a variable before assigning it a value, the program will stop with an error. If you rearrange the steps, the logic breaks. The structure of the program is not arbitrary—it reflects the logical dependencies between the tasks.

4.12.1.1 When Order Goes Wrong

To understand just how strict order matters is, it helps to look at what happens when the order is wrong.

Computers do not anticipate, infer, or rearrange instructions. They do not "look ahead" to see what you meant to do. They only know what has already been executed. If a program tries to use information that hasn't been created yet, it stops immediately and reports an error.

For example, consider the following R code.

```
print(paste("We need", total_ingredients, "ingredients total"))

flour <- 2

sugar <- 1

total_ingredients <- flour + sugar
```

At first glance, this might look harmless. But the very first line tries to print the value of total_ingredients—a variable that hasn't been created yet. Because the computer executes instructions strictly from top to bottom, it reaches the print statement before it ever sees the lines that define flour, sugar, or total_ingredients.

The result is an error. Not because the math is wrong, and not because the computer is confused, but because the program violates the fundamental rule of sequential execution: a variable must exist before it can be used.

The corrected version simply places the steps in a logical sequence:

```
flour <- 2

sugar <- 1
```

```
total_ingredients <- flour + sugar

print(paste("We need", total_ingredients, "ingredients total"))
```

```
[1] "We need 3 ingredients total"
```

Now the program works exactly as intended. The variables are created first, the calculation is performed second, and the result is printed last. Nothing else changed—only the order.

4.12.1.2 Understanding Data Types

Up to this point, we have focused on the structure of programs and the importance of execution order. But there is another foundational idea that shapes everything a program can do: data types.

Every value in a program has a type, and that type determines what operations are possible. Humans are flexible—we can add "2" and "2" whether they are written as numbers, words, or tally marks. Computers are not. They treat numbers, text, logical values, and collections as fundamentally different kinds of information.

To see how this works in practice, let's explore the major data types you will encounter in R and what you can do with each of them.

Numbers are the most straightforward data type. They represent quantities, measurements, and anything you can perform arithmetic on.

```
height_inches <- 68

weight_pounds <- 150

bmi <- (weight_pounds / (height_inches^2)) * 703

print(paste("BMI calculation:", bmi))
```

```
[1] "BMI calculation: 22.8049307958477"
```

Here, the computer treats height_inches and weight_pounds as numeric values. Because they are numbers, R can square them, divide them, and use them in formulas. If these values were stored as text, none of these operations would work.

Text—also called a string—represents names, labels, and other human-readable information. Text is not meant for math; it is meant for communication.

```
first_name <- "John"
```

```
last_name <- "Smith"

full_name <- paste(first_name, last_name)

print(paste("Full name:", full_name))
```

```
[1] "Full name: John Smith"
```

The paste() function combines pieces of text, much like joining words in a sentence. This is a different kind of "combining" than adding numbers; the computer understands that text is something to be assembled, not calculated.

Boolean values represent simple logical states: TRUE or FALSE. These values are essential for decision-making in programs.

```
is_adult <- TRUE

is_student <- FALSE

can_vote <- is_adult

print(paste("Can vote:", can_vote))
```

```
[1] "Can vote: TRUE"
```

Booleans allow programs to answer yes/no questions and make choices. Later, when we introduce conditional statements, these values will become the backbone of program logic.

Often, we need to work with more than one value at a time. A vector is a collection of values of the same type—like a list of test scores.

```
test_scores <- c(85, 92, 78, 96, 88)

average_score <- mean(test_scores)

print(paste("Average test score:", average_score))
```

```
[1] "Average test score: 87.8"
```

Because test_scores is a numeric vector, R can apply mathematical functions like mean() to the entire collection at once. This is one of the strengths of R: it is designed to work efficiently with groups of data.

Because each data type behaves differently, using the wrong operation on the wrong type leads to errors. For example:

```
name <- "Alice"

# mean(name) # Uncomment to show error

print("You can't calculate the average of a name!")
```

```
[1] "You can't calculate the average of a name!"
```

The computer cannot compute the "average" of a word because text has no numerical meaning. This kind of mismatch is one of the most common sources of beginner errors—and one of the easiest to fix once you understand data types.

Understanding data types is not just about avoiding errors. It is about learning how the computer interprets information. When you know the type of a value, you can predict:

- what operations are allowed
- what functions will work
- how the computer will treat the value
- what kinds of errors you might encounter

Data types are the grammar of programming. Just as sentences must follow grammatical rules to make sense, programs must use data in ways that match its type.

4.12.1.3 How AI Supports Learning About Program Structure

As you begin writing and reading programs, one of the most challenging parts is making sense of what each line of code is doing and why the order matters. Modern programming environments increasingly include AI assistants that can help you explore code more confidently. These tools do not replace learning; instead, they act as a guide that helps you understand the logic behind the program.

AI assistants are especially useful in the early stages of learning because they can explain unfamiliar functions, clarify confusing lines, and help you reason about errors. In other words, they reinforce the same foundational ideas introduced in this lab: programs run in order, variables must exist before they are used, and data types determine what operations are possible.

To see how AI can support this process, consider the following short script:

```
student_ages <- c(18, 19, 20, 18, 21, 19, 20)

student_names <- c("Alice", "Bob", "Carol", "David", "Eve", "Frank",
 ↪  "Grace")

average_age <- mean(student_ages)
```

```
print(paste("Average student age:", average_age))
```

```
[1] "Average student age: 19.2857142857143"
```

```
total_students <- length(student_names)

print(paste("Total students:", total_students))
```

```
[1] "Total students: 7"
```

A beginner might wonder:

- What does mean() actually do?
- Why do we use c() to create a vector?
- What does length() count?
- How do I know whether my variable names are clear?
- What happens if I misspell a variable or use the wrong data type?

An AI assistant can answer these questions directly in the context of the code you are looking at. For example, you can highlight mean(student_ages) and ask, "Explain what this line does." You can ask the assistant to walk through the script line by line, or to describe why an error occurred if you intentionally break the code.

This kind of immediate, contextual explanation helps you build intuition about how programs work. When the assistant explains that mean() only works on numeric data, it reinforces your understanding of data types. When it points out that a variable is being used before it is defined, it reinforces the importance of execution order. When it suggests clearer variable names, it models good programming style.

AI does not replace the need to think through a program yourself. Instead, it acts as a learning companion that helps you check your understanding, explore alternatives, and get unstuck when something doesn't make sense. As you continue learning, AI becomes one more tool—alongside examples, diagrams, and experimentation—that helps you understand how programs behave and why structure matters.

4.12.2 Practice

Directions: Complete each task in R. Run every line of code and observe what happens. Fix errors when they occur.

1. Create three variables representing information about a student (for example: age, GPA, credits). Print each variable on its own line.

2. Write code that calculates a student's total credits using the following lines, in this order:

```
total_credits <- fall + spring

fall <- 12

spring <- 15
```

Run the code. Then reorder the lines so the script runs without error.

3. Create two numeric variables and compute a result using them (any calculation you choose). Then change one of the variables to text (for example, "20"). Run the script again and observe what happens.

4. Create a vector of five ages. Print the vector. Then use mean() to print the average age. Then use length() to print how many ages are in the vector.

5. Create a vector of five course names. Print the vector. Then try running mean() on this vector. Observe the error and add a comment in your script explaining why it fails.

6. Write a script that creates two variables, then creates a third variable that depends on the first two, and then prints all three variables. Run the script. Next, move the print line to the top of the script so it runs before the variables are created. Run it again and observe the error.

7. Create a vector of exam scores. Use c() to add one more score to the vector. Print the updated vector. Then use mean() to print the new average score.

8. Create a Boolean variable called passed that is TRUE if a score is greater than or equal to 70 and FALSE otherwise. Print the value of passed.

9. Create a vector of numbers. Use indexing to print the first value in the vector. Then print the last value in the vector. Then print the third value in the vector.

10. Write a script that intentionally misspells a variable name. Run the script and read the error message. Then correct the spelling and run it again.

11. Create a vector of ages and a vector of names. Use length() to confirm that both vectors have the same length. Then remove one name from the names vector. Run length() again on both vectors and observe the difference. Try printing the ages and names together and observe what happens.

12. Create a numeric vector. Change one element of the vector to text (for example, "18"). Then run mean() on the vector and observe what happens. Add a comment in your script explaining the result.

13. Write a short script that calculates a simple statistic (for example, the sum, average,

or difference of some numbers). Then use an AI assistant to ask one question about a specific line in your script (for example, "What does this line do?"). In your R script, add a comment that describes the question you asked and the answer you received.

14. Break your own code on purpose by writing a script that uses a variable before defining it, mixes text and numbers in a calculation, and misspells a function name. Run the script and read each error message. Then add comments in your script explaining what each error means.

15. Take any script you wrote in this lab and ask an AI assistant to suggest clearer variable names or a better organization of the code. Make at least one change based on the suggestion. Add a comment in your script summarizing what you changed.

Chapter 5

Data as the Central Object

5.1 Learning Outcomes

5-1: Explain what a computer program is and describe how code functions as a sequence of instructions executed from top to bottom.

5-2: Distinguish between statements and expressions and explain how execution order affects program behavior and results.

5-3: Explain the purpose of variables as labeled values and describe how variable values change over the course of program execution.

5-4: Identify and describe major conceptual data types, including numbers, text, logical values, and collections, and explain why data types matter in data analysis.

5-5: Describe what happens when code runs, explain why small errors can cause programs to fail, and recognize how modern tools and AI assistance support debugging and learning.

5.2 Introduction

If you've made it through the previous chapters, you now understand what programming is, why it's useful for data analysis, how to organize your workspace, and how code is structured. But here's where we make a crucial shift in perspective: in data analysis, programming isn't really about programming at all. It's about data.

This might seem like an obvious statement, but it represents a fundamental change in how you should think about what you're doing when you write code for data analysis. Instead of thinking "I need to learn programming commands," start thinking "I need to understand my data and figure out how to transform it to answer my questions."

This chapter is about making that mental shift from command-focused thinking to data-focused thinking. We'll explore what data actually looks like in the programming world, understand why most data analysis revolves around tables, and learn to think in terms of data transformations rather than programming steps. Most importantly, we'll see how this perspective makes programming for data analysis much more intuitive and purposeful.

The key insight of this chapter is that most programming for data analysis is really data manipulation. Once you understand this, you'll stop seeing code as mysterious commands and start seeing it as a toolkit for reshaping, filtering, summarizing, and exploring your data.

5.3 What Tabular Data Really Is

When most people think about data, they think about numbers in spreadsheets. This intuition is actually quite accurate—the vast majority of data analysis does indeed work with information organized in tables. But to work effectively with data in programming environments, we need to understand what these tables really represent and why they're so fundamental to analytical thinking.

The Spreadsheet Connection

If you've ever used Excel or Google Sheets, you already understand the basic idea of tabular data. A table organizes information into rows and columns, where each row represents a single case, observation, or record, each column represents a variable, characteristic, or measurement, and each cell contains one piece of information about one case. This structure isn't arbitrary; it mirrors the way we naturally think about collecting and organizing information.

A Concrete Example: Student Survey Data

Imagine you've conducted a survey of 100 students about their study habits. Your data might look like this:

Student_ID	Age	Major	Study_Hours	GPA	Graduated
001	20	Biology	15	3.2	FALSE
002	22	Psychology	20	3.8	TRUE
003	19	Mathematics	25	3.9	FALSE
004	21	Biology	12	2.9	FALSE

Each row tells the complete story of a single student, while each column shows one characteristic across all students. This organization makes it easy to ask questions such as: What is the average GPA of Biology majors? Do students who study more hours have higher GPAs? How many students have graduated?

Why Tables Work So Well

Tables are powerful because they match the way we naturally organize information. They provide consistency, since every row has the same structure with the same variables measured in the same way. They allow comparability, because all rows follow the same pattern, making it easy to compare across cases. They offer flexibility, letting you examine data row by row to focus on individual cases or column by column to focus on variables. And they scale effortlessly—the same principles work whether you have ten rows or ten million.

Beyond Simple Tables

While the basic table structure is fundamental, real-world data can be more complex. Related information might be split across multiple tables, some cells may contain lists or other nested data, and time-series data collected over time or hierarchical data with natural groupings require special organization. Even so, these more complex structures are usually built on the same basic table concept.

5.4 Rows, Columns, and Observations

Understanding the relationship between rows, columns, and observations is crucial for thinking clearly about data analysis. This isn't just a technical detail—it's a fundamental way of organizing your analytical thinking.

Rows: The Unit of Analysis

Each row in a data table represents the unit of analysis—the "thing" you are studying. This could be individual people in survey research, companies in business analysis, countries in comparative studies, time periods in longitudinal analysis, or experimental trials in scientific research. The unit of analysis determines the questions you can ask and the conclusions you can draw. For example, if each row represents a student, you can examine student-level characteristics; if each row represents a school, you can study patterns at the school level.

Columns: Variables and Measurements

Each column in a data table represents a variable—a characteristic or measurement recorded for each unit of analysis. Variables come in different types. Identifier variables provide unique labels for each row, such as Student_ID or Company_Name. Demographic variables capture basic characteristics like age, gender, or location. Behavioral variables track actions or choices, such as study hours or purchase amounts. Outcome variables represent results or dependent measures, like GPA or sales revenue. Categorical variables divide data into groups or categories, such as major, department, or treatment group.

The Observation Concept

An observation is the complete set of information about a single unit of analysis—essentially, one full row in a data table. Each observation should be complete, containing all the variables being measured; independent, representing a separate case that does not depend on other rows; and consistent, measured using the same methods and definitions as all other observations.

A Practical Example: Course Evaluation Data

Consider data from course evaluations:

Course_ID	Instructor	Department	Enrollment	Avg_Rating	Semester
STAT101	Dr. Smith	Statistics	45	4.2	Fall2024
BIOL200	Dr. Jones	Biology	32	3.8	Fall2024
PSYC150	Dr. Brown	Psychology	28	4.5	Fall2024

For example, if the unit of analysis is individual courses, each row (observation) represents one course offering, and each column (variable) records a course characteristic such as instructor, enrollment, or rating. This structure makes it easy to ask questions like: "Do smaller classes receive higher ratings?" or "Which departments offer the highest-rated courses?"

Common Organizational Mistakes

Common organizational mistakes include mixing units of analysis, such as having some rows represent students and others represent schools in the same table; duplicate observations, where the same case appears multiple times without reason; collecting data at the wrong level for your research question; and inconsistent variables, where the same concept is measured differently across observations.

5.5 Data Frames in R and Python

Now that we understand what tabular data represents conceptually, let's see how programming languages handle this structure. Both R and Python have specific ways of working with tabular data that reflect the principles we've discussed.

R's Data Frame Approach

In R, tabular data is stored in objects called "data frames." Think of a data frame as R's version of a spreadsheet specifically designed to handle the row-and-column structure that's fundamental to data analysis.

Here's what a simple data frame creation might look like in R:

```
# Create a data frame
student_data <- data.frame(
  student_id = c(1, 2, 3, 4),
  age = c(20, 22, 19, 21),
  major = c("Biology", "Psychology", "Math", "Biology"),
  gpa = c(3.2, 3.8, 3.9, 2.9)
)
```

R's data frames are special because they allow mixed data types, so each column can hold numbers, text, or logical values. Columns are named, letting you refer to variables by name rather than by position. Each row maintains its integrity as a complete observation, and R treats the data frame as a statistical object, providing built-in tools for analysis.

Python's DataFrame Approach

Python handles tabular data through the pandas library, which provides DataFrame objects that work similarly to R's data frames:

```
import pandas as pd

# Create a DataFrame
student_data = pd.DataFrame({
```

```
    'student_id': [1, 2, 3, 4],
    'age': [20, 22, 19, 21],
    'major': ['Biology', 'Psychology', 'Math', 'Biology'],
    'gpa': [3.2, 3.8, 3.9, 2.9]
})
```

Both approaches accomplish the same goal: they create a structured way to store and work with tabular data that preserves the relationship between rows and columns.

Why This Structure Matters

This structure matters because data frames are designed to support the analytical workflow. You can easily load data from CSV files, databases, or other sources, explore it through summaries and structural checks, and filter rows based on conditions. You can select specific variables, transform data by creating new variables or recoding existing ones, and aggregate information. Finally, you can apply statistical methods that understand the table's structure, making analysis more straightforward and reliable.

What makes data frames powerful isn't just that they store data—it's that they preserve the meaning and relationships in your data. When you perform operations on a data frame, the programming language understands that you're working with structured, meaningful information, not just random numbers and text.

5.6 Why Most Data Analysis Starts with Tables

Understanding why tabular data is central to data analysis helps explain why data manipulation is such a core skill. It's not because tables are the only way to store information, but because they are the most effective way to organize information for analytical thinking. Most data analysis follows a predictable workflow: collecting information about cases and variables, organizing it into a structured format, cleaning and preparing the data, exploring patterns and relationships, applying statistical methods, and communicating findings. Tables support every step of this workflow by providing a consistent, flexible structure.

They also enable comparison, which is the heart of most analytical questions. When you ask "Do students who study more have higher GPAs?" you're comparing study hours across different levels of academic performance. Tables make these comparisons natural and systematic.

The Analysis Pipeline

Most data analysis projects follow a similar pattern:

1. **Data Collection**: Gathering information about your units of analysis
2. **Data Organization**: Structuring information into tables with clear rows and columns

3. **Data Cleaning**: Handling missing values, correcting errors, and standardizing formats
4. **Data Exploration**: Examining patterns, distributions, and relationships
5. **Data Analysis**: Applying statistical methods to answer research questions
6. **Data Communication**: Presenting findings through visualizations and reports

Tables support each of these steps because they provide a consistent framework for organizing and manipulating information.

Why Tables Beat Other Formats

While data can be stored in many formats—lists, hierarchical structures, networks, or unstructured text—tables have unique advantages for analysis. They enforce consistency by requiring the same variables for each observation, support comparison by organizing similar information in columns, enable aggregation by grouping rows with similar characteristics, and facilitate visualization by providing clear mappings between variables and visual elements.

5.7 Data Manipulation as the Core Skill

Once you understand that data analysis is fundamentally about working with tables, you can see why data manipulation becomes such a central skill. Most of what you do in data analysis involves transforming tables: filtering rows, selecting columns, creating new variables, summarizing information, and combining datasets.

The Five Core Operations

Almost all data manipulation can be broken down into five fundamental operations:

1. **Filter**: Select specific rows based on conditions
2. **Select**: Choose specific columns or variables
3. **Mutate**: Create new variables or modify existing ones
4. **Summarize**: Calculate statistics across groups of observations
5. **Arrange**: Sort rows based on variable values

These operations can be combined in countless ways to answer analytical questions.

A Practical Example

Suppose you want to answer: "What is the average GPA of Biology majors who study more than 15 hours per week?"

This question involves several data manipulation steps:

1. **Filter** to Biology majors: Keep only rows where Major = "Biology"
2. **Filter** to high study hours: Keep only rows where Study_Hours > 15
3. **Summarize**: Calculate the mean of the GPA variable

The power of thinking in terms of data manipulation is that complex questions become sequences of simple, logical steps.

Beyond Basic Operations

While the five core operations handle most situations, real data analysis often requires additional manipulations:

- **Joining**: Combining information from multiple tables
- **Reshaping**: Converting between wide and long formats
- **Grouping**: Performing operations within subsets of data
- **Handling Missing Data**: Dealing with incomplete observations

5.8 Thinking in Terms of Data Transformations

The most important mental shift for effective data analysis is learning to think in terms of data transformations rather than programming commands. Instead of asking "What code do I need to write?" ask "How do I need to transform my data to answer this question?"

The Transformation Mindset

When you approach data analysis with a transformation mindset, you focus on the logical flow of data manipulation rather than the specific syntax of programming languages. This approach has several advantages: it makes your analysis more systematic and reproducible, helps you break complex problems into manageable steps, makes it easier to communicate your approach to others, and allows you to work effectively across different programming languages and tools.

From Questions to Transformations

Every analytical question can be translated into a series of data transformations. Here are some examples:

- "Which students have the highest GPAs?" → Arrange data by GPA in descending order, then select the top rows
- "How does average study time vary by major?" → Group by major, then summarize study hours with mean
- "Are there differences in graduation rates between majors?" → Group by major, then calculate the proportion of graduated students

Planning Your Analysis

Before writing any code, sketch out the transformations you need:

1. **Start with your question**: What do you want to know?
2. **Identify your target**: What should the final result look like?
3. **Map the steps**: What transformations will get you from raw data to the answer?

4. **Consider the order**: In what sequence should these transformations happen?

This planning process makes the actual coding much more straightforward because you have a clear roadmap to follow.

5.9 Data Types and Their Analytical Implications

Understanding data types isn't just a technical requirement—it's fundamental to thinking clearly about what kinds of analysis make sense with your data. Different types of data support different operations and lead to different insights.

Numerical Data: The Foundation of Quantitative Analysis

Numerical data supports mathematical operations and statistical analysis. With numerical variables, you can calculate means, medians, and standard deviations, create histograms and scatter plots, perform correlation analysis, and apply regression models. However, not all numbers are the same analytically. Count data (like number of students) behaves differently from continuous measurements (like GPA), and understanding these distinctions helps you choose appropriate analytical methods.

Categorical Data: Groups and Classifications

Categorical data divides observations into groups or categories. This type of data supports different operations: you can count frequencies within categories, calculate proportions and percentages, create bar charts and pie charts, and perform chi-square tests. Categorical data is essential for comparing groups and understanding how outcomes vary across different classifications.

Logical Data: Yes/No Decisions

Logical (boolean) data represents binary choices or conditions. This data type is crucial for filtering operations, conditional analysis, and creating indicator variables. Logical data often emerges from comparisons (Is GPA > 3.5?) and becomes the basis for subsetting and grouping operations.

Text Data: Beyond Simple Categories

Text data can contain rich information but requires special handling. While you can't perform mathematical operations on text, you can search for patterns, extract information, categorize content, and convert text to other data types when appropriate.

Mixed Data Types in Practice

Real datasets typically contain multiple data types, and understanding how they interact is crucial for effective analysis. For example, you might use categorical data to group observations, numerical data to calculate statistics within groups, and logical data to filter the results.

5.10 Conclusion

Understanding data as the central object of analysis transforms how you approach programming for data analysis. Instead of focusing on learning programming commands, you focus on understanding your data structure and the transformations needed to answer your questions. Tables provide the fundamental organizing principle for most data analysis, with rows representing observations and columns representing variables. The core skills of data analysis—filtering, selecting, creating variables, summarizing, and arranging—are really data manipulation skills that work the same way regardless of the programming language you use.

This data-centric perspective makes programming more intuitive and purposeful. When you understand that code is simply a tool for transforming data, you can focus on the logical flow of analysis rather than getting lost in syntax details. Combined with AI assistance, this approach allows you to work effectively with data from day one, building your analytical thinking skills while the AI handles the technical implementation details.

5.11 Review Questions

1. How does thinking about programming as "data manipulation" change your approach to learning code for data analysis?
2. What makes tabular data so fundamental to data analysis, and why do most analytical workflows start with tables?
3. What is the relationship between rows, columns, and observations in a data table, and why does this structure matter for analysis?
4. How do data frames in R and Python preserve the meaning and relationships in your data beyond just storing numbers and text?
5. What are the five core data manipulation operations, and how do they combine to answer analytical questions?
6. How do you translate an analytical question into a series of data transformations?
7. Why is it important to understand different data types (numerical, categorical, logical, text) for data analysis?
8. What advantages does thinking in terms of data transformations provide over focusing on programming syntax?
9. How does the unit of analysis (what each row represents) determine the kinds of questions you can ask about your data?
10. Why does the chapter argue that "programming for data analysis is really data manipulation"?

5.12 Ch 5 Lab Data as the Central Object

This lab accompanies Chapter 5 and focuses on understanding data as the central object in programming for data analysis. You'll learn to think in terms of data transformations rather than programming commands, understand tabular data structures, and practice the fundamental operations that form the basis of most data analysis work.

5.12.1 Demonstration

5.12.1.1 Understanding Tabular Data Structure

Most real-world data analysis is built on a single, powerful idea: information is organized in tables. A table is more than a convenient layout—it is a structured way of representing data so that each piece of information has a clear meaning and a predictable place.

In a tabular dataset, each row represents one complete observation, and each column represents one variable describing those observations. This structure allows us to compare individuals, summarize patterns, and perform analysis systematically. Whether you are working in R, Python, SQL, or a spreadsheet, this same idea appears everywhere.

To see how this works in practice, let's build a small dataset of students and examine its structure in both R and Python.

R Approach

In this example, the dataset contains five students. Each row corresponds to one student, and each column describes a characteristic of those students—such as age, major, GPA, or weekly study hours. When you print the dataset, you can see the entire table at once. When you print a single row, you see one complete observation. When you print a single column, you see one variable measured across all students.

```
# ============================================
# Demo 1: Tabular Data Structure (R)
# Understanding rows, columns, and observations
# ============================================

# Create a simple student dataset
student_data <- data.frame(
  student_id = c(1001, 1002, 1003, 1004, 1005),
  age = c(20, 22, 19, 21, 20),
  major = c("Biology", "Psychology", "Math", "Biology", "Psychology"),
  gpa = c(3.2, 3.8, 3.9, 2.9, 3.5),
  study_hours = c(15, 25, 30, 12, 18)
)

# Examine the structure
print("Student Dataset:")
```

```
[1] "Student Dataset:"
```

```r
print(student_data)
```

```
  student_id age      major gpa study_hours
1       1001  20    Biology 3.2          15
2       1002  22 Psychology 3.8          25
3       1003  19       Math 3.9          30
4       1004  21    Biology 2.9          12
5       1005  20 Psychology 3.5          18
```

```r
print("Dataset dimensions:")
```

```
[1] "Dataset dimensions:"
```

```r
print(paste("Rows (observations):", nrow(student_data)))
```

```
[1] "Rows (observations): 5"
```

```r
print(paste("Columns (variables):", ncol(student_data)))
```

```
[1] "Columns (variables): 5"
```

```r
# Each row is one complete observation (one student)
print("First student (complete observation):")
```

```
[1] "First student (complete observation):"
```

```r
print(student_data[1, ])
```

```
  student_id age   major gpa study_hours
1       1001  20 Biology 3.2          15
```

```r
# Each column is one variable across all observations
print("All GPAs (one variable):")
```

```
[1] "All GPAs (one variable):"
```

```r
print(student_data$gpa)
```

```
[1] 3.2 3.8 3.9 2.9 3.5
```

Python Approach

Python's pandas library uses the same conceptual structure as R's data frames. The syntax is different, but the underlying ideas are identical. Rows represent individual students. Columns represent variables describing those students. This consistency across languages is one of the reasons tabular data is so central to data analysis.

```
# ============================================
# Demo 1: Tabular Data Structure (Python)
# Understanding rows, columns, and observations
# ============================================

import pandas as pd

# Create a simple student dataset
student_data = pd.DataFrame({
    'student_id': [1001, 1002, 1003, 1004, 1005],
    'age': [20, 22, 19, 21, 20],
    'major': ['Biology', 'Psychology', 'Math', 'Biology',
     ↪ 'Psychology'],
    'gpa': [3.2, 3.8, 3.9, 2.9, 3.5],
    'study_hours': [15, 25, 30, 12, 18]
})

# Examine the structure
print("Student Dataset:")
```

```
Student Dataset:
```

```
print(student_data)
```

```
   student_id  age       major  gpa  study_hours
0        1001   20     Biology  3.2           15
1        1002   22  Psychology  3.8           25
2        1003   19        Math  3.9           30
3        1004   21     Biology  2.9           12
4        1005   20  Psychology  3.5           18
```

```
print("Dataset dimensions:")
```

```
Dataset dimensions:
```

```
print(f"Rows (observations): {len(student_data)}")
```

```
Rows (observations): 5
```

```
print(f"Columns (variables): {len(student_data.columns)}")
```

```
Columns (variables): 5
```

```
# Each row is one complete observation (one student)
print("First student (complete observation):")
```

```
First student (complete observation):
```

```
print(student_data.iloc[0])
```

```
student_id        1001
age                 20
major          Biology
gpa                3.2
study_hours         15
Name: 0, dtype: object
```

```
# Each column is one variable across all observations
print("All GPAs (one variable):")
```

```
All GPAs (one variable):
```

```
print(student_data['gpa'])
```

```
0    3.2
1    3.8
2    3.9
3    2.9
4    3.5
Name: gpa, dtype: float64
```

A tabular dataset gives you a predictable way to work with information. When each row is one observation and each column is one variable, you can:

- compare individuals
- summarize patterns
- calculate statistics
- filter or group data
- visualize relationships

This structure is the foundation for everything from simple summaries to advanced machine learning models. Once you understand how rows and columns represent information, you can work confidently in any data analysis environment.

5.12.1.2 Data Frames as Programming Objects

Once you understand that tabular data is organized into rows and columns, the next step is to see how programming languages represent this structure internally. In both R and Python, a data frame is not just a table you print to the screen. It is a programming object designed specifically to store tabular data while preserving the meaning of that structure.

A data frame knows how many rows and columns it has. It knows the names of its variables. It knows the data type of each column. It even knows how to summarize itself. This is what makes data frames powerful: they carry both the data and the information needed to analyze it.

Below, we examine how R and Python treat data frames as structured objects.

R Approach

In R, the str() function reveals the internal structure of the data frame: how many rows it contains, how many variables it stores, and the data type of each variable. The names() function lists the column names, and sapply(…, class) shows the type of data stored in each column. Because data frames preserve the relationship between rows and columns, functions like summary() can automatically compute meaningful statistics for each variable.

```
# ============================================
# Demo 2: Data Frames as Programming Objects (R)
# How programming languages handle tabular data
# ============================================

# Examine data frame properties
print("Data frame structure:")
```

```
[1] "Data frame structure:"
```

```
str(student_data)
```

```
'data.frame':   5 obs. of  5 variables:
 $ student_id : num  1001 1002 1003 1004 1005
 $ age        : num  20 22 19 21 20
 $ major      : chr  "Biology" "Psychology" "Math" "Biology" ...
 $ gpa        : num  3.2 3.8 3.9 2.9 3.5
 $ study_hours: num  15 25 30 12 18
```

```
print("Variable names:")
```

```
[1] "Variable names:"
```

```
names(student_data)
```

```
[1] "student_id"  "age"         "major"       "gpa"         "study_hours"
```

```
print("Data types in each column:")
```

```
[1] "Data types in each column:"
```

```
sapply(student_data, class)
```

```
 student_id         age       major         gpa study_hours 
  "numeric"   "numeric" "character"   "numeric"   "numeric" 
```

```
# Data frames preserve relationships
print("Summary statistics:")
```

```
[1] "Summary statistics:"
```

```
summary(student_data[,1:4])
```

```
   student_id        age           major                gpa       
 Min.   :1001   Min.   :19.0   Length:5           Min.   :2.90  
 1st Qu.:1002   1st Qu.:20.0   Class :character   1st Qu.:3.20  
 Median :1003   Median :20.0   Mode  :character   Median :3.50  
 Mean   :1003   Mean   :20.4                      Mean   :3.46  
 3rd Qu.:1004   3rd Qu.:21.0                      3rd Qu.:3.80  
 Max.   :1005   Max.   :22.0                      Max.   :3.90  
```

```
summary(student_data[,5])
```

```
   Min. 1st Qu.  Median    Mean 3rd Qu.    Max. 
     12      15      18      20      25      30 
```

Python Approach

Python's pandas library provides similar tools. The info() method displays the structure of the DataFrame, including row count, column count, and data types. The columns attribute lists the variable names, and dtypes shows the type of each column. Like R, pandas understands that each column represents a variable, so describe() automatically generates summary statistics for all numeric columns.

```
# ============================================
# Demo 2: Data Frames as Programming Objects (Python)
# How programming languages handle tabular data
# ============================================

# Examine DataFrame properties
print("DataFrame structure:")
```

```
DataFrame structure:
```

```
print(student_data.info())
```

```
<class 'pandas.DataFrame'>
RangeIndex: 5 entries, 0 to 4
```

```
Data columns (total 5 columns):
 #   Column       Non-Null Count  Dtype
---  ------       --------------  -----
 0   student_id   5 non-null      int64
 1   age          5 non-null      int64
 2   major        5 non-null      str
 3   gpa          5 non-null      float64
 4   study_hours  5 non-null      int64
dtypes: float64(1), int64(3), str(1)
memory usage: 332.0 bytes
None
```

```
print("Variable names:")
```

```
Variable names:
```

```
print(student_data.columns.tolist())
```

```
['student_id', 'age', 'major', 'gpa', 'study_hours']
```

```
print("Data types in each column:")
```

```
Data types in each column:
```

```
print(student_data.dtypes)
```

```
student_id       int64
age              int64
major              str
gpa            float64
study_hours      int64
dtype: object
```

```
# DataFrames preserve relationships
print("Summary statistics:")
```

```
Summary statistics:
```

```
print(student_data.describe())
```

```
        student_id        age       gpa  study_hours
count     5.000000   5.000000  5.000000     5.000000
mean   1003.000000  20.400000  3.460000    20.000000
std       1.581139   1.140175  0.415933     7.382412
min    1001.000000  19.000000  2.900000    12.000000
25%    1002.000000  20.000000  3.200000    15.000000
```

```
50%     1003.000000  20.000000  3.500000    18.000000
75%     1004.000000  21.000000  3.800000    25.000000
max     1005.000000  22.000000  3.900000    30.000000
```

A data frame is more than a container for numbers and text. It is a structured object that preserves the analytical meaning of the data:

- each row remains a complete observation
- each column remains a variable
- each variable keeps its own data type
- the relationships between rows and columns stay intact

Because of this structure, both R and Python can provide built-in tools for summarizing, inspecting, and analyzing tabular data. Although the syntax differs between languages, the underlying concept is the same: a data frame is the central object for working with structured data.

5.12.1.3 Basic Data Manipulation Operations

Once you understand how data frames store tabular data, the next step is learning how to work with that data. Most data analysis—regardless of the language or tool—relies on a small set of core operations. These operations allow you to extract the rows you need, choose the variables you want to work with, create new variables, sort the data, and compute summaries.

Although different programming languages use different syntax, the underlying ideas are the same. In this section, we explore the five fundamental operations that appear in nearly every data analysis workflow: filter, select, mutate, arrange, and summarize. These operations form the backbone of data manipulation in both R and Python.

R Approach

In R, each operation works directly on the data frame. Filtering extracts only the rows that meet a condition. Selecting chooses specific columns. Mutating adds new variables derived from existing ones. Arranging sorts the data based on one or more variables. Summarizing computes aggregate statistics, such as counts or averages, often grouped by a category like major. These operations can be combined to answer increasingly complex questions.

```r
# ============================================
# Demo 3: Core Data Manipulation Operations (R)
# The five fundamental operations
# ============================================

print("=== FILTER: Select rows that meet criteria ===")
```

```
[1] "=== FILTER: Select rows that meet criteria ==="
```

```
# Find students with GPA > 3.5
high_gpa <- student_data[student_data$gpa > 3.5, ]
print("High GPA students:")
```

```
[1] "High GPA students:"
```

```
print(high_gpa)
```

```
  student_id age      major gpa study_hours
2       1002  22 Psychology 3.8          25
3       1003  19       Math 3.9          30
```

```
print("=== SELECT: Choose specific columns ===")
```

```
[1] "=== SELECT: Choose specific columns ==="
```

```
# Get just ID, major, and GPA
basic_info <- student_data[, c("student_id", "major", "gpa")]
print("Basic student info:")
```

```
[1] "Basic student info:"
```

```
print(basic_info)
```

```
  student_id      major gpa
1       1001    Biology 3.2
2       1002 Psychology 3.8
3       1003       Math 3.9
4       1004    Biology 2.9
5       1005 Psychology 3.5
```

```
print("=== MUTATE: Create new variables ===")
```

```
[1] "=== MUTATE: Create new variables ==="
```

```
# Create a study category variable
student_data$study_category <- ifelse(student_data$study_hours > 20,
 ↪  "High", "Moderate")
print("Data with new variable:")
```

```
[1] "Data with new variable:"
```

```
print(student_data[, c("student_id", "study_hours", "study_category")])
```

```
  student_id study_hours study_category
1       1001          15       Moderate
```

```
2        1002          25          High
3        1003          30          High
4        1004          12      Moderate
5        1005          18      Moderate
```

```
print("=== ARRANGE: Sort data ===")
```

```
[1] "=== ARRANGE: Sort data ==="
```

```
# Sort by GPA (highest first)
sorted_data <- student_data[order(-student_data$gpa), ]
print("Students sorted by GPA:")
```

```
[1] "Students sorted by GPA:"
```

```
print(sorted_data[, c("student_id", "major", "gpa")])
```

```
  student_id      major gpa
3       1003       Math 3.9
2       1002 Psychology 3.8
5       1005 Psychology 3.5
1       1001    Biology 3.2
4       1004    Biology 2.9
```

```
print("=== SUMMARIZE: Calculate aggregate statistics ===")
```

```
[1] "=== SUMMARIZE: Calculate aggregate statistics ==="
```

```
# Calculate averages by major

major_summary <- aggregate(gpa ~ major, data = student_data,
                          FUN = function(x) c(count = length(x), avg =
                           ↪  round(mean(x), 2)))
print("GPA by major:")
```

```
[1] "GPA by major:"
```

```
print(major_summary)
```

```
       major gpa.count gpa.avg
1    Biology      2.00    3.05
2       Math      1.00    3.90
3 Psychology      2.00    3.65
```

Python Approach

Python's pandas library provides the same operations using different syntax. Filtering uses Boolean conditions inside brackets. Selecting uses a list of column names. Mutating uses assignment and functions like apply(). Arranging uses sort_values(). Summarizing uses groupby() and aggregation functions. Even though the commands look different from R, the logic is identical.

```
# ============================================
# Demo 3: Core Data Manipulation Operations (Python)
# The five fundamental operations
# ============================================

print("=== FILTER: Select rows that meet criteria ===")
```

```
=== FILTER: Select rows that meet criteria ===
```

```
# Find students with GPA > 3.5
high_gpa = student_data[student_data['gpa'] > 3.5]
print("High GPA students:")
```

```
High GPA students:
```

```
print(high_gpa)
```

```
   student_id  age       major  gpa  study_hours
1        1002   22  Psychology  3.8           25
2        1003   19        Math  3.9           30
```

```
print("=== SELECT: Choose specific columns ===")
```

```
=== SELECT: Choose specific columns ===
```

```
# Get just ID, major, and GPA
basic_info = student_data[['student_id', 'major', 'gpa']]
print("Basic student info:")
```

```
Basic student info:
```

```
print(basic_info)
```

```
   student_id       major  gpa
0        1001     Biology  3.2
1        1002  Psychology  3.8
2        1003        Math  3.9
3        1004     Biology  2.9
4        1005  Psychology  3.5
```

```
print("=== MUTATE: Create new variables ===")
```

```
=== MUTATE: Create new variables ===
```

```python
# Create a study category variable
student_data['study_category'] = student_data['study_hours'].apply(
    lambda x: 'High' if x > 20 else 'Moderate')
print("Data with new variable:")
```

```
Data with new variable:
```

```python
print(student_data[['student_id', 'study_hours', 'study_category']])
```

```
   student_id  study_hours study_category
0        1001           15       Moderate
1        1002           25           High
2        1003           30           High
3        1004           12       Moderate
4        1005           18       Moderate
```

```python
print("=== ARRANGE: Sort data ===")
```

```
=== ARRANGE: Sort data ===
```

```python
# Sort by GPA (highest first)
sorted_data = student_data.sort_values('gpa', ascending=False)
print("Students sorted by GPA:")
```

```
Students sorted by GPA:
```

```python
print(sorted_data[['student_id', 'major', 'gpa']])
```

```
   student_id       major  gpa
2        1003        Math  3.9
1        1002  Psychology  3.8
4        1005  Psychology  3.5
0        1001     Biology  3.2
3        1004     Biology  2.9
```

```python
print("=== SUMMARIZE: Calculate aggregate statistics ===")
```

```
=== SUMMARIZE: Calculate aggregate statistics ===
```

```python
# Calculate averages by major
major_summary = student_data.groupby('major')['gpa'].agg(['count',
 ↪  'mean']).round(2)
print("GPA by major:")
```

```
GPA by major:
```

```
print(major_summary)
```

```
            count  mean
major
Biology         2  3.05
Math            1  3.90
Psychology      2  3.65
```

These five operations—filter, select, mutate, arrange, and summarize—form the core of almost every data analysis task. They allow you to narrow down your data, focus on the variables you care about, create new insights, reorder information, and compute meaningful summaries. Once you understand these operations, you can combine them to answer complex analytical questions in both R and Python.

5.12.1.4 Data Transformation Thinking

Up to this point, we have focused on understanding data structures and learning the core operations used to manipulate them. But successful data analysis is not about memorizing commands. It is about learning to think in terms of transformations—how to reshape, filter, summarize, or reorganize data so that it answers a specific analytical question.

Every analysis begins with a question. The role of programming is to transform the data into a form where that question can be answered clearly. This mindset shifts the focus away from syntax and toward reasoning: What does my data look like now? What do I need it to look like? What steps will get me there?

To illustrate this approach, let's walk through a simple analytical question using both R and Python.

R Approach

In R, the transformation begins by identifying the variables involved—major and study hours. To answer the question, we need to compute the average study hours for each major. This requires grouping the data by major, calculating the mean, and then sorting the results to see which major studies the most. The final output is not just a number; it is the result of a sequence of transformations guided by the analytical question.

```
# ============================================
# Demo 4: Data Transformation Thinking (R)
# From question to data transformation
# ============================================

print("=== ANALYTICAL QUESTION ===")
```

```
[1] "=== ANALYTICAL QUESTION ==="
```

```
print("Question: Which major has students who study the most on
↪  average?")
```

```
[1] "Question: Which major has students who study the most on average?"
```

```
print("=== TRANSFORMATION APPROACH ===")
```

```
[1] "=== TRANSFORMATION APPROACH ==="
```

```
print("Step 1: Current data structure")
```

```
[1] "Step 1: Current data structure"
```

```
print(head(student_data[, c("major", "study_hours")], 3))
```

```
       major study_hours
1    Biology          15
2 Psychology          25
3       Math          30
```

```
print("Step 2: What do we need? Average study hours by major")
```

```
[1] "Step 2: What do we need? Average study hours by major"
```

```
print("Step 3: Apply transformations")
```

```
[1] "Step 3: Apply transformations"
```

```
# Group by major and calculate averages
study_by_major <- aggregate(study_hours ~ major, data = student_data,
↪  FUN = mean)
study_by_major$avg_study_hours <- round(study_by_major$study_hours, 1)

# Sort to find highest
study_by_major <-
↪  study_by_major[order(-study_by_major$avg_study_hours), ]

print("Result - Average study hours by major:")
```

```
[1] "Result - Average study hours by major:"
```

```
print(study_by_major[, c("major", "avg_study_hours")])
```

```
       major avg_study_hours
2       Math            30.0
3 Psychology            21.5
1    Biology            13.5
```

Python Approach

Python follows the same reasoning. The syntax differs, but the thought process is identical: identify the relevant variables, group the data, compute the averages, and sort the results. The transformation steps mirror the analytical steps.

```
# ============================================
# Demo 4: Data Transformation Thinking (Python)
# From question to data transformation
# ============================================

print("=== ANALYTICAL QUESTION ===")
```

```
=== ANALYTICAL QUESTION ===
```

```
print("Question: Which major has students who study the most on
↪  average?")
```

```
Question: Which major has students who study the most on average?
```

```
print("=== TRANSFORMATION APPROACH ===")
```

```
=== TRANSFORMATION APPROACH ===
```

```
print("Step 1: Current data structure")
```

```
Step 1: Current data structure
```

```
print(student_data[['major', 'study_hours']].head(3))
```

```
        major  study_hours
0     Biology           15
1  Psychology           25
2        Math           30
```

```
print("Step 2: What do we need? Average study hours by major")
```

```
Step 2: What do we need? Average study hours by major
```

```
print("Step 3: Apply transformations")
```

```
Step 3: Apply transformations
```

```
# Group by major and calculate averages
study_by_major =
↪  student_data.groupby('major')['study_hours'].mean().round(1)
study_by_major = study_by_major.sort_values(ascending=False)
```

```
print("Result - Average study hours by major:")
```

```
Result - Average study hours by major:
```

```
print(study_by_major)
```

```
major
Math          30.0
Psychology    21.5
Biology       13.5
Name: study_hours, dtype: float64
```

```
print("Answer: Math majors study the most on average")
```

```
Answer: Math majors study the most on average
```

This example highlights a key idea: data analysis is a process of moving from the data you have to the data you need. The commands you use are simply tools that carry out the transformations you have already reasoned through.

When you approach analysis this way, programming becomes clearer. Instead of asking “What command do I use?”, you begin asking:

- What does my data look like right now?
- What form does it need to be in to answer my question?
- What sequence of transformations will get me there?

This mindset makes your work more systematic, more accurate, and easier to explain.

5.12.1.5 Using AI to Support Transformation Thinking

Modern tools like Positron’s AI assistant can help reinforce this way of thinking. Instead of asking for a specific command, you can ask the AI to help you reason through the transformation steps. For example, you might ask: “I want to find which major has the highest average study hours. What transformations do I need?”

The AI can help you identify the steps—grouping, averaging, sorting—and then show you how to express those steps in code. You can also ask it to verify your results or explain why a particular transformation works.

AI becomes a guide that supports your reasoning, not a shortcut that replaces it. By helping you think through the transformations, it strengthens your understanding of how data analysis works.

5.12.2 Practice

Use the dataset below for all questions. You may use either R or Python.

R version

```r
student_data <- data.frame(
  student_id = c(1001, 1002, 1003, 1004, 1005),
  age = c(20, 22, 19, 21, 20),
  major = c("Biology", "Psychology", "Math", "Biology", "Psychology"),
  gpa = c(3.2, 3.8, 3.9, 2.9, 3.5),
  study_hours = c(15, 25, 30, 12, 18)
)
```

Python version (pandas)

```python
import pandas as pd

student_data = pd.DataFrame({
    'student_id': [1001, 1002, 1003, 1004, 1005],
    'age': [20, 22, 19, 21, 20],
    'major': ['Biology', 'Psychology', 'Math', 'Biology',
     ↪ 'Psychology'],
    'gpa': [3.2, 3.8, 3.9, 2.9, 3.5],
    'study_hours': [15, 25, 30, 12, 18]
})
```

5.12.3 Questions

1. How many rows (observations) are in the dataset?
2. How many columns (variables) are in the dataset?
3. What does each row in this dataset represent?
4. What does each column represent?
5. Print the first row of the dataset. What information does this single observation contain?
6. Print only the "gpa" column. What type of information does this variable store?
7. Print the structure or info summary of the dataset. What data types do you see for each column?
8. Select only the student_id, major, and gpa columns. What does this smaller table show you?

9. Filter the dataset to show only students with a GPA greater than 3.5. How many students meet this condition?
10. Create a new variable that categorizes students as “High” or “Moderate” based on study_hours. Describe how the categories were assigned.
11. Sort the dataset by GPA from highest to lowest. Which student has the highest GPA?
12. Compute the average GPA for each major. Which major has the highest average GPA?
13. Ask an AI assistant: “What transformations do I need to compare average study hours by major?” Write down the explanation you received.
14. Use the AI’s guidance to compute the average study_hours for each major. Which major studies the most on average?
15. Based on your results, write a short conclusion that answers the question: “Which major has students who study the most on average?”

Chapter 6

Writing Code Humans Can Read

6.1 Learning Outcomes

6-1: Explain why code readability is a fundamental requirement for effective data analysis and why it matters more than clever or compact solutions.

6-2: Apply clear and consistent naming conventions for variables and objects to improve code clarity and communication.

6-3: Use comments strategically to explain reasoning, context, and intent rather than restating obvious code behavior.

6-4: Organize code visually through spacing, indentation, and sectioning to make logical structure and execution flow easy to follow.

6-5: Combine code with narrative text using tools such as R Markdown to present data analyses as clear, reproducible, and interpretable stories.

6.2 Introduction

If you've been following along through the previous chapters, you now understand what programming is, how to organize your workspace, how code is structured, and how to think about data as the central object of analysis. But here's where we address a crucial aspect that many beginners overlook: writing code that humans can understand.

You might think this seems premature—after all, shouldn't you focus on getting code to work before worrying about how it looks? This intuition is understandable but misguided. The truth is that readable code is not a luxury or an advanced skill—it's a fundamental requirement for effective data analysis.

This chapter is about establishing good habits early, before you develop bad ones that are hard to break. We'll explore why readability matters more than cleverness, learn practical techniques for clear communication through code, and discover how treating your analysis as a story makes everything more understandable.

The key insight of this chapter is both simple and profound: your future self is your most important audience. The code you write today will be read by you weeks or months from now, when you've forgotten the details. Writing readable code isn't about impressing others—it's about being kind to your future self.

6.3 Readability Matters More Than Cleverness

When people first start programming, they often focus solely on getting their code to work, regardless of how it looks. This is natural—there's something satisfying about solving a problem, even if the solution is messy. But making code work is only the first step. Making it understandable is equally important.

The Maintenance Reality

Here's a truth that might surprise you: most code is read far more often than it's written. You write a piece of code once, but you'll read it many times when you need to modify, debug, or explain your analysis.

Consider these two approaches to calculating average GPA by major:

Hard to read:

```
d<-read.csv("data.csv")
r<-aggregate(d$gpa,by=list(d$major),FUN=mean)
```

Easy to read:

```
student_data <- read.csv("student_survey.csv")
gpa_by_major <- aggregate(student_data$gpa,
                          by = list(student_data$major),
                          FUN = mean)
```

Both produce the same result, but the second tells a clear story. You can understand what's happening without decoding cryptic variable names.

The Cleverness Trap

Beginning programmers sometimes assume that shorter, more compact code is better, trying to accomplish as much as possible in a single line. This is known as the "cleverness trap," where brevity is prioritized over clarity. Clever code can create significant problems. It makes debugging difficult because when something breaks, it is hard to locate the source of the problem. Modifying the code becomes challenging, as changing one part might unexpectedly break something else. Additionally, others may struggle to understand the logic, making knowledge transfer and collaboration more difficult.

6.4 Naming Things Clearly

One of the most important aspects of readable code is choosing good names for your variables and functions. Names are how you communicate your intentions to anyone reading your code.

The difference between unclear and clear names is dramatic:

Unclear:

```
d <- read.csv("survey.csv")
x <- mean(d$age)
n <- nrow(d)
```

Clear:

```
student_survey <- read.csv("survey.csv")
average_age <- mean(student_survey$age)
```

```
total_responses <- nrow(student_survey)
```

The second version immediately tells you what each variable represents.

Naming Guidelines That Work

- **Be descriptive:** `student_count` beats `n`
- **Use full words:** `average_gpa` beats `avg_gpa`
- **Be consistent:** If you use `student_count`, also use `teacher_count`
- **Avoid abbreviations:** `psychology_majors` beats `psyc_maj`

Context Matters

Good names depend on your analysis scope. In a short GPA-focused script, `gpa` works fine. In a longer analysis with multiple scores, `cumulative_gpa` provides better clarity.

Here's how naming can tell your analysis story:

```
# Each name explains the data transformation process
raw_survey_responses <- read.csv("student_survey_2024.csv")
complete_responses <- raw_survey_responses[
complete.cases(raw_survey_responses),
]

undergraduate_responses <- complete_responses[
complete_responses$class_year <= 4,
]

# Results are clearly labeled
average_study_hours <- mean(undergraduate_responses$weekly_study_hours)
final_results <- data.frame(
  major = gpa_by_major$Group.1,
  mean_gpa = round(gpa_by_major$x, 2)
)
```

Just reading the variable names reveals the analysis flow: loading, filtering, calculating, and organizing results.

6.5 Comments as Explanations

Comments are lines that explain your code to human readers—they're ignored by the computer. Learning to write good comments is crucial, but many beginners either avoid them or use them poorly.

The key principle: explain **why** you're doing something, not just **what** you're doing.

Good vs. Poor Comments

Poor (states the obvious):

```
# Calculate the mean
average_gpa <- mean(student_data$gpa)
```

Good (explains context and reasoning):

```
# Calculate average GPA for comparison with national benchmarks
# Excludes students with incomplete grades
average_gpa <- mean(student_data$gpa, na.rm = TRUE)
```

Strategic Comment Placement

Use comments at three key levels:

Script overview:

```
# Student Performance Analysis
# Data: Fall 2024 survey (n=847)
# Purpose: Identify relationships between study habits and outcomes
```

Section headers:

```
# Data cleaning and preparation
# Remove incomplete responses and standardize formats
```

Complex operations:

```
# Convert study hours to z-scores within each major
# Accounts for different baseline patterns across disciplines
standardized_hours <- scale(study_hours)
```

This creates a natural bridge to our next topic: how visual structure supports understanding.

6.6 Visual Structure and Organization

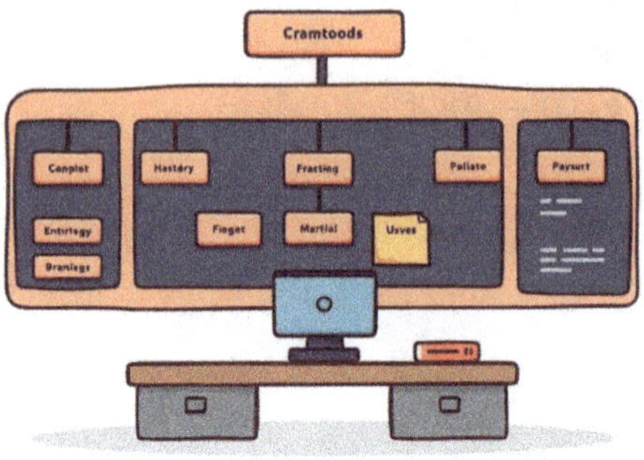

Just as you rely on paragraphs and headings to understand a book's organization, code structure helps readers follow your logical flow. Good visual organization makes relationships between code elements immediately apparent.

Start Simple: Basic Indentation

```
# Poor structure - everything runs together
if(gpa>=3.5){status<-"Dean's List"}else{status<-"Regular"}

# Good structure - logic is visible
if (gpa >= 3.5) {
  status <- "Dean's List"
} else {
  status <- "Regular"
}
```

Progress to Complex: Function Organization

Once you're comfortable with basic structure, you can handle more complex formatting:

```
# Simple version first
plot(data$x, data$y)

# Then build complexity with clear structure
ggplot(data, aes(x = study_hours, y = gpa)) +
  geom_point() +
  geom_smooth(method = "lm") +
  labs(
    title = "Study Hours vs GPA",
```

```
    x = "Weekly Study Hours",
    y = "Cumulative GPA"
  )
```

Section Organization

Use consistent patterns to organize major sections:

```
# ==========================================================
# DATA PREPARATION
# ==========================================================

student_data <- read.csv("survey.csv")
clean_data <- student_data[complete.cases(student_data), ]

# ==========================================================
# ANALYSIS
# =========================================================

summary_stats <- clean_data %>%
  group_by(major) %>%
  summarize(mean_gpa = mean(gpa))
```

This systematic approach to organization naturally leads us to combining code with explanatory text.

6.7 Combining Code with Narrative

One of the most powerful ways to make analysis readable is to combine code with narrative text that explains your thinking. This approach treats your analysis like a story, integrating computation with explanation so that others can understand not just what you did, but why you did it. For beginners, looking at code alone can be confusing, because the actions have no context. By adding narrative, you clarify the purpose of each step, the structure of the dataset, and the meaning of the results.

Markdown is a simple way to format text using plain symbols, like # for headings, so your analysis is organized and easy to read. In R, Markdown is used in **R Markdown documents**, which let you combine narrative text, headings, and R code in the same file. When you “knit” the document, R runs the code and produces a report with the results embedded alongside your explanations. This lets you tell a clear story: your narrative explains what the code does, the code performs the calculations, and the output shows the results—all in one readable document.

6.8 Conclusion

The habits you develop while learning programming often stick with you throughout your career. Starting with good practices—such as using clear variable names, adding helpful comments, and organizing your code logically—makes these approaches natural and automatic. Before considering any code finished, ask yourself: "If I returned to this in six months, would I understand what I was doing and why?" Investing a few extra minutes for clarity pays off. These skills are highly valued in professional settings, where employers seek people who can solve problems and communicate solutions clearly. As you advance, readable code becomes essential for teamwork and collaboration. A simple way to practice is to take any piece of code you've written and improve it by applying one technique from this chapter: giving variables descriptive names, adding comments, reorganizing the structure, or including a brief narrative explanation. Even small changes can dramatically improve your ability to understand and share your work.

6.9 Review Questions

1. Why is writing readable code considered a fundamental requirement rather than an advanced skill in data analysis?
2. What does it mean to say that your "future self" is the most important audience for your code?
3. Why is code typically read far more often than it is written, and how does this affect how code should be written?
4. What is the "cleverness trap," and why can clever but compact code be harmful in practice?
5. How do clear and descriptive variable names improve understanding and reduce errors in analysis?
6. What guidelines help analysts choose effective names for variables and objects?
7. What is the primary purpose of comments, and why should they focus on *why* rather than *what*?
8. How does visual structure—such as spacing, indentation, and sectioning—support code readability?
9. Why is combining code with narrative text an effective way to communicate data analysis?
10. How do tools like R Markdown support treating an analysis as a readable story rather than a collection of commands?

6.10 Ch 6 Lab Writing Readable Code

This lab accompanies Chapter 6 and focuses on one of the most important skills in programming: writing code that other people can understand. Readable code is easier to debug, easier to maintain, and easier for future you to revisit. In this lab, you will practice choosing clear names, writing meaningful comments, organizing code visually, and combining narrative with code to explain your thinking.

6.10.1 Demonstration

6.10.1.1 Readability

Programming is not just about getting code to run. It's about writing code that another human can understand — including your future self. Readable code is easier to debug, easier to maintain, and easier to build on. In this lab, you will learn how to write code that communicates clearly: code with meaningful names, helpful comments, and a visual structure that makes the logic easy to follow.

Readable code is not about being fancy or compact. It's about being clear. A few extra lines, a descriptive variable name, or a short comment can make the difference between code that is immediately understandable and code that requires deciphering.

Below are two versions of the same task: calculating the average score for students who earned an A. The first version is technically correct but difficult to read. The second version expresses the same logic in a way that is easy to follow.

R Approach — Unclear Version

```
# ============================================
# Demo 1: Readability vs. Compression (R)
# Unclear version
# ============================================

d<-data.frame(x=c(85,92,78,88,95),y=c("A","A","C","B","A"))
r<-d[d$y=="A",]$x
m<-mean(r)
print(paste("Result:",m))
```

```
[1] "Result: 90.6666666666667"
```

This code works, but the meaning is buried in short variable names and compressed expressions. Someone reading it must decode what d, r, and m represent.

R Approach — Clear Version

```
# ============================================
# Demo 1: Readability vs. Clarity (R)
# Clear version
```

```
# ============================================

# Create student grade data
student_grades <- data.frame(
  score = c(85, 92, 78, 88, 95),
  letter_grade = c("A", "A", "C", "B", "A")
)

# Filter for A-grade students
a_grade_students <- student_grades[student_grades$letter_grade == "A",
↪  ]

# Calculate average score for A-grade students
average_a_grade_score <- mean(a_grade_students$score)

# Display the result
print(paste("Average score for A-grade students:",
↪  average_a_grade_score))
```

```
[1] "Average score for A-grade students: 90.6666666666667"
```

This version uses descriptive names, clear steps, and comments that explain the purpose of each block.

Python Approach — Unclear Version

```
# ============================================
# Demo 1: Readability vs. Compression (Python)
# Unclear version
# ============================================

import pandas as pd
d=pd.DataFrame({'x':[85,92,78,88,95],'y':['A','A','C','B','A']})
r=d[d['y']=='A']['x'].mean()
print(f"Result: {r}")
```

```
Result: 90.66666666666667
```

Again, the logic is compressed into a single line, and the variable names do not communicate meaning.

Python Approach — Clear Version

```
# ============================================
# Demo 1: Readability vs. Clarity (Python)
# Clear version
```

```
# ==============================================

import pandas as pd

# Create student grade data
student_grades = pd.DataFrame({
    'score': [85, 92, 78, 88, 95],
    'letter_grade': ['A', 'A', 'C', 'B', 'A']
})

# Filter for A-grade students
a_grade_students = student_grades[student_grades['letter_grade'] ==
 ↪  'A']

# Calculate average score for A-grade students
average_a_grade_score = a_grade_students['score'].mean()

# Display the result
print(f"Average score for A-grade students: {average_a_grade_score}")
```

```
Average score for A-grade students: 90.66666666666667
```

Readable code makes the logic obvious: create data, filter it, compute a statistic, print the result.

AI Integration

AI tools can support the process of writing readable code by helping you see your work the way another programmer would. Instead of asking an AI to rewrite your logic, you can use it to evaluate clarity, naming choices, structure, and the overall readability of your script. This mirrors the kind of peer review that happens in real development environments.

Here are examples of prompts that encourage constructive, readability-focused feedback:

"Review this code and suggest improvements for readability." "How can I make this code easier to understand?" "Are my variable names clear and descriptive?" "Does the structure of this script make the logic easy to follow?"

The goal is not to make the code shorter or more "clever," but to make it easier for a human reader to understand the intent behind each step. AI can highlight unclear naming, missing comments, overly compact expressions, or places where the logic would benefit from clearer structure.

Used this way, AI becomes a tool for reflection — a second set of eyes that helps you communicate your thinking more effectively. Readable code communicates your thinking. It shows intent, not just mechanics. It makes your work easier to understand, easier to debug, and easier to extend.

6.10.1.2 Naming Things Clearly

One of the simplest ways to make code easier to understand is to choose names that communicate meaning. Good names reduce the need for comments, make the logic easier to follow, and help readers understand the purpose of each variable or function at a glance. When names are vague or overly short, the reader must mentally decode what each symbol represents. When names are descriptive, the code becomes self-explanatory.

Clear naming is especially important in data analysis, where variables often represent measurements, categories, or derived values. A name like x forces the reader to remember what the value stands for. A name like daily_temperatures_celsius or average_daily_temperature tells the story directly. Consistent naming patterns also help: using similar structures for similar concepts makes your code predictable and easier to navigate.

The examples below show how naming choices affect readability in both R and Python.

R Approach

```
# ============================================
# Demo 2: Clear Naming Conventions (R)
# ============================================

# BAD NAMING - Unclear and confusing
x <- c(23, 45, 67, 34, 56, 78, 23, 45)
y <- length(x)
z <- sum(x)
a <- z / y
print(paste("Result:", a))
```

```
[1] "Result: 46.375"
```

```
# GOOD NAMING - Clear and descriptive
daily_temperatures_celsius <- c(23, 45, 67, 34, 56, 78, 23, 45)
number_of_days <- length(daily_temperatures_celsius)
total_temperature <- sum(daily_temperatures_celsius)
average_daily_temperature <- total_temperature / number_of_days
print(paste("Average daily temperature:", average_daily_temperature,
 ↪  "°C"))
```

```
[1] "Average daily temperature: 46.375 °C"
```

```r
# NAMING PATTERNS FOR DATA ANALYSIS
# Use descriptive prefixes
student_count <- 150
course_enrollment <- 45
survey_response_rate <- 0.85

# Use consistent naming conventions
calculate_mean_gpa <- function(gpa_values) {
  return(mean(gpa_values, na.rm = TRUE))
}

calculate_median_age <- function(age_values) {
  return(median(age_values, na.rm = TRUE))
}
```

Python Approach

```python
# ================================================
# Demo 2: Clear Naming Conventions (Python)
# ================================================

# BAD NAMING - Unclear and confusing
x = [23, 45, 67, 34, 56, 78, 23, 45]
y = len(x)
z = sum(x)
a = z / y
print(f"Result: {a}")
```

```
Result: 46.375
```

```python
# GOOD NAMING - Clear and descriptive
daily_temperatures_celsius = [23, 45, 67, 34, 56, 78, 23, 45]
number_of_days = len(daily_temperatures_celsius)
total_temperature = sum(daily_temperatures_celsius)
average_daily_temperature = total_temperature / number_of_days
print(f"Average daily temperature: {average_daily_temperature}°C")
```

```
Average daily temperature: 46.375°C
```

```python
# NAMING PATTERNS FOR DATA ANALYSIS
# Use descriptive prefixes
student_count = 150
course_enrollment = 45
survey_response_rate = 0.85
```

```
# Use consistent naming conventions


def calculate_mean_gpa(gpa_values):
    """Calculate mean GPA, handling missing values."""
    clean_values = [x for x in gpa_values if x is not None]
    return sum(clean_values) / len(clean_values)

def calculate_median_age(age_values):
    """Calculate median age, handling missing values."""
    clean_ages = [x for x in age_values if x is not None]
    clean_ages.sort()
    n = len(clean_ages)

    if n % 2 == 1:
        return clean_ages[n // 2]
    else:
        return (clean_ages[n // 2 - 1] + clean_ages[n // 2]) / 2
```

Names are one of the most powerful tools for making code understandable. Clear, descriptive naming reduces cognitive load, makes your intent obvious, and helps your code communicate its purpose without relying on comments. Consistent naming patterns turn your scripts into readable, maintainable documents that others — and your future self — can navigate with ease.

AI Integration

AI tools can help you evaluate whether your names are clear and consistent. Instead of asking an AI to rewrite your code, you can ask it to review your naming choices and suggest improvements. Prompts such as:

"Suggest better variable names for this code." "What naming conventions should I follow for data analysis?" "Are these function names descriptive enough?"

encourage feedback that strengthens clarity without changing your logic. AI can help you spot vague names, inconsistent patterns, or places where a more descriptive term would make the code easier to read.

6.10.1.3 Comments as Explanations

Comments are most useful when they explain the thinking behind your code. A comment that simply repeats what the code already shows adds no value. But a comment that explains why you made a decision, what assumptions you're making, or what limitations the data has — that kind of comment turns code into a clear, communicative analysis.

In data analysis, comments often carry important context: where the data came from, why a particular method was chosen, what potential biases exist, or what the next steps should be. These explanations help future readers understand not just the mechanics of the code, but the reasoning that shaped the analysis. Good comments make your work easier to maintain, easier to revisit, and easier for others to trust.

The examples below show the difference between comments that state the obvious and comments that provide meaningful context.

R Approach

```
# ============================================
# Demo 3: Effective Comments (R)
# ============================================

# BAD COMMENTS - State the obvious
# Create a data frame
survey_data <- data.frame(
  age = c(22, 25, 30, 28, 35), # Age column
  income = c(45000, 52000, 68000, 58000, 75000) # Income column
)

# Calculate mean of age
mean_age <- mean(survey_data$age)

# GOOD COMMENTS - Explain the reasoning and context
# Survey data from our Q3 2024 customer satisfaction study
# Note: Income data is self-reported and may have response bias
survey_data <- data.frame(
  age = c(22, 25, 30, 28, 35),
  income = c(45000, 52000, 68000, 58000, 75000)
)

# Calculate mean age to determine if our sample skews young
# This will inform our marketing strategy recommendations
mean_age <- mean(survey_data$age)

# COMMENT TYPES FOR DATA ANALYSIS

# 1. Data source and context comments
# Data downloaded from company database on 2024-02-18
# Excludes customers who opted out of research participation

# 2. Analytical decision comments
# Using median instead of mean due to outliers in income distribution
```

```
median_income <- median(survey_data$income)

# 3. Assumption and limitation comments
# Assumes all survey responses are truthful
# Sample size (n=5) is too small for statistical significance

# 4. Next steps and TODO comments
# TODO: Expand sample size to at least 30 respondents
# TODO: Add demographic weighting to match population
```

Python Approach

```
# ============================================
# Demo 3: Effective Comments (Python)
# ============================================

import pandas as pd

# BAD COMMENTS - State the obvious
# Create a dataframe
survey_data = pd.DataFrame({
    'age': [22, 25, 30, 28, 35], # Age column
    'income': [45000, 52000, 68000, 58000, 75000] # Income column
})

# Calculate mean of age
mean_age = survey_data['age'].mean()

# GOOD COMMENTS - Explain the reasoning and context
# Survey data from our Q3 2024 customer satisfaction study
# Note: Income data is self-reported and may have response bias
survey_data = pd.DataFrame({
    'age': [22, 25, 30, 28, 35],
    'income': [45000, 52000, 68000, 58000, 75000]
})

# Calculate mean age to determine if our sample skews young
# This will inform our marketing strategy recommendations
mean_age = survey_data['age'].mean()

# COMMENT TYPES FOR DATA ANALYSIS

# 1. Data source and context comments
# Data downloaded from company database on 2024-02-18
```

```
# Excludes customers who opted out of research participation

# 2. Analytical decision comments
# Using median instead of mean due to outliers in income distribution
median_income = survey_data['income'].median()

# 3. Assumption and limitation comments
# Assumes all survey responses are truthful
# Sample size (n=5) is too small for statistical significance

# 4. Next steps and TODO comments
# TODO: Expand sample size to at least 30 respondents
# TODO: Add demographic weighting to match population
```

Comments should explain the reasoning behind your code, not restate what the code already shows. Good comments document context, decisions, assumptions, and next steps — the parts of your analysis that aren't visible in the code itself. These explanations make your work easier to maintain and easier for others to understand.

AI Integration

AI tools can help you refine your comments by identifying where additional explanation would make your analysis clearer. Useful prompts include:

"Review my comments and suggest improvements." "What should I explain in comments for this analysis?" "Are there assumptions or limitations I should document?"

AI can help you spot missing context, unclear reasoning, or places where a short explanation would make the code more understandable.

6.10.1.4 Visual Structure and Code Organization

Readable code is not only about naming and comments — it's also about how the code looks on the page. Visual structure plays a major role in how easily someone can follow your logic. When code is tightly packed together with no spacing, no sectioning, and no clear flow, even simple tasks become harder to understand. But when code is organized into meaningful blocks, separated by whitespace, and introduced with short section headers, the structure guides the reader through the analysis.

Good organization mirrors the way you would explain your work out loud: start with setup, move to data preparation, then modeling or analysis, and finally visualization or results. Grouping related steps together and adding visual cues helps the reader see the progression of your thinking. This is especially important in data analysis, where scripts often combine multiple stages of work.

Visual organization is part of communication. Spacing, indentation, and sectioning guide the reader through your code and make your analysis easier to follow. When your code is visually clear, the logic becomes clearer too — and that clarity pays off every time you return to the script or share it with someone else.

AI Integration

AI tools can help you improve the visual structure of your code by suggesting clearer formatting, better grouping, or more consistent spacing. Prompts such as:

"Format this code for better readability." "Suggest ways to organize this analysis more clearly." "Where should I add section headers or spacing?"

can help you refine the layout of your script so that the structure reflects the logic of your analysis.

Use the code below for all questions. You may choose R or Python, but the questions are the same.

6.10.2 Practice

6.10.2.1 R Version

```
# ORIGINAL CODE (INTENTIONALLY HARD TO READ)
d<-c(78,85,92,88,76,94,89,83,91,87)
n<-length(d)
s<-sum(d)
m<-s/n
v<-sum((d-m)^2)/(n-1)
sd<-sqrt(v)
print(paste("M:",m,"SD:",sd))
```

6.10.2.2 Python

```
# ORIGINAL CODE (INTENTIONALLY HARD TO READ)
import math
d=[78,85,92,88,76,94,89,83,91,87]
n=len(d)
s=sum(d)
m=s/n
v=sum([(x-m)**2 for x in d])/(n-1)
sd=math.sqrt(v)
print(f"M: {m}, SD: {sd}")
```

6.10.2.3 Questions

1. What do you think this code is trying to calculate?

2. Which variable names are unclear or uninformative? List at least three.
3. Rewrite the variable names in a way that makes the purpose of each one obvious.
4. Add comments that explain why each calculation is being done, not just what the code does.
5. Add spacing and line breaks to make the code easier to read.
6. Rewrite the final print statement so the output is more descriptive and readable.
7. Identify one place where a section header (e.g., "# Calculate variance") would improve clarity.
8. Explain how you would reorganize the code into logical sections.
9. Ask an AI assistant to review your rewritten code. Summarize one suggestion it gave you.
10. Based on your improved version, describe how readability changed your understanding of the code.

Chapter 7

Functions and Reuse

7.1 Learning Outcomes

7-1: Recognize repeated code patterns as signals for abstraction and explain why repetition reduces efficiency, reliability, and clarity.

7-2: Explain the conceptual purpose of functions as reusable tools that package analytical logic into consistent, repeatable operations.

7-3: Describe how functions handle inputs (arguments), outputs, and assumptions, and explain why understanding this contract is essential for correct use.

7-4: Distinguish between built-in functions, user-defined functions, and library functions, and identify appropriate use cases for each.

7-5: Apply functions and libraries to reduce duplication, improve readability, and create more maintainable and scalable data analysis workflows.

7.2 Introduction

By now, you've learned to write readable code that tells clear stories about your data analysis. But as you work on more projects, you'll start noticing something: you're writing the same types of code repeatedly. You calculate means, create similar plots, and perform the same statistical tests across different datasets.

This repetition isn't just tedious—it's a signal pointing toward one of programming's most powerful concepts: functions. This chapter explains abstraction without intimidation, showing you how functions naturally solve common problems.

The key insight is both practical and profound: **functions package ideas into reusable tools**. Instead of viewing functions as advanced programming concepts, think of them as a natural way to organize your analytical thinking.

7.3 Why Repetition Is a Warning Sign

When you first start programming, repetition feels normal. You calculate summary statistics for one group, then another, then another. But experienced programmers view repetition differently—as an opportunity for improvement.

7.3.1 Recognizing the Pattern

Imagine analyzing student data and calculating statistics for different majors:

```
# Psychology majors
psych_students <- student_data[student_data$major == "Psychology", ]
psych_mean_gpa <- mean(psych_students$gpa, na.rm = TRUE)
psych_count <- nrow(psych_students)
```

```
# Biology majors
bio_students <- student_data[student_data$major == "Biology", ]
bio_mean_gpa <- mean(bio_students$gpa, na.rm = TRUE)
bio_count <- nrow(bio_students)

# Mathematics majors
math_students <- student_data[student_data$major == "Mathematics", ]
math_mean_gpa <- mean(math_students$gpa, na.rm = TRUE)
math_count <- nrow(math_students)
```

Notice the pattern: filter for a major, calculate statistics, count students. The logic is identical, but you're writing it completely each time.

7.3.2 Why Repetition Creates Problems

Repetition in code creates several significant problems that can impact both efficiency and reliability. When the same logic or structure is duplicated across multiple places, maintaining the code becomes burdensome, because any change must be carefully applied to every copy. This increases the risk of errors, as it is easy to update one instance but forget another, leading to inconsistencies and bugs. Repetitive code also makes extending functionality more difficult, since adding new cases often requires rewriting or copying code multiple times, which is tedious and error prone. Additionally, repetition increases cognitive overhead, as developers expend mental energy on repetitive typing rather than focusing on problem-solving or improving the logic, reducing overall productivity and code quality.

7.3.3 The "Three Times Rule"

Many programmers follow this guideline: if you write similar code three times, consider creating a function. This isn't absolute, but it's useful for recognizing when repetition becomes worth solving.

7.4 What a Function Is Conceptually

The word "function" might sound intimidating, but you use functions in everyday life constantly—you just don't call them that.

7.4.1 Functions as Familiar Concepts

Functions in programming can be thought of like recipes or tools. Like a recipe, a function takes ingredients, or inputs, follows a defined set of steps, and produces a result, or output. For example, a "chocolate chip cookies" recipe always follows the same process, but you can adjust the ingredients to create different variations. Similarly, functions are tools designed for specific computational tasks. Just as you use a hammer for nails and a screwdriver for screws, you use different functions for different purposes: mean() calculates averages, plot() creates visualizations, and read.csv() loads data from files. By using functions, you can perform tasks efficiently, consistently, and with less repetitive effort.

7.4.2 A Simple Function Solution

Let's solve our repetitive code problem:

```
# Create a function that captures the pattern
summarize_major <- function(data, major_name) {
  major_students <- data[data$major == major_name, ]

  results <- list(
    mean_gpa = mean(major_students$gpa, na.rm = TRUE),
    count = nrow(major_students)
  )

  return(results)
}

# Now use it consistently
psych_summary <- summarize_major(student_data, "Psychology")
bio_summary <- summarize_major(student_data, "Biology")
math_summary <- summarize_major(student_data, "Mathematics")
```

The function captures the pattern and applies it consistently to different inputs.

7.5 How Functions Handle Information

Every function operates on a simple contract: you provide inputs, the function processes them, and returns an output. Understanding this contract is crucial for using functions effectively.

7.5.1 Function Inputs (Arguments)

Functions need raw materials to do their work:

Simple inputs:

```
mean(c(85, 92, 78, 96, 88))        # One input: numbers
student_data <- read.csv("survey.csv")  # One input: filename
```

Multiple inputs:

```
plot(x = student_data$study_hours,
```

```
    y = student_data$gpa,
    main = "Study Hours vs GPA")
```

7.5.2 Function Outputs

Functions return results in predictable ways:

Single values:

```
average_gpa <- mean(student_data$gpa)  # Returns one number
```

Complex results:

```
correlation_test <- cor.test(student_data$study_hours, student_data$gpa)
# Returns correlation, p-value, confidence interval
```

7.5.3 Function Assumptions

Every function operates based on certain assumptions about the inputs it receives. These expectations ensure that the function can run correctly and produce meaningful results. For example, mean() assumes that its input consists of numbers rather than text, while other functions may expect specific data structures, such as an entire data frame or just a single column. Functions also differ in how they handle missing data: some can process missing values automatically, while others require explicit instructions to manage them. Understanding these assumptions is essential for using functions effectively and avoiding errors in your code.

7.6 Built-in vs User-Defined Functions

You'll encounter two main types of functions: those built into the programming language and those created for specific purposes.

7.6.1 Built-in Functions: Your Standard Toolkit

These handle common tasks everyone needs:

Mathematical operations:

```
mean(student_data$gpa)      # Calculate average
max(student_data$age)       # Find maximum
round(3.14159, 2)          # Round numbers
```

Data operations:

```
nrow(student_data)         # Count rows
names(student_data)        # Get column names
```

7.6.2 User-Defined Functions: Custom Solutions

These solve specific problems you encounter:

```
# Custom function for coefficient of variation
coefficient_of_variation <- function(numbers) {
  cv <- sd(numbers, na.rm = TRUE) / mean(numbers, na.rm = TRUE)
  return(cv)
}

# Use it like any built-in function
gpa_variability <- coefficient_of_variation(student_data$gpa)
```

7.6.3 When to Use Each Type

Knowing when to use different types of functions helps keep code efficient and manageable. Built-in functions are ideal when they already perform exactly what you need, saving time and reducing errors. Custom functions become valuable when you find yourself repeating complex operations, allowing you to encapsulate that logic once and reuse it consistently. It's best to start simply by mastering built-in functions before creating your own, ensuring a solid foundation and avoiding unnecessary complexity in your code.

7.7 Libraries: Collections of Specialized Tools

In R, individual functions are useful, but the real power comes from libraries, also called packages. A library is a collection of related functions that work together to make specific tasks easier, similar to a specialized toolbox. For example, the library dplyr provides functions for manipulating data, ggplot2 offers functions for creating visualizations, and readr includes tools for importing data. Using libraries allows you to access a set of well-designed, tested, and consistent tools without having to write everything from scratch.

7.7.1 Installing and Loading Libraries

To use a library, you first need to install it once. For example, running install.packages("dplyr") downloads and installs the dplyr library onto your computer. Similarly, install.packages("ggplot2") installs the visualization library ggplot2. After installation, you must load the library each time you start R by using library(dplyr) or library(ggplot2). Loading a library makes all its functions available for use in your current R session.

7.7.2 Examples in Action

Once a library is loaded, you can use its functions to perform tasks efficiently. For instance, using dplyr, you can manipulate data with readable, step-by-step commands. In the code

```
student_summary <- student_data %>%
  filter(gpa > 2.0) %>%
  group_by(major) %>%
  summarize(avg_gpa = mean(gpa))
```

we first take a dataset called student_data and filter it to include only students with a GPA greater than 2.0. Then, we group the data by each student's major and calculate the average GPA within each group. The result is stored in a new dataset called student_summary.

Similarly, with ggplot2, you can create visualizations easily. In the code

```
ggplot(student_data, aes(x = study_hours, y = gpa)) +
  geom_point() +
  geom_smooth(method = "lm")
```

we create a scatterplot of study hours versus GPA using the student_data dataset. The geom_point() function adds the individual data points, while geom_smooth(method = "lm") overlays a trend line using a linear model to show the overall relationship between study time and GPA.

7.7.3 Why Libraries Matter

Libraries are important because they save time and reduce errors. The functions within a library are designed to work together consistently, they are created by experts who have solved complex problems, and they are widely used, so bugs are quickly identified and fixed. Libraries also come with extensive documentation and examples, making it easier to learn and apply new techniques. For beginners, a good way to start is by installing and exploring a library like dplyr for data manipulation or ggplot2 for visualization to see how much they can simplify your work in R.

7.8 Choosing the Right Functions

With so many functions in R, it helps to focus on your goals first. Ask yourself what you want to learn from your data, what output you need, and who will use it. Start with built-in functions, which are reliable and require no setup. Then explore popular libraries like dplyr or ggplot2, and later specialized libraries for specific tasks. Custom functions should come last, only when nothing else fits.

Learn gradually: master essential built-ins, then one major library, add specialized tools as needed, and create custom functions for repetitive or unique tasks. Before learning something new, check if it solves a real problem, is well-documented, fits your workflow, and is worth the effort. Reviewing which functions you use most can help you focus your learning and work more efficiently in R.

7.9 Conclusion

Functions represent a fundamental shift in how you approach programming problems. Instead of writing everything from scratch each time, you begin building and using tools that capture your analytical thinking.

In the next chapter, we'll explore how functions are organized into larger ecosystems—comprehensive libraries that provide complete solutions to analytical challenges. We'll see how the function concept scales up to entire communities working together.

Remember that learning functions is gradual. Start by recognizing repetition, then experiment with simple functions for your most common operations. Over time, you'll develop an intuitive sense for when and how functions make your analysis more efficient and reliable.

The journey from repetitive code to elegant, reusable solutions is one of the most satisfying aspects of learning to program. Each function you master represents a new tool in your analytical toolkit and a new way of thinking about problems.

7.10 Review Questions

1. Why is repeated code considered a warning sign in programming, and what problems can it create?
2. Explain the "Three Times Rule" and how it helps identify when to create a function.

3. Conceptually, what is a function, and how can it be compared to everyday examples like recipes or tools?
4. What are the key components of a function's "contract" in programming?
5. What is the difference between built-in functions and user-defined functions, and when should each be used?
6. How do function inputs (arguments) and outputs differ in complexity, and why is it important to understand them?
7. What assumptions do functions make about the data they receive, and what can go wrong if these assumptions are violated?
8. How do libraries (packages) extend the power of functions, and why are they important for efficient programming?
9. Describe a practical scenario where creating a custom function reduces repetition and improves code clarity.
10. What is the recommended approach for gradually learning and using functions and libraries effectively in R?

7.11 Ch 7 Lab Functions and Reuse

In programming, repetition is often a signal that your code needs structure. When you find yourself copying and pasting the same steps, or rewriting the same calculation with only small changes, it becomes harder to maintain your work and easier to introduce mistakes. Functions solve this problem by giving you a way to bundle a task into a reusable tool. Instead of repeating code, you define the logic once and then call it whenever you need it.

Functions are central to how modern data analysis works. Every time you calculate a mean, load a dataset, create a plot, or fit a model, you are using functions written by someone else. In this lab, you will learn how functions operate conceptually, how they take information in and return results, and how to create your own functions to make your code cleaner and more reusable. You will also explore the difference between built-in functions, user-defined functions, and functions that come from external libraries.

By learning to think in terms of functions, you gain the ability to write code that is easier to read, easier to test, and easier to extend. This lab will help you recognize when a function is needed, design one effectively, and use it as part of a larger analysis.

7.11.1 Demonstration

7.11.1.1 Repetition and the "Three Times Rule"

One of the clearest signs that your code needs structure is repetition. When you find yourself writing the same pattern of calculations over and over — even with different data — it becomes harder to maintain your work and easier to make mistakes. In data analysis, this often shows up when you compute the same set of statistics for multiple groups, run the same transformation on several variables, or repeat the same plotting steps across different datasets.

A helpful guideline is the "three times rule": if you repeat the same pattern three times, it's time to turn that pattern into a function. This isn't a strict rule, but a way of noticing when your code is telling you it needs organization. A function lets you define the logic once and reuse it whenever you need it, making your analysis cleaner, shorter, and easier to understand.

The examples below show how repetition appears in real code and how a function can eliminate it entirely.

R Approach - Repetitive Code Problem

```
# ============================================
# Demo 1: Recognizing Repetition (R)
# BAD EXAMPLE - Repetitive code
# ============================================

# Student grade analysis - repetitive approach
math_scores <- c(85, 92, 78, 88, 95)
english_scores <- c(82, 89, 91, 76, 88)
science_scores <- c(90, 85, 83, 92, 87)

# Calculate statistics for math - lots of repetition!
math_mean <- mean(math_scores)
math_median <- median(math_scores)
math_sd <- sd(math_scores)
math_min <- min(math_scores)
math_max <- max(math_scores)

print("Math Statistics:")
```

```
[1] "Math Statistics:"
```

```
print(paste("Mean:", round(math_mean, 2)))
```

```
[1] "Mean: 87.6"
```

```
print(paste("Median:", math_median))
```

```
[1] "Median: 88"
```

```
print(paste("SD:", round(math_sd, 2)))
```

```
[1] "SD: 6.58"
```

```
print(paste("Range:", math_min, "-", math_max))
```

```
[1] "Range: 78 - 95"
```

```
# Calculate statistics for English - same pattern repeated!
english_mean <- mean(english_scores)
english_median <- median(english_scores)
english_sd <- sd(english_scores)
english_min <- min(english_scores)
english_max <- max(english_scores)

print("English Statistics:")
```

```
[1] "English Statistics:"
```

```
print(paste("Mean:", round(english_mean, 2)))
```

```
[1] "Mean: 85.2"
```

```
print(paste("Median:", english_median))
```

```
[1] "Median: 88"
```

```
print(paste("SD:", round(english_sd, 2)))
```

```
[1] "SD: 6.14"
```

```
print(paste("Range:", english_min, "-", english_max))
```

```
[1] "Range: 76 - 91"
```

```
# Calculate statistics for Science - pattern repeated again!
science_mean <- mean(science_scores)
science_median <- median(science_scores)
science_sd <- sd(science_scores)
science_min <- min(science_scores)
science_max <- max(science_scores)

print("Science Statistics:")
```

```
[1] "Science Statistics:"
```

```
print(paste("Mean:", round(science_mean, 2)))
```

```
[1] "Mean: 87.4"
```

```
print(paste("Median:", science_median))
```

```
[1] "Median: 87"
```

```
print(paste("SD:", round(science_sd, 2)))
```

```
[1] "SD: 3.65"
```

```
print(paste("Range:", science_min, "-", science_max))
```

```
[1] "Range: 83 - 92"
```

R Approach - Function Solution

```
# =============================================
# Demo 1: Function Solution (R)
# GOOD EXAMPLE - Using a function to eliminate repetition
# =============================================

# Create a function to calculate subject statistics
calculate_subject_stats <- function(scores, subject_name) {
  # Calculate all statistics
  mean_score <- mean(scores)
  median_score <- median(scores)
  sd_score <- sd(scores)
  min_score <- min(scores)
  max_score <- max(scores)

  # Display results
  print(paste(subject_name, "Statistics:"))
  print(paste("Mean:", round(mean_score, 2)))
  print(paste("Median:", median_score))
  print(paste("SD:", round(sd_score, 2)))
  print(paste("Range:", min_score, "-", max_score))
  print("") # Empty line for readability
}

# Now use the function - no repetition!
calculate_subject_stats(math_scores, "Math")
```

```
[1] "Math Statistics:"
```

```
[1] "Mean: 87.6"
[1] "Median: 88"
[1] "SD: 6.58"
[1] "Range: 78 - 95"
[1] ""
```

```
calculate_subject_stats(english_scores, "English")
```

```
[1] "English Statistics:"
[1] "Mean: 85.2"
[1] "Median: 88"
[1] "SD: 6.14"
[1] "Range: 76 - 91"
[1] ""
```

```
calculate_subject_stats(science_scores, "Science")
```

```
[1] "Science Statistics:"
[1] "Mean: 87.4"
[1] "Median: 87"
[1] "SD: 3.65"
[1] "Range: 83 - 92"
[1] ""
```

Python Approach - Repetitive Code Problem

```
# ============================================
# Demo 1: Recognizing Repetition (Python)
# BAD EXAMPLE - Repetitive code
# ============================================

import statistics

# Student grade analysis - repetitive approach
math_scores = [85, 92, 78, 88, 95]
english_scores = [82, 89, 91, 76, 88]
science_scores = [90, 85, 83, 92, 87]

# Calculate statistics for math - lots of repetition!
math_mean = statistics.mean(math_scores)
math_median = statistics.median(math_scores)
math_sd = statistics.stdev(math_scores)
math_min = min(math_scores)
math_max = max(math_scores)
```

```
print("Math Statistics:")
```

```
Math Statistics:
```

```
print(f"Mean: {math_mean:.2f}")
```

```
Mean: 87.60
```

```
print(f"Median: {math_median}")
```

```
Median: 88
```

```
print(f"SD: {math_sd:.2f}")
```

```
SD: 6.58
```

```
print(f"Range: {math_min} - {math_max}")
```

```
Range: 78 - 95
```

```
# Calculate statistics for English - same pattern repeated!
english_mean = statistics.mean(english_scores)
english_median = statistics.median(english_scores)
english_sd = statistics.stdev(english_scores)
english_min = min(english_scores)
english_max = max(english_scores)

print("English Statistics:")
```

```
English Statistics:
```

```
print(f"Mean: {english_mean:.2f}")
```

```
Mean: 85.20
```

```
print(f"Median: {english_median}")
```

```
Median: 88
```

```
print(f"SD: {english_sd:.2f}")
```

```
SD: 6.14
```

```
print(f"Range: {english_min} - {english_max}")
```

```
Range: 76 - 91
```

```
# Calculate statistics for Science - pattern repeated again!
science_mean = statistics.mean(science_scores)
science_median = statistics.median(science_scores)
science_sd = statistics.stdev(science_scores)
science_min = min(science_scores)
science_max = max(science_scores)

print("Science Statistics:")
```

```
Science Statistics:
```

```
print(f"Mean: {science_mean:.2f}")
```

```
Mean: 87.40
```

```
print(f"Median: {science_median}")
```

```
Median: 87
```

```
print(f"SD: {science_sd:.2f}")
```

```
SD: 3.65
```

```
print(f"Range: {science_min} - {science_max}")
```

```
Range: 83 - 92
```

Python Approach - Function Solution

```
# ============================================
# Demo 1: Function Solution (Python)
# GOOD EXAMPLE - Using a function to eliminate repetition
# ============================================

import statistics

def calculate_subject_stats(scores, subject_name):
    """Calculate and display statistics for a subject."""
    # Calculate all statistics
    mean_score = statistics.mean(scores)
    median_score = statistics.median(scores)
    sd_score = statistics.stdev(scores)
    min_score = min(scores)
    max_score = max(scores)

    # Display results
```

```
    print(f"{subject_name} Statistics:")
    print(f"Mean: {mean_score:.2f}")
    print(f"Median: {median_score}")
    print(f"SD: {sd_score:.2f}")
    print(f"Range: {min_score} - {max_score}")
    print() # Empty line for readability

# Now use the function - no repetition!
calculate_subject_stats(math_scores, "Math")
```

```
Math Statistics:
Mean: 87.60
Median: 88
SD: 6.58
Range: 78 - 95
```

```
calculate_subject_stats(english_scores, "English")
```

```
English Statistics:
Mean: 85.20
Median: 88
SD: 6.14
Range: 76 - 91
```

```
calculate_subject_stats(science_scores, "Science")
```

```
Science Statistics:
Mean: 87.40
Median: 87
SD: 3.65
Range: 83 - 92
```

Repetition in your code is often a sign that the logic should be wrapped in a function, and the "three times rule" is a helpful way to notice when that moment has arrived. Functions allow you to define a process once and reuse it whenever needed, reducing errors and making your analysis easier to maintain. Although R and Python use different syntax, the underlying idea is the same: functions help you organize your work, eliminate duplication, and express your analysis more clearly.

AI Integration

AI tools can play a useful role in helping you recognize when your code would benefit from a function. Because repetition can be easy to overlook when you're focused on getting results, an AI assistant can act as a second set of eyes, pointing out patterns that appear multiple times and suggesting ways to consolidate them into a single reusable function. You can ask the AI to examine your script for repeated logic, help you think through what inputs and outputs a function should have, or propose clearer names that make the function's purpose obvious. Prompts such as "I have repetitive code—how can I turn this into a function?" or "What patterns in my code suggest I need a function?" encourage the AI to focus on structure rather than rewriting your logic. Used this way, AI becomes a design partner that helps you build cleaner, more maintainable code.

7.11.1.2 Function Inputs, Outputs, and Assumptions

Functions are most powerful when you understand how they handle information. Every function receives inputs, performs some internal work, and produces an output. These inputs — often called arguments — allow you to pass different data into the same reusable logic. The output is the value the function returns, which you can store, print, or use in further calculations. Along the way, every function makes assumptions about the data it receives: that it's numeric, that it's not empty, that it doesn't contain missing values, or that the inputs are the same length. Good functions make these assumptions clear and, when possible, check them directly.

Thinking about functions in terms of inputs, outputs, and assumptions helps you design tools that are reliable and predictable. When a function clearly states what it expects and what it returns, it becomes easier to reuse and easier to trust. The examples below show how R and Python handle these ideas, from simple one-argument functions to functions with defaults and functions that validate their inputs before proceeding.

R Approach

```
# ============================================
# Demo 2: Function Inputs, Outputs, Assumptions (R)
# ============================================

# FUNCTION INPUTS (ARGUMENTS)
# Functions receive information through arguments

# Simple function with one input
calculate_gpa <- function(grades) {
  return(mean(grades))
}

# Function with multiple inputs
calculate_weighted_gpa <- function(grades, credit_hours) {
  weighted_sum <- sum(grades * credit_hours)
  total_credits <- sum(credit_hours)
  return(weighted_sum / total_credits)
}
```

```
# Function with default arguments
summarize_grades <- function(grades, include_median = TRUE,
↪  round_digits = 2) {
  mean_grade <- round(mean(grades), round_digits)
  if (include_median) {
    median_grade <- round(median(grades), round_digits)
    return(list(mean = mean_grade, median = median_grade))
  } else {
    return(list(mean = mean_grade))
  }
}

# FUNCTION OUTPUTS
# Functions return values that can be stored and used
student_grades <- c(3.2, 3.8, 3.5, 3.9, 3.1)
credit_hours <- c(3, 4, 3, 4, 3)

# Store function output in variables
simple_gpa <- calculate_gpa(student_grades)
weighted_gpa <- calculate_weighted_gpa(student_grades, credit_hours)
grade_summary <- summarize_grades(student_grades)

print(paste("Simple GPA:", simple_gpa))
```

```
[1] "Simple GPA: 3.5"
```

```
print(paste("Weighted GPA:", round(weighted_gpa, 2)))
```

```
[1] "Weighted GPA: 3.54"
```

```
print("Grade Summary:")
```

```
[1] "Grade Summary:"
```

```
print(grade_summary)
```

```
$mean
[1] 3.5

$median
[1] 3.5
```

```
# FUNCTION ASSUMPTIONS
# Functions make assumptions about their inputs
# This function assumes:
```

```r
# 1. Input is numeric
# 2. Input contains no missing values
# 3. Input has at least one value

safe_mean <- function(values) {
  # Check assumptions and handle violations
  if (!is.numeric(values)) {
    stop("Input must be numeric")
  }
  if (length(values) == 0) {
    stop("Input cannot be empty")
  }

  # Handle missing values
  clean_values <- values[!is.na(values)]
  if (length(clean_values) == 0) {
    warning("All values are missing")
    return(NA)
  }

  return(mean(clean_values))
}

# Test the function with different inputs
test_grades <- c(3.2, 3.8, NA, 3.5, 3.9)
result <- safe_mean(test_grades)
print(paste("Safe mean result:", result))
```

```
[1] "Safe mean result: 3.6"
```

Python Approach

```python
# ==============================================
# Demo 2: Function Inputs, Outputs, Assumptions (Python)
# ==============================================

import statistics

# FUNCTION INPUTS (ARGUMENTS)
# Functions receive information through arguments

# Simple function with one input
def calculate_gpa(grades):
    """Calculate simple GPA from grades."""
```

```
    return statistics.mean(grades)

# Function with multiple inputs
def calculate_weighted_gpa(grades, credit_hours):
    """Calculate weighted GPA using grades and credit hours."""
    weighted_sum = sum(g * c for g, c in zip(grades, credit_hours))
    total_credits = sum(credit_hours)
    return weighted_sum / total_credits

# Function with default arguments
def summarize_grades(grades, include_median=True, round_digits=2):
    """Summarize grades with optional median calculation."""
    mean_grade = round(statistics.mean(grades), round_digits)
    if include_median:
        median_grade = round(statistics.median(grades), round_digits)
        return {'mean': mean_grade, 'median': median_grade}
    else:
        return {'mean': mean_grade}

# FUNCTION OUTPUTS
# Functions return values that can be stored and used
student_grades = [3.2, 3.8, 3.5, 3.9, 3.1]
credit_hours = [3, 4, 3, 4, 3]

# Store function output in variables
simple_gpa = calculate_gpa(student_grades)
weighted_gpa = calculate_weighted_gpa(student_grades, credit_hours)
grade_summary = summarize_grades(student_grades)

print(f"Simple GPA: {simple_gpa:.2f}")
```

```
Simple GPA: 3.50
```

```
print(f"Weighted GPA: {weighted_gpa:.2f}")
```

```
Weighted GPA: 3.54
```

```
print(f"Grade Summary: {grade_summary}")
```

```
Grade Summary: {'mean': 3.5, 'median': 3.5}
```

```
# FUNCTION ASSUMPTIONS
# Functions make assumptions about their inputs
def safe_mean(values):
    """
```

```
    Calculate mean with error checking.
    Assumptions:
    1. Input is a list/array of numbers
    2. Function handles missing values (None)
    3. Function validates input type
    """
    # Check if input is a list or similar
    if not hasattr(values, '__iter__'):
        raise TypeError("Input must be iterable")

    # Convert to list and filter out None values
    clean_values = [v for v in values if v is not None]

    if len(clean_values) == 0:
        raise ValueError("No valid values provided")

    # Check if all values are numeric
    if not all(isinstance(v, (int, float)) for v in clean_values):
        raise TypeError("All values must be numeric")

    return statistics.mean(clean_values)

# Test the function with different inputs
test_grades = [3.2, 3.8, None, 3.5, 3.9]
result = safe_mean(test_grades)
print(f"Safe mean result: {result:.2f}")
```

```
Safe mean result: 3.60
```

Functions receive information through their inputs, perform a task, and return outputs that can be stored or reused. Good functions make their assumptions clear and validate them when possible, which helps prevent errors and makes the code more reliable. Default arguments add flexibility, allowing the same function to handle multiple scenarios. Although R and Python use different syntax, both languages follow the same core ideas about how functions operate and how they support reusable, maintainable code.

AI Integration

AI tools can help you design functions that are clearer, safer, and easier to reuse. When you're unsure how many inputs a function should take, what to return, or what assumptions to check, an AI assistant can help you think through the structure. Asking questions like "Help me design a function that takes these inputs and returns this output" or "What assumptions should my function make about its inputs?" encourages the AI to focus on the design rather than rewriting your logic. This kind of feedback can help you create functions that are more robust and easier for others to understand.

7.11.1.3 Built-in vs User-Defined Functions

Every programming language gives you a set of built-in functions — tools that handle common tasks like calculating means, sorting values, or summarizing data. These functions are efficient, reliable, and optimized by the language designers, which makes them the first place you should look when you need to perform a standard operation. But real data analysis often requires more than the basics. When you need to perform a specialized calculation, apply a custom rule, or repeat a specific workflow across multiple datasets, built-in functions are no longer enough. That's where user-defined functions come in.

User-defined functions allow you to create your own tools tailored to the needs of your analysis. They encapsulate logic that is unique to your workflow — whether that's a custom quality check, a domain-specific calculation, or a multi-step process you want to reuse. Good programming involves knowing when to rely on the built-ins and when to extend the language with your own functions. Built-ins give you a foundation; user-defined functions let you build on top of it.

The examples below show how R and Python combine both types of functions in real analysis: using built-ins for standard tasks and custom functions for deeper, more specific work.

R Approach

```
# ============================================
# Demo 3: Built-in vs User-Defined Functions (R)
# ============================================

# BUILT-IN FUNCTIONS: Your Standard Toolkit
# R comes with many built-in functions for common tasks
survey_data <- c(22, 25, 30, 28, 35, 24, 27, 32, 29, 26)

# Mathematical built-ins
print("Built-in Mathematical Functions:")
```

```
[1] "Built-in Mathematical Functions:"
```

```
print(paste("Mean:", mean(survey_data)))
```

```
[1] "Mean: 27.8"
```

```
print(paste("Median:", median(survey_data)))
```

```
[1] "Median: 27.5"
```

```
print(paste("Standard Deviation:", round(sd(survey_data), 2)))
```

```
[1] "Standard Deviation: 3.88"
```

```
print(paste("Length:", length(survey_data)))
```

```
[1] "Length: 10"
```

```
print(paste("Sum:", sum(survey_data)))
```

```
[1] "Sum: 278"
```

```
# Statistical built-ins
print("Built-in Statistical Functions:")
```

```
[1] "Built-in Statistical Functions:"
```

```
print("Summary:")
```

```
[1] "Summary:"
```

```
print(summary(survey_data))
```

```
   Min. 1st Qu.  Median    Mean 3rd Qu.    Max.
  22.00   25.25   27.50   27.80   29.75   35.00
```

```
# Data manipulation built-ins
print("Built-in Data Manipulation:")
```

```
[1] "Built-in Data Manipulation:"
```

```
print(paste("Sorted:", paste(sort(survey_data), collapse = ", ")))
```

```
[1] "Sorted: 22, 24, 25, 26, 27, 28, 29, 30, 32, 35"
```

```
print(paste("Unique values:", paste(unique(survey_data), collapse = ",
↪  ")))
```

```
[1] "Unique values: 22, 25, 30, 28, 35, 24, 27, 32, 29, 26"
```

```
# USER-DEFINED FUNCTIONS: Custom Solutions
# Create functions for specific analysis needs

# Custom function for detailed age analysis
analyze_age_distribution <- function(ages, group_name = "Sample") {
  # Calculate comprehensive statistics
  n <- length(ages)
  mean_age <- mean(ages)
  median_age <- median(ages)
  sd_age <- sd(ages)
```

```
  # Create age categories
  young <- sum(ages < 25)
  middle <- sum(ages >= 25 & ages < 30)
  older <- sum(ages >= 30)

  # Return comprehensive analysis
  cat("Age Analysis for", group_name, "\n")
  cat("Sample size:", n, "\n")
  cat("Mean age:", round(mean_age, 1), "years\n")
  cat("Median age:", median_age, "years\n")
  cat("Standard deviation:", round(sd_age, 1), "years\n")
  cat("Age distribution:\n")
  cat(" Under 25:", young, "(", round(young/n*100, 1), "%)\n")
  cat(" 25-29:", middle, "(", round(middle/n*100, 1), "%)\n")
  cat(" 30+:", older, "(", round(older/n*100, 1), "%)\n")
  cat("\n")
}

# Custom function for data quality check
check_data_quality <- function(data, variable_name) {
  missing_count <- sum(is.na(data))
  total_count <- length(data)
  missing_percent <- round(missing_count / total_count * 100, 1)

  # Check for outliers (values more than 2 SD from mean)
  if (is.numeric(data)) {
    clean_data <- data[!is.na(data)]
    mean_val <- mean(clean_data)
    sd_val <- sd(clean_data)
    outliers <- sum(abs(clean_data - mean_val) > 2 * sd_val)

    cat("Data Quality Report for", variable_name, "\n")
    cat("Total observations:", total_count, "\n")
    cat("Missing values:", missing_count, "(", missing_percent, "%)\n")
    cat("Potential outliers:", outliers, "\n")
    cat("Data range:", min(clean_data), "to", max(clean_data), "\n\n")
  }
}

# Use both built-in and user-defined functions
analyze_age_distribution(survey_data, "Survey Respondents")
```

```
Age Analysis for Survey Respondents
```

```
Sample size: 10
Mean age: 27.8 years
Median age: 27.5 years
Standard deviation: 3.9 years
Age distribution:
 Under 25: 2 ( 20 %)
 25-29: 5 ( 50 %)
 30+: 3 ( 30 %)
```

```
check_data_quality(survey_data, "Age")
```

```
Data Quality Report for Age
Total observations: 10
Missing values: 0 ( 0 %)
Potential outliers: 0
Data range: 22 to 35
```

```
# WHEN TO USE EACH TYPE
print("When to use built-in functions:")
```

```
[1] "When to use built-in functions:"
```

```
print("- Common mathematical operations")
```

```
[1] "- Common mathematical operations"
```

```
print("- Standard statistical calculations")
```

```
[1] "- Standard statistical calculations"
```

```
print("- Basic data manipulation")
```

```
[1] "- Basic data manipulation"
```

```
print("")
```

```
[1] ""
```

```
print("When to create user-defined functions:")
```

```
[1] "When to create user-defined functions:"
```

```
print("- Specific analysis workflows")
```

```
[1] "- Specific analysis workflows"
```

```
print("- Complex calculations not available built-in")
```

```
[1] "- Complex calculations not available built-in"
```

```
print("- Repetitive custom operations")
```

```
[1] "- Repetitive custom operations"
```

Python Approach

```
# ================================================
# Demo 3: Built-in vs User-Defined Functions (Python)
# ================================================

import statistics
import math

# BUILT-IN FUNCTIONS: Your Standard Toolkit
# Python comes with many built-in functions for common tasks
survey_data = [22, 25, 30, 28, 35, 24, 27, 32, 29, 26]

# Mathematical built-ins
print("Built-in Mathematical Functions:")
```

```
Built-in Mathematical Functions:
```

```
print(f"Mean: {statistics.mean(survey_data):.1f}")
```

```
Mean: 27.8
```

```
print(f"Median: {statistics.median(survey_data)}")
```

```
Median: 27.5
```

```
print(f"Standard Deviation: {statistics.stdev(survey_data):.2f}")
```

```
Standard Deviation: 3.88
```

```
print(f"Length: {len(survey_data)}")
```

```
Length: 10
```

```
print(f"Sum: {sum(survey_data)}")
```

```
Sum: 278
```

```
# Statistical built-ins
print("\nBuilt-in Statistical Functions:")
```

```
Built-in Statistical Functions:
```

```
print(f"Min: {min(survey_data)}")
```

```
Min: 22
```

```
print(f"Max: {max(survey_data)}")
```

```
Max: 35
```

```
print(f"Range: {max(survey_data) - min(survey_data)}")
```

```
Range: 13
```

```
# Data manipulation built-ins
print("\nBuilt-in Data Manipulation:")
```

```

Built-in Data Manipulation:
```

```
print(f"Sorted: {sorted(survey_data)}")
```

```
Sorted: [22, 24, 25, 26, 27, 28, 29, 30, 32, 35]
```

```
print(f"Unique values: {sorted(set(survey_data))}")
```

```
Unique values: [22, 24, 25, 26, 27, 28, 29, 30, 32, 35]
```

```
# USER-DEFINED FUNCTIONS: Custom Solutions
# Create functions for specific analysis needs

def analyze_age_distribution(ages, group_name="Sample"):
    """Comprehensive age distribution analysis."""
    # Calculate comprehensive statistics
    n = len(ages)
    mean_age = statistics.mean(ages)
    median_age = statistics.median(ages)
    sd_age = statistics.stdev(ages)

    # Create age categories
    young = sum(1 for age in ages if age < 25)
    middle = sum(1 for age in ages if 25 <= age < 30)
    older = sum(1 for age in ages if age >= 30)

    # Display comprehensive analysis
    print(f"Age Analysis for {group_name}")
    print(f"Sample size: {n}")
```

```
    print(f"Mean age: {mean_age:.1f} years")
    print(f"Median age: {median_age} years")
    print(f"Standard deviation: {sd_age:.1f} years")
    print("Age distribution:")
    print(f" Under 25: {young} ({young/n*100:.1f}%)")
    print(f" 25-29: {middle} ({middle/n*100:.1f}%)")
    print(f" 30+: {older} ({older/n*100:.1f}%)")
    print()

def check_data_quality(data, variable_name):
    """Check data quality including missing values and outliers."""
    # Handle None values
    clean_data = [x for x in data if x is not None]
    missing_count = len(data) - len(clean_data)
    total_count = len(data)
    missing_percent = missing_count / total_count * 100 if total_count
↪   > 0 else 0

    if clean_data and all(isinstance(x, (int, float)) for x in
     ↪  clean_data):
        mean_val = statistics.mean(clean_data)
        sd_val = statistics.stdev(clean_data) if len(clean_data) > 1
↪   else 0
        outliers = sum(1 for x in clean_data if abs(x - mean_val) > 2
↪   * sd_val)

        print(f"Data Quality Report for {variable_name}")
        print(f"Total observations: {total_count}")
        print(f"Missing values: {missing_count}
         ↪  ({missing_percent:.1f}%)")
        print(f"Potential outliers: {outliers}")
        print(f"Data range: {min(clean_data)} to {max(clean_data)}")
        print()

# Use both built-in and user-defined functions
analyze_age_distribution(survey_data, "Survey Respondents")
```

```
Age Analysis for Survey Respondents
Sample size: 10
Mean age: 27.8 years
Median age: 27.5 years
Standard deviation: 3.9 years
Age distribution:
```

```
 Under 25: 2 (20.0%)
 25-29: 5 (50.0%)
 30+: 3 (30.0%)
```

```
check_data_quality(survey_data, "Age")
```

```
Data Quality Report for Age
Total observations: 10
Missing values: 0 (0.0%)
Potential outliers: 0
Data range: 22 to 35
```

```
# WHEN TO USE EACH TYPE
print("When to use built-in functions:")
```

```
When to use built-in functions:
```

```
print("- Common mathematical operations")
```

```
- Common mathematical operations
```

```
print("- Standard statistical calculations")
```

```
- Standard statistical calculations
```

```
print("- Basic data manipulation")
```

```
- Basic data manipulation
```

```
print()
```

```
print("When to create user-defined functions:")
```

```
When to create user-defined functions:
```

```
print("- Specific analysis workflows")
```

```
- Specific analysis workflows
```

```
print("- Complex calculations not available built-in")
```

```
- Complex calculations not available built-in
```

```
print("- Repetitive custom operations")
```

```
- Repetitive custom operations
```

Built-in functions give you fast, reliable tools for common tasks, while user-defined functions let you create custom solutions tailored to your analysis. Good programming involves using both effectively: relying on built-ins for standard operations and writing your own functions when you need specialized logic or want to eliminate repetition. User-defined functions should complement built-ins, not replace them, and together they form a flexible toolkit for writing clear, reusable, and maintainable code.

AI Integration

AI tools can help you decide whether a task is best handled with a built-in function or whether it requires a custom solution. When you're unsure what built-ins are available, an AI assistant can point you toward the right tool and help you avoid reinventing something the language already provides. When your task is more specialized, AI can help you design a user-defined function that fits your workflow, clarifies your inputs and outputs, and handles edge cases gracefully. Asking questions like "Should I use a built-in function or create my own for this task?" or "What built-in functions are available for statistical analysis?" encourages the AI to guide you toward efficient, well-structured code.

7.11.1.4 Libraries and Specialized Tools

Programming languages are designed to be flexible, but no language includes every tool you might need for real-world data analysis. Instead, languages like R and Python rely on libraries — collections of specialized functions created by experts and communities — to extend their capabilities. Libraries allow you to work efficiently in domains such as data manipulation, visualization, statistical modeling, and machine learning without reinventing complex tools from scratch. They provide optimized, well-tested functions with consistent interfaces, making it easier to write reliable and expressive code.

In data analysis, libraries are essential. They let you filter and summarize data with a single line of code, create publication-quality visualizations, or run advanced statistical models that would be impractical to implement yourself. Learning to use libraries effectively is a core skill: it helps you write cleaner code, avoid unnecessary complexity, and take advantage of the collective expertise built into the language ecosystem. The examples below show how R and Python use libraries to transform raw data into meaningful insights.

7.11.2 Practice

Use the code below for all questions. You may choose R or Python, but the questions are the same.

7.11.2.1 R Version

```
# Repetitive grade statistics (intentionally not optimized)
math_scores <- c(85, 92, 78, 88, 95)
```

```r
english_scores <- c(82, 89, 91, 76, 88)
science_scores <- c(90, 85, 83, 92, 87)

math_mean <- mean(math_scores)
math_sd <- sd(math_scores)
english_mean <- mean(english_scores)
english_sd <- sd(english_scores)
science_mean <- mean(science_scores)
science_sd <- sd(science_scores)

print(paste("Math mean:", math_mean, "SD:", math_sd))
print(paste("English mean:", english_mean, "SD:", english_sd))
print(paste("Science mean:", science_mean, "SD:", science_sd))

# Simple function with assumptions
safe_mean <- function(values) {
  if (!is.numeric(values)) stop("Input must be numeric")
  clean <- values[!is.na(values)]
  if (length(clean) == 0) return(NA)
  return(mean(clean))
}

# Using a library function
library(dplyr)
high_math <- data.frame(score = math_scores) %>% filter(score > 85)
```

7.11.2.2 Python Version

```python
import statistics
import pandas as pd

# Repetitive grade statistics (intentionally not optimized)
math_scores = [85, 92, 78, 88, 95]
english_scores = [82, 89, 91, 76, 88]
science_scores = [90, 85, 83, 92, 87]

math_mean = statistics.mean(math_scores)
math_sd = statistics.stdev(math_scores)
english_mean = statistics.mean(english_scores)
english_sd = statistics.stdev(english_scores)
science_mean = statistics.mean(science_scores)
science_sd = statistics.stdev(science_scores)
```

```
print("Math mean:", math_mean, "SD:", math_sd)
print("English mean:", english_mean, "SD:", english_sd)
print("Science mean:", science_mean, "SD:", science_sd)

# Simple function with assumptions
def safe_mean(values):
    clean = [v for v in values if v is not None]
    if len(clean) == 0:
        return None
    return statistics.mean(clean)

# Using a library function
df = pd.DataFrame({'score': math_scores})
high_math = df[df['score'] > 85]
```

7.11.3 Questions

1. Identify one place in the code where repetition suggests the need for a function.
2. Rewrite the repeated grade-statistics pattern as a single reusable function.
3. Explain what inputs your new function should take and what output it should return.
4. Describe one assumption the original code makes about the score data.
5. Describe one assumption the safe_mean function checks for.
6. Rewrite the safe_mean function to include one additional assumption check of your choice.
7. Explain how using a library function (such as dplyr or pandas) improves the clarity or efficiency of the code.
8. Identify one part of the code that would benefit from clearer naming and explain why.
9. Ask an AI assistant to review your rewritten function. Summarize one suggestion it gave you.
10. In your own words, explain how functions help make code more reusable and maintainable.

Chapter 8

The Premade Code Ecosystem

8.1 Learning Outcomes

8-1: Explain why modern data analysis relies on shared ecosystems of pre-built functions and libraries rather than writing all code from scratch.

8-2: Describe what packages and libraries are, how they are organized, and the benefits they provide in terms of efficiency, reliability, and consistency.

8-3: Compare major data analysis ecosystems in R and Python, including the tidyverse and Python's core data stack (NumPy, pandas, matplotlib, seaborn).

8-4: Explain how coordinated library design improves readability, workflow integration, and analytical thinking across tools.

8-5: Interpret library version numbers and explain why versioning and compatibility matter for reproducible and reliable analysis.

8-6: Evaluate the quality and trustworthiness of libraries using criteria such as documentation, maintenance, community support, and standards.

8-7: Apply a systematic approach to selecting, learning, and integrating new libraries into a data analysis workflow.

8.2 Introduction

In the previous chapter, we explored how functions package ideas into reusable tools. But here's where the story gets even more interesting: you don't have to create all these tools yourself. There's an entire world of pre-built, tested, and refined tools waiting for you to use.

This might feel overwhelming at first. How do you know which tools to trust? How do you learn what's available? How do you avoid getting lost in an endless sea of options? This chapter is about making external tools feel normal and approachable.

We'll explore why analysts don't write everything from scratch, understand what packages and libraries really are, and see how entire ecosystems of tools have evolved to support data analysis. Most importantly, we'll learn how to navigate these ecosystems confidently.

The key insight is both liberating and practical: **modern analysis is built on shared ecosystems**. You're not expected to reinvent every analytical tool—you're expected to learn how to choose, use, and combine the excellent tools that others have created.

8.3 Why Analysts Don't Write Everything from Scratch

When you first start programming, you might think that "real" programmers write everything themselves. This is a common misconception that can actually hold back your progress.

8.3.1 The Reinvention Problem

Imagine if every time you wanted to cook, you had to grow your own vegetables, mill your own flour, make your own utensils, and even build your own stove. You would spend so much time on these basic preparations that you would hardly have any time left to actually cook. Programming works in the same way: if you had to write every small function or tool from scratch, you would waste most of your time on setup instead of solving the real problem. Libraries and built-in functions exist to handle these "basic tasks" for you, so you can focus on the important work.

8.3.2 What "From Scratch" Really Means

Inefficient approach:

```
# Writing your own mean function
calculate_mean <- function(numbers) {
  total <- 0
  count <- 0
  for (i in 1:length(numbers)) {
    if (!is.na(numbers[i])) {
      total <- total + numbers[i]
      count <- count + 1
    }
  }
  return(total / count)
}

my_mean <- calculate_mean(student_data$gpa)
```

Practical approach:

```
# Using the built-in function
my_mean <- mean(student_data$gpa, na.rm = TRUE)
```

The second approach isn't "cheating"—it's smart. It lets you focus on your analytical questions rather than basic computational mechanics.

8.3.3 Standing on the Shoulders of Giants

Using existing tools in programming is like benefiting from a division of labor. Popular tools and libraries are reliable because they have been tested by thousands of users, and they are efficient since experts have optimized them for performance. They often include features you might not think to create on your own, and they come with documentation that provides examples and clear explanations. Additionally, these tools are supported by a community of users who share knowledge and help solve problems, making it easier for you to learn and work effectively.

This collaborative approach leads us naturally to understanding what packages and libraries actually are.

8.4 What Packages and Libraries Are

The terms "packages" and "libraries" are often used interchangeably, but they represent a simple, powerful concept: collections of related functions organized for easy use.

Think of a library in programming like a well-organized toolbox. A basic toolbox might contain a hammer, screwdriver, and wrench all mixed together, which works for simple tasks but can be messy and hard to manage. A professional toolbox, on the other hand, organizes tools by type: electrical tools like wire strippers and voltage testers, plumbing tools like pipe wrenches and fittings, and carpentry tools like saws and chisels, each in their own section. Programming libraries work the same way—they group related functions together, making it easier to find and use the right tools for a specific task efficiently.

8.4.1 Simple Library Example

Without libraries (basic approach):

```
# Using built-in functions individually
student_summary <- aggregate(student_data$gpa,
                             by = list(student_data$major),
                             FUN = mean)
filtered_data <- student_data[student_data$gpa > 3.0, ]
```

With libraries (organized approach):

```
library(dplyr)

# Functions designed to work together
student_summary <- student_data %>%
  filter(gpa > 3.0) %>%
  group_by(major) %>%
  summarize(mean_gpa = mean(gpa))
```

8.4.2 What Libraries Provide

Libraries in programming provide several important benefits. They offer consistent syntax, meaning the functions within a library are designed to work together smoothly. They provide comprehensive solutions by including complete sets of tools for specific tasks, saving you from having to build everything yourself. Libraries are also tested and refined by many users, which improves reliability and reduces errors. In addition, they come with documentation, including tutorials, examples, and help files, making it easier to learn and apply their functions. Finally, libraries often have strong community support, with forums, tutorials, and shared knowledge that can help you solve problems and learn best practices.

8.4.3 How Libraries Are Created

Libraries in programming don't appear out of nowhere—they are created by people and communities addressing real needs. Researchers develop libraries to share solutions to problems they've studied. Practitioners create them to have better tools for their everyday work. Software developers often build libraries simply because they enjoy creating useful tools. In addition, communities come together to collaborate on common challenges, contributing improvements, testing, and documentation. Together, these efforts result in the libraries that programmers rely on today.

Understanding what libraries are prepares us to explore specific ecosystems, starting with R's tidyverse.

8.5 The Tidyverse

The tidyverse represents one of the most successful examples of a coordinated library ecosystem. Understanding its philosophy helps you see how well-designed tools can work together seamlessly.

8.5.1 What the Tidyverse Is

The tidyverse is a collection of R packages designed around a shared philosophy of data analysis. Unlike using many unrelated tools, the tidyverse provides a coordinated system where the packages work seamlessly together. Its core packages include dplyr for data manipulation, ggplot2 for data visualization, readr for importing data, tidyr for reshaping data, purrr for functional programming, and tibble for modern, user-friendly data frames.

The philosophy behind the tidyverse emphasizes consistency and readability. All packages follow consistent grammar, so learning one package helps you use others more easily. Functions are pipe-friendly, meaning you can chain them together in a clear sequence of steps. The code is designed to be human-readable, often reading like plain English, and it encourages tidy data practices, where data is structured in a consistent and predictable way. This makes data analysis more intuitive, efficient, and less error prone.

8.5.2 Seeing the Philosophy in Action

The tidyverse makes R code more readable and consistent compared with traditional approaches. For example, suppose you want to filter students with a GPA above 3.0 and calculate the average study hours by major. In traditional R, you might write:

```
# Traditional R approach
filtered_data <- subset(student_data, gpa > 3.0)
grouped_data <- aggregate(filtered_data$study_hours,
```

```
                        by = list(filtered_data$major),
                        FUN = mean)
names(grouped_data) <- c("major", "avg_hours")
```

Here, you first create a filtered dataset, then aggregate the study hours using aggregate(), and finally rename the columns. Each step uses a separate variable, which can make the code longer and harder to follow.

Using the tidyverse, the same task becomes much simpler and more readable:

```
# Tidyverse approach
library(dplyr)
result <- student_data %>%
  filter(gpa > 3.0) %>%
  group_by(major) %>%
  summarize(avg_hours = mean(study_hours))
```

The %>% pipe operator passes the dataset from one function to the next. You filter the rows, group by major, and summarize the average study hours in one flowing sequence, avoiding intermediate variables and making the logic easy to follow.

Consistency is another benefit of the tidyverse. Once you learn a pattern in dplyr, you can apply it in other packages. For example, filtering and selecting columns:

```
# Data manipulation example
student_data %>%
  filter(gpa > 3.0) %>%
  select(major, gpa, study_hours)
```

And filtering before visualizing with ggplot2:

```
# Data visualization example
library(ggplot2)
student_data %>%
  filter(gpa > 3.0) %>%
  ggplot(aes(x = study_hours, y = gpa)) +
  geom_point()
```

Notice how both examples use the same %>% pipe operator and logical flow.

To get started with the tidyverse, install it with:

```
install.packages("tidyverse") # Installs all core tidyverse packages
library(tidyverse) # Loads dplyr, ggplot2, readr, and others
```

A practical learning path is to first master dplyr for data manipulation, ggplot2 for visualization, and readr for importing data. Then gradually add tidyr for reshaping data, purrr for applying functions systematically, and stringr for working with text. This approach helps you build a consistent, readable, and efficient workflow in R.

This coordinated approach in R has parallels in Python's data ecosystem, which we'll explore next.

8.6 Python's Data Stack: pandas, NumPy, matplotlib

Python's approach to data analysis is different from R's tidyverse but equally powerful. Instead of one coordinated system, Python has several foundational libraries that work together to create a comprehensive data analysis environment.

8.6.1 The Foundation: NumPy

NumPy (Numerical Python) provides the mathematical foundation for everything else:

```
import numpy as np

# Efficient numerical operations
grades = np.array([85, 92, 78, 96, 88])
average = np.mean(grades)
std_dev = np.std(grades)
```

NumPy is a fundamental library in Python for numerical computing. It provides efficient arrays that allow fast mathematical operations on large datasets, far faster than using regular Python lists. NumPy also includes a wide range of mathematical functions, such as statistics, linear algebra operations, and random number generation, making it easier to perform complex calculations. Beyond its own capabilities, NumPy serves as a foundation layer for many other libraries, such as pandas, SciPy, and scikit-learn, which build on its efficient array structures and functions.

8.6.2 Data Manipulation: pandas

pandas provides data structures and tools for practical data analysis:

```
import pandas as pd

# Read and manipulate data
student_data = pd.read_csv("student_survey.csv")

# Data manipulation that feels familiar
summary = (student_data
           .query("gpa > 3.0")
           .groupby("major")
           .agg({"gpa": "mean", "study_hours": "mean"}))
```

Pandas is a Python library designed for working with structured data. Its core data structure is the DataFrame, which works like a spreadsheet, making it easy to store and manipulate tabular data. Pandas provides tools for cleaning data, including handling missing values, removing duplicates, and correcting inconsistencies. It also supports powerful grouping and aggregation operations, often called split-apply-combine, which let you summarize and analyze data efficiently. Additionally, pandas makes it simple to read from and write to a variety of file formats, such as CSV, Excel, and even databases, allowing smooth integration with other data sources.

8.6.3 Visualization: matplotlib and seaborn

Python offers multiple options for creating visualizations, with matplotlib serving as the foundational library and seaborn providing a higher-level, easier-to-use interface.

Using matplotlib, you can create detailed plots by specifying each component of the graph. For example:

```
import matplotlib.pyplot as plt

plt.scatter(student_data['study_hours'], student_data['gpa'])
plt.xlabel('Study Hours')
plt.ylabel('GPA')
plt.show()
```

This code creates a scatterplot of study hours versus GPA. plt.scatter() plots the points, plt.xlabel() and plt.ylabel() add axis labels, and plt.show() displays the plot. Matplotlib gives you full control over each element of your visualization, but it can require more code.

Seaborn, on the other hand, builds on matplotlib and provides simpler syntax for creating attractive plots with additional features. For instance:

```
import seaborn as sns

sns.scatterplot(data=student_data, x='study_hours', y='gpa', hue='major')
```

Here, sns.scatterplot() automatically handles coloring by major using the hue argument and applies default styling for a cleaner look. Seaborn makes it easy to create informative, visually appealing plots with less code.

8.6.4 How They Work Together

Python's data stack—NumPy, pandas, matplotlib, and seaborn—works seamlessly. Each library complements the others:

```
import numpy as np
import pandas as pd
import matplotlib.pyplot as plt
```

```
# NumPy for mathematical operations
standardized_gpa = (student_data['gpa']
    - np.mean(student_data['gpa'])) / np.std(student_data['gpa'])

summary_stats = (
    student_data.groupby('major')['gpa_standardized']
    .describe()
)

# matplotlib for visualization
plt.hist(student_data['gpa_standardized'], bins=20)
plt.title('Distribution of Standardized GPA')
```

In this example, NumPy calculates the standardized GPA using mathematical operations. Pandas stores the result in a DataFrame and allows grouping by major to generate summary statistics. Finally, matplotlib creates a histogram to visualize the distribution of standardized GPAs. By combining these tools, Python lets you efficiently process, analyze, and visualize data in a consistent workflow.

8.6.5 Getting Started with Python's Data Stack

To use Python for data analysis, you need several key libraries: NumPy for numerical calculations, pandas for data manipulation, and matplotlib and seaborn for visualization. You can install these individually using pip by running:

```
pip install numpy pandas matplotlib seaborn
```

This installs each package one by one.

Alternatively, a simpler approach—especially for beginners—is to use a complete Python distribution like **Anaconda** or **Miniconda**. Anaconda comes with all the core data science packages pre-installed, along with additional tools for managing environments and packages. Miniconda is a smaller, minimal version that lets you add only the packages you need. Using a distribution can save time and reduce setup problems, making it easier to start working with Python's data stack immediately.

8.7 Versioning and Compatibility

One of the challenges of using external libraries is that they're constantly being updated and improved. Understanding how versioning works helps you avoid compatibility problems and choose stable tools.

8.7.1 Why Versions Matter

Software libraries are constantly evolving and using the right version matters. Updates often include bug fixes that correct errors, new features that add capabilities, and performance improvements that make code run faster. However, updates can also introduce breaking changes, where older ways of doing things no longer work as before. Being aware of library versions ensures your code runs reliably and takes advantage of improvements without unexpected problems.

8.7.2 Understanding Version Numbers

Library version numbers, like "2.1.3," help you understand the type of changes included in an update. The first number, the **major version** (2), indicates big changes that might break existing code. The second number, the **minor version** (1), signals new features that are usually backward compatible, meaning your existing code should still work. The third number, the **patch version** (3), represents bug fixes and small improvements that are generally safe to update without affecting your code. Understanding these numbers helps you manage updates and maintain stable, reliable projects.

8.7.3 Practical Examples

R package versions:

```
# Check what version you have
packageVersion("dplyr")

# Install a specific version if needed
install.packages("dplyr", version = "1.0.7")
```

Python package versions:

```
# Check versions
import pandas as pd
print(pd.__version__)

# Install specific version
# pip install pandas==1.3.0
```

8.7.4 Managing Library Versions

To avoid version-related problems, it's important to document the versions you're using, test updates carefully, stick to stable releases for critical work, and use virtual environments to isolate project dependencies. Compatibility issues can occur when code stops working, functions are renamed or removed, or default behaviors change. Solutions include checking changelogs, following migration guides, or staying with older versions for stability. For learning, recent stable versions are best; for important projects, prioritize reliability over the newest features; and for exploration, you can experiment with cutting-edge releases. Regularly reviewing your library versions and their documentation helps maintain trust and ensures your code remains reliable.

8.8 Trust, Maintenance, and Community Standards

With thousands of available libraries, how do you know which ones to trust? Understanding how the open-source ecosystem works helps you make good choices.

8.8.1 Evaluating Library Quality

A trustworthy library is actively maintained with regular updates and bug fixes, has clear documentation with examples, a large user base, responsive maintainers, and a clear license for legal use. Warning signs include no recent updates, poor or confusing documentation, many unresolved issues, unclear licensing, or relying on a single maintainer. Checking these factors helps ensure you choose reliable, safe, and well-supported libraries for your projects.

8.8.2 Community Standards and Best Practices

High-quality libraries follow established community standards. In R, CRAN packages meet strict quality checks, use consistent naming, provide documentation and examples, and include automated tests for reliability. In Python, well-designed libraries are distributed via PyPI, follow PEP guidelines, include type hints, and use testing frameworks like pytest. Adhering to these standards ensures libraries are reliable, maintainable, and easier for users to adopt.

8.8.3 Library Maintenance and Contribution

Most libraries are maintained by individual developers, research groups, companies, or user communities, ensuring that tools stay reliable, updated, and improved over time. You don't need to be an expert to contribute to this ecosystem. Simple contributions like reporting bugs, suggesting improvements, sharing usage examples, or answering questions in forums help strengthen the community and improve the tools for everyone.

When choosing libraries, consider your purpose: for learning, prioritize popular and well-documented libraries; for production work, focus on stability and active maintenance; for exploration, try newer tools that solve specific problems; and for collaboration, use tools your team already knows.

As you gain experience, you can build your reputation in the community by documenting your work, contributing to discussions, creating useful tools, and maintaining high-quality standards in your own projects. This approach helps you both benefit from and contribute to the shared ecosystem of libraries.

8.9 Conclusion

With so many tools available, the key is to develop a systematic approach. Start by building a core toolkit: in R, focus on the tidyverse packages like dplyr, ggplot2, and readr; in Python, start with pandas, numpy, and matplotlib. Expand gradually, adding libraries for specific tasks, specialized domains, or advanced techniques only when needed.

When discovering new tools, look for task-based solutions, community recommendations, course materials, or examples from colleagues and conferences. Evaluate quickly by asking if the tool solves your problem, is actively maintained, is well-documented, and fits your workflow. For deeper evaluation, try simple examples with your own data and review documentation and community discussions.

Adopt new tools systematically: learn the basics, practice on small projects, explore features gradually, and integrate them into your workflow. It's okay to stick with tools that work, learn gradually, and match tools to specific projects rather than chasing every new trend. Focus on solving real problems, building deep expertise, and maintaining quality in your analysis.

Modern data analysis is collaborative: every project builds on the work of statisticians, programmers, domain experts, educators, and community contributors. As you develop skills, you move from being a user and learner to eventually contributing and creating tools yourself. This collaborative ecosystem ensures continuous improvement, shared knowledge, and higher-quality work.

8.10 Review Questions

1. Why don't professional analysts write all their code from scratch, and what is the "reinvention problem"?
2. How does using pre-built functions or libraries save time and improve reliability in programming?
3. What is the difference between a package and a library in programming, and why are they useful?

4. Explain the analogy of a programming library as a "professional toolbox."
5. What is the tidyverse in R, and what are its core packages?
6. How does the tidyverse improve code readability and consistency compared with traditional R approaches?
7. In Python, what are the main libraries used for data analysis, and what roles do NumPy, pandas, matplotlib, and seaborn play?
8. How do Python's data libraries complement each other in a typical workflow?
9. Why is understanding library versioning important, and what do the major, minor, and patch version numbers indicate?
10. What factors help you determine whether a library is trustworthy and suitable for your project?
11. How can you contribute to library ecosystems, even as a beginner?
12. Describe a systematic approach to discovering, learning, and integrating new libraries into your workflow.

8.11 Ch 8 Lab The Premade Code Ecosystem

Modern data analysis is built on an enormous foundation of premade code. Analysts rarely write everything from scratch because the tools they need already exist — optimized, tested, and refined by large communities over many years. Instead of reinventing basic operations like reading data, calculating statistics, or creating visualizations, analysts rely on packages and libraries that provide these capabilities out of the box. This ecosystem of shared code allows you to focus on the logic of your analysis rather than the mechanics of implementation.

In R, ecosystems like the Tidyverse provide a coherent set of tools for data manipulation, visualization, and modeling. In Python, libraries such as NumPy, pandas, and matplotlib form the core of the scientific computing stack. These ecosystems give analysts a common language and workflow, making it easier to collaborate, learn from examples, and build analyses that are both powerful and readable. Understanding how these tools fit together — and how to choose the right one for the task — is a key part of becoming an effective data analyst.

This lab introduces the major ecosystems you'll use throughout the course. You'll learn why premade code is essential, how packages extend the capabilities of a language, and how to install, load, and use these tools in both R and Python. You'll also explore how Positron can help you discover new libraries, understand their purpose, and integrate them into your workflow.

8.11.1 Demonstration

8.11.1.1 Don't Write Everything from Scratch

A core idea in modern data analysis is that you are never starting from a blank slate. The tools you use — whether in R or Python — sit on top of decades of mathematical, statistical, and computational work. Trying to reimplement these tools yourself is not only inefficient, it's unnecessary. Understanding what "from scratch" actually looks like helps you appreciate why packages and libraries exist, and why analysts rely on them every day.

When you write code from scratch, you take responsibility for every detail: the formulas, the edge cases, the performance, the error handling, and the correctness of the results. Even something as simple as a correlation coefficient requires multiple steps: computing means, centering values, summing products, and normalizing by squared deviations. Doing this once is manageable. Doing it for every statistical operation you need — standard deviation, regression, visualization, file reading — quickly becomes overwhelming. This is why analysts build on existing, tested code rather than reinventing it.

The examples below show the contrast clearly. First, you'll see what it looks like to compute correlation manually. Then you'll see how a single built-in function or library call replaces all of that work, while also handling missing values, edge cases, and performance optimizations automatically. This is the essence of the premade code ecosystem: standing on the shoulders of giants so you can focus on the analysis, not the mechanics.

R Approach - Writing from Scratch

```
# ============================================
# Demo 1: The Reinvention Problem (R)
# BAD EXAMPLE - Writing everything from scratch
# ============================================

# Imagine trying to calculate correlation without built-in functions
calculate_correlation_from_scratch <- function(x, y) {
  # Calculate means
  n <- length(x)
  mean_x <- sum(x) / n
  mean_y <- sum(y) / n

  # Calculate numerator and denominators
  numerator <- sum((x - mean_x) * (y - mean_y))
  sum_sq_x <- sum((x - mean_x)^2)
  sum_sq_y <- sum((y - mean_y)^2)
  denominator <- sqrt(sum_sq_x * sum_sq_y)
```

```
  # Return correlation
  return(numerator / denominator)
}

# Create sample data
study_hours <- c(10, 15, 20, 25, 30, 35, 40)
gpa <- c(2.5, 2.8, 3.2, 3.5, 3.8, 3.9, 4.0)

# Calculate correlation the hard way
correlation_manual <- calculate_correlation_from_scratch(study_hours,
 ↪  gpa)
print(paste("Manual correlation:", round(correlation_manual, 3)))
```

```
[1] "Manual correlation: 0.978"
```

```
# Now imagine doing this for every statistical operation!
# - Standard deviation from scratch
# - Linear regression from scratch
# - Data visualization from scratch
# - File reading from scratch

print("Problems with writing from scratch:")
```

```
[1] "Problems with writing from scratch:"
```

```
print("1. Time-consuming and error-prone")
```

```
[1] "1. Time-consuming and error-prone"
```

```
print("2. Likely to have bugs")
```

```
[1] "2. Likely to have bugs"
```

```
print("3. Not optimized for performance")
```

```
[1] "3. Not optimized for performance"
```

```
print("4. Missing edge case handling")
```

```
[1] "4. Missing edge case handling"
```

```
print("5. Reinventing solved problems")
```

```
[1] "5. Reinventing solved problems"
```

R Approach - Using Built-in Functions

```
# ============================================
# Demo 1: Standing on Shoulders of Giants (R)
# GOOD EXAMPLE - Using existing, tested code
# ============================================

# Using built-in correlation function
correlation_builtin <- cor(study_hours, gpa)
print(paste("Built-in correlation:", round(correlation_builtin, 3)))
```

```
[1] "Built-in correlation: 0.978"
```

```
# Verify they're the same
print(paste("Results match:", round(correlation_manual, 6) ==
↪  round(correlation_builtin, 6)))
```

```
[1] "Results match: TRUE"
```

```
# But built-in functions offer much more:
# - Handle missing values
# - Multiple correlation methods
# - Error checking
# - Optimized performance

# Example with missing data
study_hours_missing <- c(10, 15, NA, 25, 30, 35, 40)
gpa_missing <- c(2.5, 2.8, 3.2, NA, 3.8, 3.9, 4.0)

# Built-in handles this gracefully
correlation_with_na <- cor(study_hours_missing, gpa_missing, use =
↪  "complete.obs")
print(paste("Correlation with missing data:",
↪  round(correlation_with_na, 3)))
```

```
[1] "Correlation with missing data: 0.985"
```

```
# Our manual function would break!
# correlation_manual_broken <-
↪  calculate_correlation_from_scratch(study_hours_missing,
↪  gpa_missing)
```

Python Approach - Writing from Scratch

```
# ============================================
# Demo 1: The Reinvention Problem (Python)
# BAD EXAMPLE - Writing everything from scratch
```

```
# ============================================

import math

def calculate_correlation_from_scratch(x, y):
    """Calculate correlation coefficient manually."""
    # Calculate means
    n = len(x)
    mean_x = sum(x) / n
    mean_y = sum(y) / n

    # Calculate numerator and denominators
    numerator = sum((x[i] - mean_x) * (y[i] - mean_y) for i in
    ↪ range(n))
    sum_sq_x = sum((x[i] - mean_x)**2 for i in range(n))
    sum_sq_y = sum((y[i] - mean_y)**2 for i in range(n))
    denominator = math.sqrt(sum_sq_x * sum_sq_y)

    # Return correlation
    return numerator / denominator

# Create sample data
study_hours = [10, 15, 20, 25, 30, 35, 40]
gpa = [2.5, 2.8, 3.2, 3.5, 3.8, 3.9, 4.0]

# Calculate correlation the hard way
correlation_manual = calculate_correlation_from_scratch(study_hours,
↪ gpa)
print(f"Manual correlation: {correlation_manual:.3f}")
```

```
Manual correlation: 0.978
```

```
print("\nProblems with writing from scratch:")
```

```

Problems with writing from scratch:
```

```
print("1. Time-consuming and error-prone")
```

```
1. Time-consuming and error-prone
```

```
print("2. Likely to have bugs")
```

```
2. Likely to have bugs
```

```
print("3. Not optimized for performance")
```

```
3. Not optimized for performance
```

```
print("4. Missing edge case handling")
```

```
4. Missing edge case handling
```

```
print("5. Reinventing solved problems")
```

```
5. Reinventing solved problems
```

Python Approach - Using Libraries

```
# ============================================
# Demo 1: Standing on Shoulders of Giants (Python)
# GOOD EXAMPLE - Using existing, tested code
# ============================================

import numpy as np
import pandas as pd

# Using NumPy's correlation function
correlation_numpy = np.corrcoef(study_hours, gpa)[0, 1]
print(f"NumPy correlation: {correlation_numpy:.3f}")
```

```
NumPy correlation: 0.978
```

```
# Using pandas for more advanced correlation analysis
df = pd.DataFrame({
    'study_hours': study_hours,
    'gpa': gpa
})
correlation_pandas = df['study_hours'].corr(df['gpa'])
print(f"Pandas correlation: {correlation_pandas:.3f}")
```

```
Pandas correlation: 0.978
```

```
# Verify they're all the same
print(f"Results match: {abs(correlation_manual - correlation_numpy) <
↪  0.000001}")
```

```
Results match: True
```

```
# But libraries offer much more:
# - Handle missing values
# - Multiple correlation methods
```

```
# - Error checking
# - Optimized performance

# Example with missing data
study_hours_missing = [10, 15, None, 25, 30, 35, 40]
gpa_missing = [2.5, 2.8, 3.2, None, 3.8, 3.9, 4.0]

df_missing = pd.DataFrame({
    'study_hours': study_hours_missing,
    'gpa': gpa_missing
})

# Pandas handles this gracefully
correlation_with_na = df_missing['study_hours'].corr(df_missing['gpa'])
print(f"Correlation with missing data: {correlation_with_na:.3f}")
```

```
Correlation with missing data: 0.985
```

```
# Our manual function would break with None values!
```

Writing everything from scratch is slow, error-prone, and unnecessary. Existing libraries are optimized, tested, and designed to handle edge cases that manual code often overlooks. Standing on the shoulders of giants means building on the work of others so you can focus on the analysis itself. Both R and Python offer rich ecosystems of premade code that make modern data analysis possible.

AI Integration

AI tools can help you identify when you're reinventing something the ecosystem already provides. When you're unsure whether a function exists, or which library handles a particular task, an AI assistant can point you toward the right tool and help you avoid unnecessary manual work. Asking questions like "What libraries should I use instead of writing this from scratch?" or "Show me the ecosystem of packages available for data analysis" helps you discover the broader landscape of premade code and choose tools that are reliable, efficient, and well supported.

8.11.1.2 Understanding Packages and Libraries

Programming languages become powerful not because of their core features, but because of the ecosystems built around them. Packages and libraries are collections of functions, datasets, documentation, and tools that extend what the language can do. They allow analysts to work efficiently without reimplementing common tasks, and they provide specialized capabilities for everything from date handling to statistical modeling. Instead of writing low-level code, you can rely on well-tested, community-maintained tools that solve problems reliably and consistently.

Packages also shape the way analysts think. In R, packages like lubridate, broom, and the datasets collection provide ready-made solutions for working with dates, cleaning model output, and exploring example data. In Python, libraries such as datetime, seaborn, and scipy offer similar capabilities. These tools give you a shared vocabulary for analysis and make it easier to learn from examples, collaborate with others, and build analyses that are both expressive and maintainable.

Understanding what packages provide — and how they are created, installed, and used — is essential for working effectively in modern data ecosystems. The demonstrations below show how R and Python packages supply functions, datasets, and specialized tools that would be impractical to build from scratch.

R Approach - Package Ecosystem

```
# ============================================
# Demo 2: Understanding Packages (R)
# What packages provide and how they work
# ============================================

# WHAT PACKAGES PROVIDE
print("=== WHAT R PACKAGES PROVIDE ===")
```

```
[1] "=== WHAT R PACKAGES PROVIDE ==="
```

```
# 1. Functions for specific tasks
library(lubridate) # Date/time manipulation

# Example: Working with dates
date_string <- "2024-02-18"
parsed_date <- ymd(date_string)
print(paste("Parsed date:", parsed_date))
```

```
[1] "Parsed date: 2024-02-18"
```

```
print(paste("Day of week:", wday(parsed_date, label = TRUE)))
```

```
[1] "Day of week: Sun"
```

```
print(paste("Month:", month(parsed_date, label = TRUE)))
```

```
[1] "Month: Feb"
```

```
# 2. Datasets for learning and testing
library(datasets)
print("Built-in datasets available:")
```

```
[1] "Built-in datasets available:"
```

```r
items <- data(package = "datasets")$results[, "Item"]
cat(items, sep = "\n")
```

```
AirPassengers
BJsales
BJsales.lead (BJsales)
BOD
CO2
ChickWeight
DNase
EuStockMarkets
Formaldehyde
HairEyeColor
Harman23.cor
Harman74.cor
Indometh
InsectSprays
JohnsonJohnson
LakeHuron
LifeCycleSavings
Loblolly
Nile
Orange
OrchardSprays
PlantGrowth
Puromycin
Seatbelts
Theoph
Titanic
ToothGrowth
UCBAdmissions
UKDriverDeaths
UKgas
USAccDeaths
USArrests
USJudgeRatings
USPersonalExpenditure
UScitiesD
VADeaths
WWWusage
WorldPhones
ability.cov
```

```
airmiles
airquality
anscombe
attenu
attitude
austres
beaver1 (beavers)
beaver2 (beavers)
cars
chickwts
co2
crimtab
discoveries
esoph
euro
euro.cross (euro)
eurodist
faithful
fdeaths (UKLungDeaths)
freeny
freeny.x (freeny)
freeny.y (freeny)
gait
infert
iris
iris3
islands
ldeaths (UKLungDeaths)
lh
longley
lynx
mdeaths (UKLungDeaths)
morley
mtcars
nhtemp
nottem
npk
occupationalStatus
penguins
penguins_raw (penguins)
precip
presidents
pressure
```

```
quakes
randu
rivers
rock
sleep
stack.loss (stackloss)
stack.x (stackloss)
stackloss
state.abb (state)
state.area (state)
state.center (state)
state.division (state)
state.name (state)
state.region (state)
state.x77 (state)
sunspot.m2014 (sunspot.month)
sunspot.month
sunspot.year
sunspots
swiss
treering
trees
uspop
volcano
warpbreaks
women
```

```r
# Example: Using built-in mtcars dataset
print("Sample from mtcars dataset:")
```

```
[1] "Sample from mtcars dataset:"
```

```r
print(head(mtcars, 3))
```

```
               mpg cyl disp  hp drat    wt  qsec vs am gear carb
Mazda RX4     21.0   6  160 110 3.90 2.620 16.46  0  1    4    4
Mazda RX4 Wag 21.0   6  160 110 3.90 2.875 17.02  0  1    4    4
Datsun 710    22.8   4  108  93 3.85 2.320 18.61  1  1    4    1
```

```r
# 3. Specialized analysis tools
library(broom) # Tidy statistical output

# Example: Clean regression output
model <- lm(mpg ~ wt + hp, data = mtcars)
tidy_results <- tidy(model)
```

```
print("Tidy regression results:")
```

```
[1] "Tidy regression results:"
```

```
print(tidy_results)
```

```
# A tibble: 3 x 5
  term        estimate std.error statistic  p.value
  <chr>          <dbl>     <dbl>     <dbl>    <dbl>
1 (Intercept)  37.2      1.60         23.3  2.57e-20
2 wt           -3.88     0.633        -6.13 1.12e- 6
3 hp           -0.0318   0.00903      -3.52 1.45e- 3
```

```
# HOW PACKAGES ARE CREATED AND MAINTAINED
print("\n=== HOW PACKAGES WORK ===")
```

```
[1] "\n=== HOW PACKAGES WORK ==="
```

```
print("Packages contain:")
```

```
[1] "Packages contain:"
```

```
print("1. R functions (.R files)")
```

```
[1] "1. R functions (.R files)"
```

```
print("2. Documentation (.Rd files)")
```

```
[1] "2. Documentation (.Rd files)"
```

```
print("3. Data files (.rda files)")
```

```
[1] "3. Data files (.rda files)"
```

```
print("4. Tests and examples")
```

```
[1] "4. Tests and examples"
```

```
print("5. Metadata (DESCRIPTION file)")
```

```
[1] "5. Metadata (DESCRIPTION file)"
```

```
# Package installation and loading
print("\nPackage workflow:")
```

```
[1] "\nPackage workflow:"
```

```
print("1. install.packages('package_name') # Download and install")
```

```
[1] "1. install.packages('package_name') # Download and install"
```

```
print("2. library(package_name) # Load into session")
```

```
[1] "2. library(package_name) # Load into session"
```

```
print("3. Use package functions")
```

```
[1] "3. Use package functions"
```

```
print("4. ?function_name # Get help")
```

```
[1] "4. ?function_name # Get help"
```

```
# Check what packages are loaded
print("Currently loaded packages:")
```

```
[1] "Currently loaded packages:"
```

```
loaded_packages <- search()
print(loaded_packages[grepl("package:", loaded_packages)])
```

```
 [1] "package:broom"      "package:lubridate"  "package:reticulate"
 [4] "package:stats"      "package:graphics"   "package:grDevices"
 [7] "package:utils"      "package:datasets"   "package:methods"
[10] "package:base"
```

Python Approach - Package Ecosystem

```
# ============================================
# Demo 2: Understanding Packages (Python)
# What packages provide and how they work
# ============================================

import datetime
import pandas as pd
import numpy as np

# WHAT PACKAGES PROVIDE
print("=== WHAT PYTHON PACKAGES PROVIDE ===")
```

```
=== WHAT PYTHON PACKAGES PROVIDE ===
```

```
# 1. Functions for specific tasks
from datetime import datetime, timedelta
```

```
# Example: Working with dates
date_string = "2024-02-18"
parsed_date = datetime.strptime(date_string, "%Y-%m-%d")
print(f"Parsed date: {parsed_date}")
```

```
Parsed date: 2024-02-18 00:00:00
```

```
print(f"Day of week: {parsed_date.strftime('%A')}")
```

```
Day of week: Sunday
```

```
print(f"Month: {parsed_date.strftime('%B')}")
```

```
Month: February
```

```
# 2. Datasets for learning and testing
# Example: Using seaborn's built-in datasets
try:
    import seaborn as sns
    print("\nBuilt-in datasets available in seaborn:")
    datasets = sns.get_dataset_names()
    print(datasets[:4]) # Show first 4

    # Load a sample dataset
    tips = sns.load_dataset('tips')
    print("Sample from tips dataset:")
    print(tips.head(3))
except ImportError:
    print("Seaborn not available - install with: pip install seaborn")
```

```

Built-in datasets available in seaborn:
['anagrams', 'anscombe', 'attention', 'brain_networks']
Sample from tips dataset:
   total_bill   tip     sex smoker  day    time  size
0       16.99  1.01  Female     No  Sun  Dinner     2
1       10.34  1.66    Male     No  Sun  Dinner     3
2       21.01  3.50    Male     No  Sun  Dinner     3
```

```
# 3. Specialized analysis tools
from scipy import stats

# Example: Statistical tests
data1 = [1, 2, 3, 4, 5]
```

```
data2 = [2, 4, 6, 8, 10]
correlation, p_value = stats.pearsonr(data1, data2)
print(f"\nCorrelation analysis:")
```

```

Correlation analysis:
```

```
print(f"Correlation: {correlation:.3f}")
```

```
Correlation: 1.000
```

```
print(f"P-value: {p_value:.3f}")
```

```
P-value: 0.000
```

```
# HOW PACKAGES ARE CREATED AND MAINTAINED
print("\n=== HOW PYTHON PACKAGES WORK ===")
```

```

=== HOW PYTHON PACKAGES WORK ===
```

```
print("Packages contain:")
```

```
Packages contain:
```

```
print("1. Python modules (.py files)")
```

```
1. Python modules (.py files)
```

```
print("2. Documentation (docstrings, README)")
```

```
2. Documentation (docstrings, README)
```

```
print("3. Data files")
```

```
3. Data files
```

```
print("4. Tests")
```

```
4. Tests
```

```
print("5. Setup configuration (setup.py, pyproject.toml)")
```

```
5. Setup configuration (setup.py, pyproject.toml)
```

```
# Package installation and importing
print("\nPackage workflow:")
```

```
Package workflow:
```

```
print("1. pip install package_name # Download and install")
```

```
1. pip install package_name # Download and install
```

```
print("2. import package_name # Import into session")
```

```
2. import package_name # Import into session
```

```
print("3. Use package functions")
```

```
3. Use package functions
```

```
print("4. help(function_name) # Get help")
```

```
4. help(function_name) # Get help
```

```
# Check what packages are available
import sys
#print(f"\nPython version: {sys.version}")
print("Some key packages in data analysis:")
```

```
Some key packages in data analysis:
```

```
print("- numpy: Numerical computing")
```

```
- numpy: Numerical computing
```

```
print("- pandas: Data manipulation")
```

```
- pandas: Data manipulation
```

```
print("- matplotlib: Plotting")
```

```
- matplotlib: Plotting
```

```
print("- scipy: Scientific computing")
```

```
- scipy: Scientific computing
```

```
print("- scikit-learn: Machine learning")
```

```
- scikit-learn: Machine learning
```

Packages extend the capabilities of a language by providing specialized functions, datasets, documentation, and examples. They are created and maintained by communities and form the backbone of modern data analysis. Both R and Python offer thousands of packages that allow analysts to work efficiently without reinventing solutions that already exist.

AI Integration

AI tools can help you understand what a package does, how to use it, and whether it fits your analysis. When you encounter a new library, an AI assistant can summarize its purpose, show examples, or compare it with alternatives. Asking questions like "What does this package do and how do I use it?" or "Recommend packages for my data analysis task" helps you navigate the ecosystem more confidently and choose tools that match your workflow.

8.11.1.3 The Tidyverse Philosophy in Action

The Tidyverse is more than a collection of R packages — it is a shared philosophy for how data analysis should feel. Instead of treating each task as an isolated problem with its own syntax and conventions, the Tidyverse creates a unified way of working with data. Its functions follow consistent patterns, its tools are designed to fit together naturally, and its syntax emphasizes clarity over cleverness. The result is code that reads like a sequence of human-level actions: filter the data, arrange the rows, summarize the groups, visualize the results.

At the heart of the Tidyverse is the idea of tidy data, where each variable is a column and each observation is a row. This structure makes it possible for different packages — such as dplyr for manipulation, tidyr for reshaping, and ggplot2 for visualization — to operate seamlessly on the same dataset. The pipe operator reinforces this workflow by letting you express an analysis as a readable pipeline of steps, rather than a series of nested function calls. Instead of jumping back and forth across your code, you can follow the logic from top to bottom, one transformation at a time.

Seeing the Tidyverse in action highlights how much clarity this approach brings. Traditional R code often requires indexing, nested operations, and multiple temporary objects. A Tidyverse pipeline expresses the same logic in a way that is easier to read, easier to debug, and easier to extend. The examples below show how the Tidyverse transforms both simple filtering tasks and more complex grouped analyses into workflows that are expressive, consistent, and aligned with how analysts naturally think about data.

R Approach - Tidyverse Ecosystem

```r
# ==============================================
# Demo 3: The Tidyverse Philosophy (R)
# Consistent, human-readable data analysis
# ==============================================

# Load core tidyverse packages
library(tidyverse) # Loads dplyr, ggplot2, tidyr, readr, purrr, tibble
```

```
# TIDYVERSE PHILOSOPHY PRINCIPLES
print("=== TIDYVERSE PHILOSOPHY ===")
```

```
[1] "=== TIDYVERSE PHILOSOPHY ==="
```

```
print("1. Tidy data: Each variable is a column, each observation is a
↪ row")
```

```
[1] "1. Tidy data: Each variable is a column, each observation is a row"
```

```
print("2. Consistent function design: Similar syntax across packages")
```

```
[1] "2. Consistent function design: Similar syntax across packages"
```

```
print("3. Pipe operator (%>%): Chain operations together")
```

```
[1] "3. Pipe operator (%>%): Chain operations together"
```

```
print("4. Human-readable code: Functions named like verbs")
```

```
[1] "4. Human-readable code: Functions named like verbs"
```

```
# Sample student data for demonstration
student_data <- tibble(
  student_id = 1:20,
  name = paste("Student", 1:20),
  major = rep(c("Biology", "Psychology", "Math", "English"), 5),
  year = rep(c("Freshman", "Sophomore", "Junior", "Senior"), 5),
  gpa = round(runif(20, 2.0, 4.0), 2),
  study_hours = sample(10:40, 20, replace = TRUE),
  credits = sample(12:18, 20, replace = TRUE)
)

print("Original data:")
```

```
[1] "Original data:"
```

```
print(head(student_data))
```

```
# A tibble: 6 x 7
  student_id name      major      year        gpa study_hours credits
       <int> <chr>     <chr>      <chr>     <dbl>       <int>   <int>
1          1 Student 1 Biology    Freshman   3.77          25      13
2          2 Student 2 Psychology Sophomore  3.46          18      17
3          3 Student 3 Math       Junior     3.55          16      15
4          4 Student 4 English    Senior     3.56          18      14
```

```
5          5 Student 5 Biology    Freshman   3.51          38      17
6          6 Student 6 Psychology Sophomore  3.84          10      18
```

```
# SEEING THE PHILOSOPHY IN ACTION
print("\n=== TIDYVERSE IN ACTION ===")
```

```
[1] "\n=== TIDYVERSE IN ACTION ==="
```

```
# Traditional R approach (harder to read)
high_gpa_stem <- student_data[student_data$gpa > 3.5 &
↪  student_data$major %in% c("Biology", "Math"), ]
high_gpa_stem_sorted <- high_gpa_stem[order(-high_gpa_stem$gpa), ]
result_traditional <- high_gpa_stem_sorted[, c("name", "major", "gpa",
↪  "study_hours")]

print("Traditional R approach result:")
```

```
[1] "Traditional R approach result:"
```

```
print(head(result_traditional))
```

```
# A tibble: 4 x 4
  name      major     gpa study_hours
  <chr>     <chr>   <dbl>       <int>
1 Student 9 Biology  3.82          19
2 Student 1 Biology  3.77          25
3 Student 3 Math     3.55          16
4 Student 5 Biology  3.51          38
```

```
# Tidyverse approach (readable pipeline)
result_tidyverse <- student_data %>%
  filter(gpa > 3.5, major %in% c("Biology", "Math")) %>%
  arrange(desc(gpa)) %>%
  select(name, major, gpa, study_hours)

print("Tidyverse approach result:")
```

```
[1] "Tidyverse approach result:"
```

```
print(result_tidyverse)
```

```
# A tibble: 4 x 4
  name      major     gpa study_hours
  <chr>     <chr>   <dbl>       <int>
1 Student 9 Biology  3.82          19
2 Student 1 Biology  3.77          25
```

```
3 Student 3 Math     3.55           16
4 Student 5 Biology  3.51           38
```

```
# Complex analysis with tidyverse
analysis_result <- student_data %>%
  # Group by major and year
  group_by(major, year) %>%
  # Calculate summary statistics
  summarise(
    count = n(),
    avg_gpa = round(mean(gpa), 2),
    avg_study_hours = round(mean(study_hours), 1),
    high_achievers = sum(gpa > 3.5),
    .groups = 'drop'
  ) %>%
  # Filter for groups with high achievers
  filter(high_achievers > 0) %>%
  # Sort by average GPA
  arrange(desc(avg_gpa))

print("Complex analysis result:")
```

```
[1] "Complex analysis result:"
```

```
print(analysis_result)
```

```
# A tibble: 4 x 6
  major      year      count avg_gpa avg_study_hours high_achievers
  <chr>      <chr>     <int>   <dbl>           <dbl>          <int>
1 Psychology Sophomore     5    3.52            24.4              2
2 Biology    Freshman      5    3.31            26                3
3 English    Senior        5    3.3             32.2              3
4 Math       Junior        5    2.48            28.4              1
```

```
# VISUALIZATION WITH GGPLOT2
print("\n=== TIDYVERSE VISUALIZATION ===")
```

```
[1] "\n=== TIDYVERSE VISUALIZATION ==="
```

```
# Create visualization following grammar of graphics
gpa_plot <- student_data %>%
  ggplot(aes(x = study_hours, y = gpa, color = major)) +
  geom_point(size = 3, alpha = 0.7) +
  geom_smooth(method = "lm", se = FALSE) +
  facet_wrap(~year) +
  labs(
```

```
    title = "Study Hours vs GPA by Major and Year",
    x = "Study Hours per Week",
    y = "GPA",
    color = "Major"
  ) +
  theme_minimal() +
  theme(legend.position = "bottom")

print("GPA visualization created")
```

```
[1] "GPA visualization created"
```

```
print(gpa_plot)
```

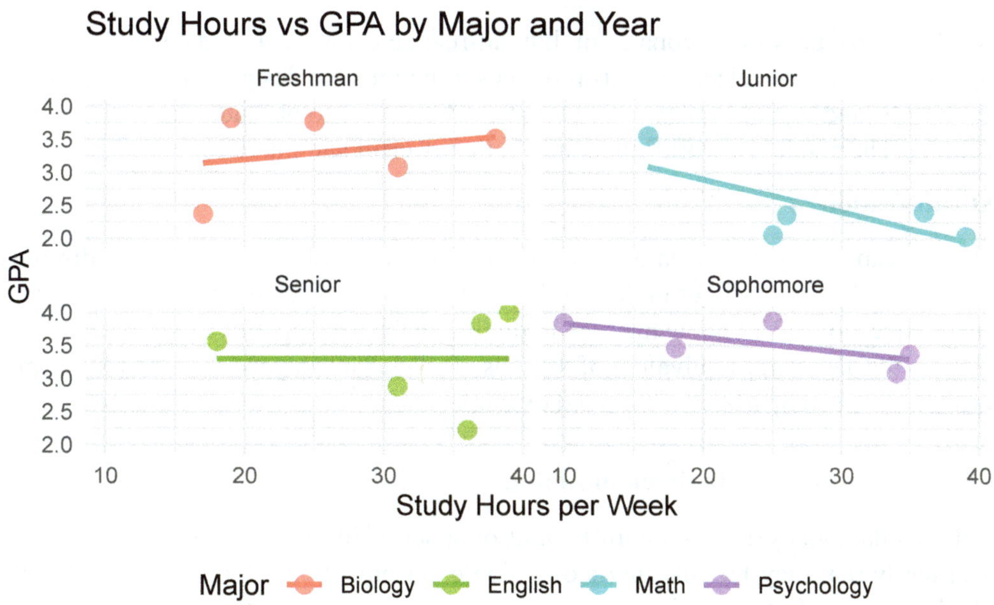


```
# WHY THE TIDYVERSE MATTERS
print("\n=== WHY TIDYVERSE MATTERS ===")
```

```
[1] "\n=== WHY TIDYVERSE MATTERS ==="
```

```
print("Benefits:")
```

```
[1] "Benefits:"
```

```
print("1. Consistent syntax across packages")
```

```
[1] "1. Consistent syntax across packages"
```

```
print("2. Readable, pipeline-based code")
```

```
[1] "2. Readable, pipeline-based code"
```

```
print("3. Designed for data analysis workflows")
```

```
[1] "3. Designed for data analysis workflows"
```

```
print("4. Excellent documentation and learning resources")
```

```
[1] "4. Excellent documentation and learning resources"
```

```
print("5. Active community and development")
```

```
[1] "5. Active community and development"
```

The Tidyverse provides a consistent, human-readable approach to data analysis. The pipe operator creates clear analysis pipelines, functions are designed to work together seamlessly, and ggplot2 follows the grammar of graphics to produce expressive visualizations. The result is a workflow that is both powerful and intuitive.

AI Integration

AI tools can help you translate traditional R code into Tidyverse pipelines, discover the right verbs for a task, or understand how different Tidyverse functions fit together. Asking questions like "Show me how to do this analysis using Tidyverse functions" or "What's the Tidyverse equivalent of this base R code" helps you learn the philosophy through direct comparison and guided examples.

8.11.1.4 Python's Data Stack in Action

Python's data analysis ecosystem is built on a set of libraries that work together so seamlessly that they feel like parts of a single system. At the foundation is NumPy, which provides fast numerical arrays and mathematical operations. On top of that sits pandas, which adds labeled data structures and a rich set of tools for cleaning, transforming, and analyzing datasets. For visualization, matplotlib provides the core plotting engine, while seaborn builds on top of it with higher-level statistical graphics. Additional libraries like SciPy and scikit-learn extend the stack into scientific computing and machine learning.

What makes this ecosystem powerful is not just the individual libraries, but the way they interoperate. A NumPy array can flow directly into a pandas DataFrame; a DataFrame can be passed into seaborn for visualization; and matplotlib can render the final output. Each library handles a different part of the workflow, but they share conventions, data structures, and design principles that make the transitions feel natural. This layered architecture allows analysts to move from raw numerical data to cleaned tables, grouped summaries, and polished visualizations without switching tools or rewriting code.

The demonstration below shows how these components fit together in practice. You'll see NumPy handling numerical operations, pandas managing structured data, and matplotlib and seaborn producing visualizations — all using the same dataset. This integration is what makes Python such a flexible and widely adopted language for data analysis.

Python Approach - Data Stack Integration

```
# =============================================
# Demo 4: Python's Data Stack (Python)
# NumPy, pandas, matplotlib working together
# =============================================

import numpy as np
import pandas as pd
import matplotlib.pyplot as plt
import seaborn as sns

# PYTHON DATA STACK COMPONENTS
print("=== PYTHON DATA STACK ===")
```

```
=== PYTHON DATA STACK ===
```

```
print("1. NumPy: Foundation for numerical computing")
```

```
1. NumPy: Foundation for numerical computing
```

```
print("2. pandas: Data manipulation and analysis")
```

```
2. pandas: Data manipulation and analysis
```

```
print("3. matplotlib: Basic plotting and visualization")
```

```
3. matplotlib: Basic plotting and visualization
```

```
print("4. seaborn: Statistical visualization")
```

```
4. seaborn: Statistical visualization
```

```
print("5. scipy: Scientific computing")
```

```
5. scipy: Scientific computing
```

```
print("6. scikit-learn: Machine learning")
```

```
6. scikit-learn: Machine learning
```

```
# THE FOUNDATION: NUMPY
print("\n=== NUMPY: THE FOUNDATION ===")
```

```
=== NUMPY: THE FOUNDATION ===
```

```
# NumPy provides efficient arrays and mathematical operations
study_hours_array = np.array([10, 15, 20, 25, 30, 35, 40, 12, 18, 28])
gpa_array = np.array([2.5, 2.8, 3.2, 3.5, 3.8, 3.9, 4.0, 2.7, 3.1,
 ↪ 3.6])

print(f"NumPy array operations:")
```

```
NumPy array operations:
```

```
print(f"Mean study hours: {np.mean(study_hours_array):.1f}")
```

```
Mean study hours: 23.3
```

```
print(f"Standard deviation: {np.std(study_hours_array):.2f}")
```

```
Standard deviation: 9.48
```

```
print(f"Correlation matrix:")
```

```
Correlation matrix:
```

```
correlation_matrix = np.corrcoef(study_hours_array, gpa_array)
print(correlation_matrix)
```

```
[[1.        0.9813651]
 [0.9813651 1.       ]]
```

```
# DATA MANIPULATION: PANDAS
print("\n=== PANDAS: DATA MANIPULATION ===")
```

```
=== PANDAS: DATA MANIPULATION ===
```

```
# Create DataFrame (pandas' main data structure)
student_data = pd.DataFrame({
    'student_id': range(1, 21),
    'name': [f'Student {i}' for i in range(1, 21)],
    'major': ['Biology', 'Psychology', 'Math', 'English'] * 5,
    'year': ['Freshman', 'Sophomore', 'Junior', 'Senior'] * 5,
    'gpa': np.round(np.random.uniform(2.0, 4.0, 20), 2),
```

```
    'study_hours': np.random.randint(10, 41, 20),
    'credits': np.random.randint(12, 19, 20)
})

# Pandas operations (similar to tidyverse philosophy)
analysis_result = (student_data
                   .query('gpa > 3.5 and major in ["Biology", "Math"]')
                   .sort_values('gpa', ascending=False)
                   .loc[:, ['name', 'major', 'gpa', 'study_hours']])

print("\nFiltered and sorted data:")
```

```
Filtered and sorted data:
```

```
print(analysis_result)
```

```
          name    major   gpa  study_hours
18  Student 19     Math  3.66           11
8    Student 9  Biology  3.62           32
```

```
# Group by operations
summary_stats = (student_data
                 .groupby(['major', 'year'])
                 .agg({
                     'gpa': ['count', 'mean'],
                     'study_hours': 'mean'
                 })
                 .round(2))

summary_stats.columns = ['count', 'avg_gpa', 'avg_study_hours']
summary_stats = summary_stats.reset_index()

print("\nSummary statistics:")
```

```
Summary statistics:
```

```
print(summary_stats)
```

```
        major       year  count  avg_gpa  avg_study_hours
0     Biology   Freshman      5     2.81             23.4
1     English     Senior      5     3.06             23.4
2        Math     Junior      5     2.78             24.2
3  Psychology  Sophomore      5     3.24             22.0
```

```
# VISUALIZATION: MATPLOTLIB AND SEABORN
print("\n=== VISUALIZATION: MATPLOTLIB & SEABORN ===")
```

```
=== VISUALIZATION: MATPLOTLIB & SEABORN ===
```

```
# Set up the plotting area
fig, axes = plt.subplots(2, 2, figsize=(15, 12))

# 1. Basic matplotlib scatter plot
axes[0, 0].scatter(student_data['study_hours'], student_data['gpa'],
 ↪  alpha=0.6, s=60)
axes[0, 0].set_xlabel('Study Hours')
axes[0, 0].set_ylabel('GPA')
axes[0, 0].set_title('Study Hours vs GPA (matplotlib)')
axes[0, 0].grid(True, alpha=0.3)

# 2. Seaborn scatter plot with categories
sns.scatterplot(data=student_data, x='study_hours', y='gpa',
 ↪  hue='major', ax=axes[0, 1])
axes[0, 1].set_title('Study Hours vs GPA by Major (seaborn)')

# 3. Box plot by major
sns.boxplot(data=student_data, x='major', y='gpa', ax=axes[1, 0])
axes[1, 0].set_title('GPA Distribution by Major')
axes[1, 0].tick_params(axis='x', rotation=45)

# 4. Correlation heatmap
correlation_data = student_data[['gpa', 'study_hours',
 ↪  'credits']].corr()
sns.heatmap(correlation_data, annot=True, cmap='coolwarm', center=0,
 ↪  ax=axes[1, 1])
axes[1, 1].set_title('Correlation Matrix')

plt.tight_layout()
plt.show()
```

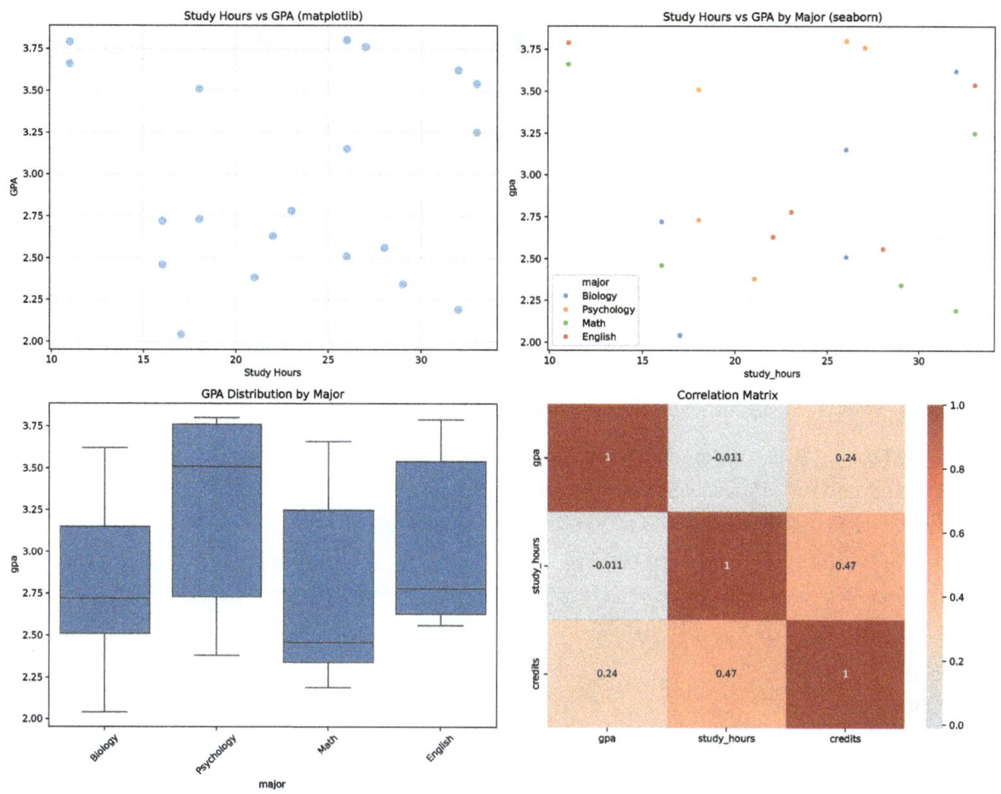


```
print("Visualizations created successfully")
```

```
Visualizations created successfully
```

```
# HOW THEY WORK TOGETHER
print("\n=== HOW THE STACK WORKS TOGETHER ===")
```

```

=== HOW THE STACK WORKS TOGETHER ===
```

```
print("Integration example:")
```

```
Integration example:
```

```
print("1. NumPy provides efficient numerical operations")
```

```
1. NumPy provides efficient numerical operations
```

```
print("2. pandas uses NumPy arrays internally for data storage")
```

```
2. pandas uses NumPy arrays internally for data storage
```

```
print("3. matplotlib creates visualizations from NumPy/pandas data")
```

```
3. matplotlib creates visualizations from NumPy/pandas data
```

```
print("4. seaborn builds on matplotlib with statistical plots")
```

```
4. seaborn builds on matplotlib with statistical plots
```

```
print("5. All packages share similar data structures and conventions")
```

```
5. All packages share similar data structures and conventions
```

```
# Example of integration
numpy_data = np.random.normal(100, 15, 1000) # NumPy generates data
pandas_series = pd.Series(numpy_data) # pandas wraps it
plt.figure(figsize=(10, 6))
plt.hist(pandas_series, bins=30, alpha=0.7) # matplotlib visualizes it
plt.title('Normal Distribution (NumPy → pandas → matplotlib)')
plt.xlabel('Value')
plt.ylabel('Frequency')
plt.show()
```

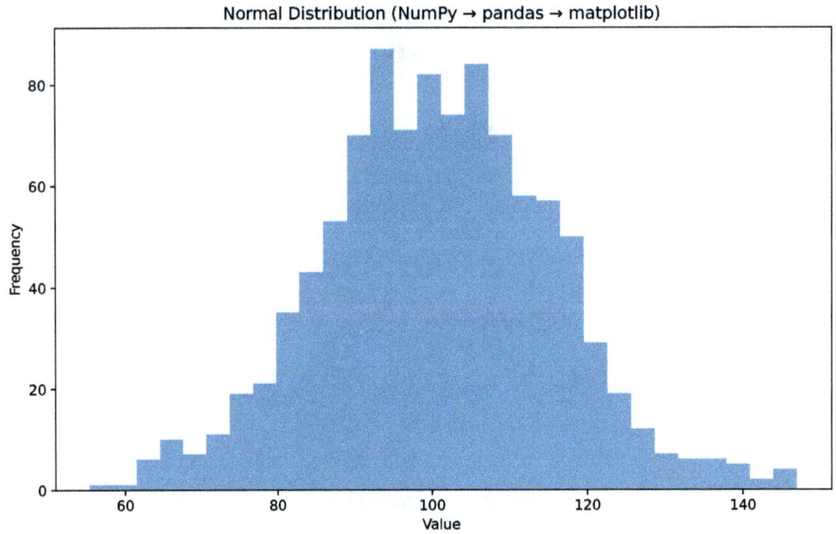


```
print("Data stack integration demonstrated")
```

```
Data stack integration demonstrated
```

NumPy provides the numerical foundation, pandas builds on NumPy for data manipulation, and matplotlib and seaborn handle visualization. These components work together seamlessly and share a common design philosophy, offering a workflow that parallels the Tidyverse in spirit while using different syntax and conventions.

AI Integration

AI tools can help you understand how Python's data stack fits together, suggest the right library for a task, or translate an R workflow into its Python equivalent. Asking questions like "How do NumPy, pandas, and matplotlib work together?" or "Show me the Python equivalent of this R analysis" helps you learn the ecosystem through guided examples and comparisons.

8.11.2 Practice

Use the code below for all questions. You may choose either the R version or the Python version. The questions are the same for both.

8.11.2.1 R Version

```
# Sample data
study_hours <- c(10, 15, 20, 25, 30, 35, 40)
gpa <- c(2.5, 2.8, 3.2, 3.5, 3.8, 3.9, 4.0)

# Manual correlation (from scratch)
calculate_correlation_from_scratch <- function(x, y) {
  n <- length(x)
  mean_x <- sum(x) / n
  mean_y <- sum(y) / n
  numerator <- sum((x - mean_x) * (y - mean_y))
  sum_sq_x <- sum((x - mean_x)^2)
  sum_sq_y <- sum((y - mean_y)^2)
  denominator <- sqrt(sum_sq_x * sum_sq_y)
  return(numerator / denominator)
}

manual_corr <- calculate_correlation_from_scratch(study_hours, gpa)

# Built-in correlation
builtin_corr <- cor(study_hours, gpa)

# Using a package
library(dplyr)
student_df <- tibble(
  hours = study_hours,
  gpa = gpa
)
```

```
filtered <- student_df %>% filter(gpa > 3.0)
```

8.11.2.2 Python Version

```
import numpy as np
import pandas as pd
import math

# Sample data
study_hours = [10, 15, 20, 25, 30, 35, 40]
gpa = [2.5, 2.8, 3.2, 3.5, 3.8, 3.9, 4.0]

# Manual correlation (from scratch)
def calculate_correlation_from_scratch(x, y):
    n = len(x)
    mean_x = sum(x) / n
    mean_y = sum(y) / n
    numerator = sum((x[i] - mean_x) * (y[i] - mean_y) for i in
    ↪ range(n))
    sum_sq_x = sum((x[i] - mean_x)**2 for i in range(n))
    sum_sq_y = sum((y[i] - mean_y)**2 for i in range(n))
    denominator = math.sqrt(sum_sq_x * sum_sq_y)
    return numerator / denominator

manual_corr = calculate_correlation_from_scratch(study_hours, gpa)

# Built-in correlation
numpy_corr = np.corrcoef(study_hours, gpa)[0, 1]

# Using a package
df = pd.DataFrame({'hours': study_hours, 'gpa': gpa})
filtered = df[df['gpa'] > 3.0]
```

8.11.3 Questions

1. Identify one part of the code where the analyst is "reinventing the wheel" by writing something from scratch.
2. Explain why the manual correlation function is more error-prone than the built-in version.
3. Describe one advantage of using a built-in function instead of a custom implementation.

4. Identify one assumption the manual correlation function makes about the input data.
5. Explain how a package (dplyr or pandas) improves the readability or efficiency of the filtering step.
6. Rewrite the filtering step using a different function from the same package ecosystem.
7. Describe one situation where writing your own function is still appropriate, even when packages exist.
8. Ask an AI assistant to recommend a package for a task you want to perform. Summarize the recommendation you received.
9. Explain how the R Tidyverse and the Python data stack are similar in their overall design philosophy.
10. In your own words, explain why modern data analysis depends on premade code ecosystems.

Chapter 9

Automating Data Tasks

9.1 Learning Outcomes

9-1: Understand the concept of automation in data analysis and recognize when it is appropriate.

9-2: Identify repetitive tasks suitable for automation and distinguish them from tasks better done manually.

9-3: Apply loops, conditional logic, and modern R tools (e.g., purrr, tidyverse) to automate workflows efficiently.

9-4: Implement safe automation practices, including input validation, error handling, and monitoring, to maintain reliable results.

9-5: Use automation to streamline multi-file processing and consistent visualizations, shifting from task-focused work to system-building.

9.2 Introduction

Here's where programming really starts to pay off. You've learned to write readable code, use functions, and navigate libraries. Now comes the moment when you stop doing repetitive tasks manually and start having the computer handle them systematically.

Sarah, a graduate student, spent every Friday afternoon creating the same five plots for her weekly lab meeting—scatter plots, histograms, and summary tables for different experimental conditions. Each week, she'd copy and paste code, change variable names, adjust titles, and save files. It took two hours every time. Then she learned about automation, and those two hours became five minutes.

This chapter shows you how to recognize when automation can transform your work and how to implement it safely. The key insight is both empowering and cautionary: **automation is powerful, but not always appropriate**.

9.3 The Automation Opportunity

9.3.1 Recognizing the Pattern

Automation opportunities usually hide in everyday work. Many analysts already repeat automatable tasks without noticing it. If you often copy and paste code and only change small parts, perform the same analysis on multiple datasets, build similar plots with different variables, generate recurring reports with the same structure, or repeatedly clean data in the same way, you are already following patterns that automation can streamline. Identifying these repeated workflows is the first step toward building more efficient, reliable, and scalable processes.

9.3.2 A Tale of Two Approaches

Maria's Manual Monday: Every week, Maria analyzes customer satisfaction surveys from five different regions. She opens each file, removes incomplete responses, calculates averages, creates charts, and saves results. Total time: 3 hours.

Maria's Automated Monday: After learning automation, Maria runs one script that processes all five files, generates standardized reports, and saves everything in organized folders. Total time: 5 minutes.

The difference isn't just time, but also consistency, accuracy, and the mental freedom to focus on interpretation rather than repetitive mechanics.

9.3.3 What Makes Tasks Automatable

Good Candidates	Poor Candidates
Repetitive processes	One-time tasks
Clear, consistent rules	Creative decisions
Predictable inputs	Highly variable situations
Time-consuming when manual	Quick manual execution
Rule-based decisions	Complex judgment calls

9.4 Understanding Automation Building Blocks

9.4.1 Conditional Logic

Conditional logic is simply "if-then" reasoning—the same type of thinking you already use in everyday decisions. In programming and data work, it means defining clear actions based on specific conditions. For example, if it is raining, you bring an umbrella; if a dataset is very large, you might start by analyzing a smaller sample; and if missing data exceeds a certain threshold, such as 20 percent, you flag it for closer review. This structured decision-making helps automate choices, maintain consistency, and ensures that your workflow adapts intelligently to different situations.

```
# Simple decision making in code
if (nrow(survey_data) > 1000) {
  print("Large dataset - using efficient methods")
  summary_method <- "sampling"
} else {
  print("Small dataset - analyzing all data")
  summary_method <- "complete"
}
```

9.4.2 Loops: The "Do This for Each Thing" Command

Loops work like giving instructions to an assembly line worker: "Take each item and apply the same process." Instead of repeating the same steps manually, a loop systematically loads each file, cleans it, analyzes it, and saves the results. You start with a list of items (such as File1 through File4), apply the same sequence of actions to each one, and end up with consistent outputs (such as Report1 through Report4). This approach saves time, reduces errors, and ensures that every item is processed in exactly the same way.

```
# Instead of writing separate code for each file
files <- c("january.csv", "february.csv", "march.csv")

for (file in files) {
  data <- read.csv(file)
  monthly_summary <- summarize_sales(data)
  save_report(monthly_summary, file)
  print(paste("Completed:", file))
}
```

9.4.3 Modern R Tools for Automation

R's modern ecosystem provides powerful and elegant ways to automate repetitive work. Instead of writing long, manual loops, tools like purrr allow you to apply functions across many files, datasets, or variables in a clean, readable way. The tidyverse makes it easy to build consistent workflows where data is imported, cleaned, transformed, and analyzed using the same structured steps.

```
library(purrr)  # Functional programming tools
library(dplyr)  # Data manipulation pipelines from tidyverse

# Traditional loop approach
results <- list()
for (i in 1:length(files)) {
  results[[i]] <- process_file(files[i])
}

# Modern purrr approach
results <- map(files, process_file)

# Pipeline approach with dplyr
summary_data <- raw_data %>%
  group_by(region, month) %>%
  summarize(
    avg_sales = mean(sales),
```

```
    total_customers = n(),
    .groups = "drop"
  ) %>%
  arrange(region, month)
```

9.5 Smart Automation Strategies

9.5.1 The Automation Investment Decision

Not every repetitive task is worth automating, so it helps to evaluate whether the effort will pay off. A simple way to think about this is as a return-on-investment calculation for your time. Start by estimating how long the task takes to do manually and how often you perform it. Then estimate how long it would take to build the automation. The break-even point is reached when the time saved by automation equals the time it took to build it. For example, if a weekly report takes two hours and you can automate it with eight hours of setup, you break even in about four weeks—clearly worthwhile. A quarterly task that takes four hours and requires twelve hours of setup may be worth it, but only if you expect to repeat it long enough to see benefits. A one-time cleanup task, on the other hand, is rarely worth automating because the automation never recovers its setup cost. This mindset helps you be strategic: automate work that repeats, saves meaningful time, and supports long-term productivity.

9.5.2 The Gradual Automation Approach

The Gradual Automation Approach begins by carefully documenting the manual process, writing down each step in detail so it becomes a clear blueprint for automation. From there, the next step is to automate the most repetitive tasks first—typically the parts you copy and paste most often, such as loading data, performing routine calculations, or generating standard plots. Once those pieces are stable, you gradually add intelligence by including conditional logic to handle different scenarios, building in error checks, and making the system more flexible. Finally, the process moves to full automation with safeguards, creating end-to-end workflows that include validation, monitoring, and graceful error handling to ensure reliability.

9.5.3 Real-World Success Story

Dr. Chen's research team collected weekly environmental data from 12 monitoring stations, and every week someone spent about four hours downloading files, checking data quality, creating standardized plots, and generating stakeholder reports. To address this, a graduate student developed an automation system that automatically downloaded data from all stations, checked for missing values and sensor errors, generated consistent visualizations, produced formatted reports, and sent alerts when any quality issues appeared. As a result, the weekly workload dropped from four hours to just fifteen minutes of review time, and the improved consistency allowed the team to detect data quality problems that had previously gone unnoticed.

9.6 When Automation Goes Wrong

Automation can save time, but if it's not implemented carefully, it can create new problems. Common pitfalls include silent failures, where errors occur but go unnoticed; assumption violations, where logic breaks when new or unexpected data appears; scale amplification, where small mistakes grow into significant issues; and maintenance neglect, where automated processes degrade or fail over time.

A cautionary example comes from a marketing team that automated their monthly customer segmentation analysis. The system worked flawlessly for six months, producing reports that guided key business decisions. Then the company changed its data collection system, adding new fields and altering formats. The automation continued to run, generating reports that were completely inaccurate. Because no one was monitoring the process, the errors went unnoticed for two months, leading to misguided marketing campaigns.

To prevent such problems, safe automation practices are essential. Start by validating inputs and checking data quality before processing. Monitor outputs regularly and include sanity checks to ensure results make sense. Build in error handling so the system responds appropriately when issues arise. Clearly document all assumptions behind your logic, and plan for ongoing maintenance so the automation can adapt to changes over time. Following these steps helps ensure that automation saves time without introducing hidden risks.

Safe automation example:

```
safe_monthly_analysis <- function(data_file) {
```

```
  # Input validation
  if (!file.exists(data_file)) {
    stop("Data file not found: ", data_file)
  }

  data <- read.csv(data_file)

  # Data quality checks
  if (nrow(data) == 0) {
    stop("Data file is empty")
  }

  if (mean(is.na(data$sales)) > 0.3) {
    warning("More than 30% of sales data is missing")
  }

  # Proceed with analysis
  results <- analyze_sales_data(data)

  # Output validation
  if (results$total_sales < 0) {
    warning("Negative total sales detected - check data")
  }

  return(results)
}
```

9.7 Practical Automation Examples

9.7.1 Example 1: Multi-File Data Processing

Scenario: You receive weekly survey files that need identical processing.

```
# Automation for consistent data processing
process_survey_batch <- function(file_pattern = "survey_week_*.csv") {
  files <- list.files(pattern = file_pattern)

  results <- map_dfr(files, function(file) {
    # Load and clean each file
    raw_data <- read.csv(file)
    clean_data <- raw_data %>%
      filter(!is.na(satisfaction_score)) %>%
      mutate(week = str_extract(file, "\\d+"))
```

```
    # Calculate summary statistics
    clean_data %>%
      group_by(department) %>%
      summarize(
        week = first(week),
        avg_satisfaction = mean(satisfaction_score),
        response_count = n(),
        .groups = "drop"
      )
  })

  return(results)
}
```

9.7.2 Example 2: Automated Visualization Pipeline

Scenario: Creating consistent plots for different variables in your dataset.

```
# Create standardized plots for multiple variables
create_variable_plots <- function(data,
    variables, output_dir = "plots") {

  # Ensure output directory exists
  if (!dir.exists(output_dir)) {
    dir.create(output_dir)
  }

  # Generate plot for each variable
  walk(variables, function(var) {
    if (var %in% names(data)) {

      # Create histogram
      p <- ggplot(data, aes_string(x = var)) +
        geom_histogram(bins = 30, fill = "steelblue", alpha = 0.7) +
        labs(
          title = paste("Distribution of", str_to_title(var)),
          x = str_to_title(var),
          y = "Count"
        ) +
        theme_minimal()

      # Save plot
      filename <- file.path(output_dir,
          paste0(var, "_distribution.png"))
```

```
        ggsave(filename, p, width = 8, height = 6)

        print(paste("Created plot:", filename))
      }
  })
}

# Usage
variables_to_plot <- c("age", "income", "satisfaction_score")
create_variable_plots(survey_data, variables_to_plot)
```

9.8 Conclusion

Learning automation changes the way you approach analytical work. Instead of focusing solely on completing individual tasks, you begin to think in terms of systems. You ask questions like, “How can I systematize this process?”, “What patterns can I extract and reuse?”, and “How can I make this more reliable and consistent?” This shift—from being a task-doer to a system-builder—is one of the most valuable skills a data analyst can develop.

Building a personal automation toolkit is a practical next step. This toolkit can include data processing functions for cleaning and validating data, visualization templates for consistent chart creation, report generators for automated, formatted outputs, and quality-check functions to ensure data and results are accurate.

The benefits of this approach compound over time. Each automation you create makes the next one easier, turning functions into reusable building blocks. Patterns you discover in one area can often be applied elsewhere, so the effort you invest in learning and building automation pays off exponentially, making your workflow faster, more reliable, and increasingly sophisticated.

9.9 Review Questions

1. What is the key insight about automation in data analysis, and why is it both empowering and cautionary?
2. How can you identify tasks in your workflow that are good candidates for automation?
3. List three characteristics of tasks that are *poor candidates* for automation.
4. Explain the role of conditional logic in automation, and give an example of its use in data processing.
5. How do loops help automate repetitive tasks in programming?

6. What advantages do modern R tools like purrr and the tidyverse provide over traditional loop-based approaches?
7. Describe the "automation investment decision" and how it relates to return on time saved.
8. What is the gradual automation approach, and why is it recommended?
9. Give an example of what can go wrong if automation is implemented without safeguards.
10. What are some safe automation practices to prevent errors and maintain reliable workflows?
11. How does multi-file data processing benefit from automation, and what R functions can help accomplish this?
12. Explain how automated visualization pipelines improve consistency and efficiency when creating multiple plots.
13. How does learning automation shift an analyst's mindset from task-doer to system-builder?

9.10 Ch 9 Lab Automating Data Tasks

Much of data analysis involves doing the same kinds of actions again and again: cleaning similar datasets, applying the same transformation to multiple variables, or running the same calculation across different groups. When these patterns start to repeat, it's a signal that your workflow can be made more efficient. Automation isn't about writing complex systems or building full applications — it's about recognizing when a task is predictable enough that the computer can handle it for you.

In this lab, you'll learn how to spot those opportunities. You'll explore the basic building blocks of automation, including conditional logic and simple loops, and see how they help you eliminate repetitive work. These tools allow you to shift your attention from mechanical steps to the reasoning behind your analysis. Instead of manually repeating the same operation ten times, you can express the logic once and let the computer carry it out.

Automation is also about making smart choices. Not every task should be automated, and part of becoming an effective analyst is learning to judge when the effort pays off. Throughout the lab, you'll use Positron's AI assistant to help identify repetitive patterns, suggest automation strategies, and troubleshoot simple logic errors. By the end, you'll have a clearer sense of how to streamline your workflow and reduce the friction in your day-to-day analysis.

9.10.1 Demonstration

9.10.1.1 Doing the Same Thing Over and Over

One of the clearest signs that a task is ready for automation is repetition. When you find yourself performing the same steps with only small changes — copying and pasting code, swapping out variable names, or running the same calculation across multiple groups — your workflow is telling you something. Repetition isn't just tedious; it increases the chance of mistakes and makes your analysis harder to update later. If you ever need to change the logic, you have to hunt down every copy of it and hope you don't miss one.

In this demonstration, you'll see what manual repetition looks like in practice. The examples start with a common scenario: checking grades for several subjects. The steps are identical — calculate an average, count how many students passed — but because the data changes, the code gets copied three times. This is the kind of pattern that quickly becomes unmanageable as your project grows.

Automation begins with noticing these patterns. Once you recognize that the same logic is being repeated, you can capture it in a single function and reuse it as many times as you need. Instead of maintaining three separate blocks of code, you maintain one. If the calculation changes, you update it once and every subject benefits. This is the essence of simple automation: write the logic once, apply it everywhere.

The R and Python examples below show this shift clearly — first the manual, repetitive approach, then the automated version that eliminates duplication and reduces the chance of errors.

9.10.1.1.1 The Problem: Manual Repetition

R Approach - The Manual Way

```r
# ============================================
# Demo 1: Spotting Repetition (R)
# The problem: doing the same thing multiple times
# ============================================

# Imagine you need to check grades for different subjects
math_grades <- c(85, 92, 78, 88, 95)
english_grades <- c(82, 89, 91, 76, 88)
science_grades <- c(90, 85, 83, 92, 87)

# Manual approach - lots of copy and paste!
print("=== MANUAL APPROACH ===")
```

```
[1] "=== MANUAL APPROACH ==="
```

```
# Check math grades
math_average <- mean(math_grades)
math_passing <- sum(math_grades >= 70)
print(paste("Math - Average:", round(math_average, 1), "Passing:",
↪  math_passing))
```

```
[1] "Math - Average: 87.6 Passing: 5"
```

```
# Check English grades (same steps, different data)
english_average <- mean(english_grades)
english_passing <- sum(english_grades >= 70)
print(paste("English - Average:", round(english_average, 1),
↪  "Passing:", english_passing))
```

```
[1] "English - Average: 85.2 Passing: 5"
```

```
# Check science grades (same steps again!)
science_average <- mean(science_grades)
science_passing <- sum(science_grades >= 70)
print(paste("Science - Average:", round(science_average, 1),
↪  "Passing:", science_passing))
```

```
[1] "Science - Average: 87.4 Passing: 5"
```

```
print("\nProblems with this approach:")
```

```
[1] "\nProblems with this approach:"
```

```
print("1. Lots of copying and pasting")
```

```
[1] "1. Lots of copying and pasting"
```

```
print("2. Easy to make mistakes")
```

```
[1] "2. Easy to make mistakes"
```

```
print("3. Hard to change if you want different calculations")
```

```
[1] "3. Hard to change if you want different calculations"
```

R Approach - Simple Automation

```
# ============================================
# Demo 1: Simple Automation Solution (R)
# ============================================

print("\n=== AUTOMATED APPROACH ===")
```

```
[1] "\n=== AUTOMATED APPROACH ==="
```

```r
# Create a simple function to do the repeated work
check_grades <- function(grades, subject_name) {
  average <- mean(grades)
  passing <- sum(grades >= 70)
  print(paste(subject_name, "- Average:", round(average, 1),
    ↪  "Passing:", passing))
}

# Now use it for all subjects - no copying and pasting!
check_grades(math_grades, "Math")
```

```
[1] "Math - Average: 87.6 Passing: 5"
```

```r
check_grades(english_grades, "English")
```

```
[1] "English - Average: 85.2 Passing: 5"
```

```r
check_grades(science_grades, "Science")
```

```
[1] "Science - Average: 87.4 Passing: 5"
```

```r
print("\nBenefits of automation:")
```

```
[1] "\nBenefits of automation:"
```

```r
print("1. Write the logic once, use it many times")
```

```
[1] "1. Write the logic once, use it many times"
```

```r
print("2. Fewer mistakes")
```

```
[1] "2. Fewer mistakes"
```

```r
print("3. Easy to change the calculation for all subjects")
```

```
[1] "3. Easy to change the calculation for all subjects"
```

Python Approach - Manual vs Automated

```python
# ============================================
# Demo 1: Manual vs Automated (Python)
# ============================================

# The same grade data
math_grades = [85, 92, 78, 88, 95]
english_grades = [82, 89, 91, 76, 88]
```

```
science_grades = [90, 85, 83, 92, 87]

print("=== MANUAL APPROACH ===")
```

```
=== MANUAL APPROACH ===
```

```
# Manual approach - lots of repetition
math_average = sum(math_grades) / len(math_grades)
math_passing = sum(1 for grade in math_grades if grade >= 70)
print(f"Math - Average: {math_average:.1f}, Passing: {math_passing}")
```

```
Math - Average: 87.6, Passing: 5
```

```
english_average = sum(english_grades) / len(english_grades)
english_passing = sum(1 for grade in english_grades if grade >= 70)
print(f"English - Average: {english_average:.1f}, Passing:
 ↪  {english_passing}")
```

```
English - Average: 85.2, Passing: 5
```

```
science_average = sum(science_grades) / len(science_grades)
science_passing = sum(1 for grade in science_grades if grade >= 70)
print(f"Science - Average: {science_average:.1f}, Passing:
 ↪  {science_passing}")
```

```
Science - Average: 87.4, Passing: 5
```

```
print("\n=== AUTOMATED APPROACH ===")
```

```

=== AUTOMATED APPROACH ===
```

```
# Simple function to avoid repetition
def check_grades(grades, subject_name):
    average = sum(grades) / len(grades)
    passing = sum(1 for grade in grades if grade >= 70)
    print(f"{subject_name} - Average: {average:.1f}, Passing:
     ↪  {passing}")

# Use it for all subjects
check_grades(math_grades, "Math")
```

```
Math - Average: 87.6, Passing: 5
```

```
check_grades(english_grades, "English")
```

```
English - Average: 85.2, Passing: 5
```

```
check_grades(science_grades, "Science")
```

```
Science - Average: 87.4, Passing: 5
```

Repetition is one of the clearest signals that a task is ready for automation. When you copy and paste code with only small changes, you increase the chance of mistakes and make your analysis harder to update later. Simple functions allow you to express the logic once and reuse it as many times as needed, reducing duplication and improving clarity. Automation doesn't have to be complex — even small steps, like wrapping repeated calculations in a function, can make your workflow more efficient and easier to maintain.

AI Integration

AI tools can play a helpful role in spotting repetition before you even realize you're doing it. When you find yourself copying and pasting code, tweaking only a variable name or a threshold, an AI assistant can point out the underlying pattern and suggest ways to automate it. You can ask the AI to review your script for repeated logic, propose a function that captures the shared steps, or help you rewrite a block of code so it scales to more subjects or datasets. This turns the AI into a kind of pattern detector — a second set of eyes that notices inefficiencies and helps you express your intent more clearly. Instead of manually repeating the same operations, you can use the AI to guide you toward a cleaner, more maintainable workflow.

9.10.1.2 Making Decisions with If-Then Logic

Automation isn't just about repeating steps — it's also about making choices. Many data tasks require different actions depending on the values you encounter: flagging low scores, categorizing students, identifying outliers, or applying different rules to different groups. This is where if-then logic comes in. It gives the computer a way to make simple decisions on your behalf, following the same reasoning you would use manually.

If-then logic is the foundation of smarter automation. Once you can express a rule — "if the score is above 90, assign an A" — you can apply that rule consistently across hundreds or thousands of values. Instead of checking each case yourself, you define the conditions once and let the computer handle the rest. This shift from manual judgment to encoded logic is what allows automation to scale.

The examples below show how a single decision can be expressed in code, and then how that same logic can be wrapped in a function and applied to many students at once. This is the moment where automation becomes more than repetition: it becomes reasoning.

R Approach - Basic If-Then Logic

```
# ============================================
# Demo 2: Simple Decision Making (R)
# ============================================

print("=== BASIC IF-THEN LOGIC ===")
```

```
[1] "=== BASIC IF-THEN LOGIC ==="
```

```
# Simple decision making
student_grade <- 85

if (student_grade >= 90) {
  print("Grade: A - Excellent work!")
} else if (student_grade >= 80) {
  print("Grade: B - Good job!")
} else if (student_grade >= 70) {
  print("Grade: C - Satisfactory")
} else {
  print("Grade: F - Needs improvement")
}
```

```
[1] "Grade: B - Good job!"
```

```
# Making this work for multiple students
print("\n=== APPLYING TO MULTIPLE STUDENTS ===")
```

```
[1] "\n=== APPLYING TO MULTIPLE STUDENTS ==="
```

```
assign_letter_grade <- function(score) {
  if (score >= 90) {
    return("A")
  } else if (score >= 80) {
    return("B")
  } else if (score >= 70) {
    return("C")
  } else {
    return("F")
  }
}

# Test with different scores
test_scores <- c(95, 67, 82, 91, 45)

for (score in test_scores) {
  letter <- assign_letter_grade(score)
```

```
  print(paste("Score", score, "gets grade", letter))
}
```

```
[1] "Score 95 gets grade A"
[1] "Score 67 gets grade F"
[1] "Score 82 gets grade B"
[1] "Score 91 gets grade A"
[1] "Score 45 gets grade F"
```

Python Approach - Basic If-Then Logic

```
# ============================================
# Demo 2: Simple Decision Making (Python)
# ============================================

print("=== BASIC IF-THEN LOGIC ===")
```

```
=== BASIC IF-THEN LOGIC ===
```

```
# Simple decision making
student_grade = 85

if student_grade >= 90:
    print("Grade: A - Excellent work!")
elif student_grade >= 80:
    print("Grade: B - Good job!")
elif student_grade >= 70:
    print("Grade: C - Satisfactory")
else:
    print("Grade: F - Needs improvement")
```

```
Grade: B - Good job!
```

```
print("\n=== APPLYING TO MULTIPLE STUDENTS ===")
```

```

=== APPLYING TO MULTIPLE STUDENTS ===
```

```
def assign_letter_grade(score):
    if score >= 90:
        return "A"
    elif score >= 80:
        return "B"
    elif score >= 70:
        return "C"
    else:
```

```
        return "F"

# Test with different scores
test_scores = [95, 67, 82, 91, 45]

for score in test_scores:
    letter = assign_letter_grade(score)
    print(f"Score {score} gets grade {letter}")
```

```
Score 95 gets grade A
Score 67 gets grade F
Score 82 gets grade B
Score 91 gets grade A
Score 45 gets grade F
```

If-then logic allows computers to make simple decisions based on conditions you define. You can combine multiple conditions to handle different cases, and once the logic is written, you can apply it to many values automatically. This makes if-then structures essential for categorizing data, flagging issues, and building smarter automation workflows.

AI Integration

AI tools can help you translate your own reasoning into clear if-then logic. If you know the rule you want to apply but aren't sure how to express it in code, you can ask the AI to draft the conditional structure, check your logic, or suggest edge cases you might have missed. This is especially useful when your conditions become more complex — multiple thresholds, nested rules, or different actions for different categories. By working with the AI, you can turn informal reasoning into precise, reliable automation.

9.10.1.3 Using Loops to "Do This for Each Thing"

Repetition shows up in many forms during data analysis. Sometimes you repeat a calculation across several variables; other times you process multiple files, run the same summary for each month, or apply the same transformation to every column in a dataset. When the structure of the task stays the same but the inputs change, a loop becomes the natural tool for the job.

Loops let you express the idea "do this for each item" without writing the same code over and over. Instead of manually typing out three nearly identical lines — "Processing student 1," "Processing student 2," "Processing student 3" — you describe the pattern once, and the loop handles the rest. This not only saves time but also reduces the chance of mistakes, especially when the number of items grows or changes.

In practice, loops are essential for tasks like processing batches of files, calculating statistics across multiple datasets, or applying the same logic to every group in your analysis. The examples below show how a simple loop replaces manual repetition and how that same structure scales to more realistic tasks, such as iterating through monthly sales data or performing calculations for each dataset in a list. Once you understand the pattern, loops become one of the most powerful building blocks of automation.

R Approach - Simple Loops

```
# ================================================
# Demo 3: Simple Loops (R)
# ================================================

print("=== BASIC LOOP CONCEPT ===")
```

```
[1] "=== BASIC LOOP CONCEPT ==="
```

```
# Instead of writing this manually:
print("Manual approach:")
```

```
[1] "Manual approach:"
```

```
print("Processing student 1")
```

```
[1] "Processing student 1"
```

```
print("Processing student 2")
```

```
[1] "Processing student 2"
```

```
print("Processing student 3")
```

```
[1] "Processing student 3"
```

```
# Use a loop:
print("\nLoop approach:")
```

```
[1] "\nLoop approach:"
```

```
for (i in 1:3) {
  print(paste("Processing student", i))
}
```

```
[1] "Processing student 1"
[1] "Processing student 2"
[1] "Processing student 3"
```

```
print("\n=== PRACTICAL EXAMPLE ===")
```

```
[1] "\n=== PRACTICAL EXAMPLE ==="
```

```
# Process multiple data files
file_names <- c("january_sales.csv", "february_sales.csv",
                "march_sales.csv")

for (filename in file_names) {
  # Simulate processing each file
  print(paste("Loading", filename))
  print(paste("Calculating totals for", filename))
  print(paste("Saving results for", filename))
  print("---")
}
```

```
[1] "Loading january_sales.csv"
[1] "Calculating totals for january_sales.csv"
[1] "Saving results for january_sales.csv"
[1] "---"
[1] "Loading february_sales.csv"
[1] "Calculating totals for february_sales.csv"
[1] "Saving results for february_sales.csv"
[1] "---"
[1] "Loading march_sales.csv"
[1] "Calculating totals for march_sales.csv"
[1] "Saving results for march_sales.csv"
[1] "---"
```

```
print("=== LOOP WITH CALCULATIONS ===")
```

```
[1] "=== LOOP WITH CALCULATIONS ==="
```

```
# Calculate statistics for multiple datasets
monthly_sales <- list(
  january = c(1200, 1500, 1800, 1300, 1600),
  february = c(1400, 1700, 1200, 1900, 1500),
  march = c(1600, 1300, 2000, 1400, 1800)
)

for (month_name in names(monthly_sales)) {
  sales_data <- monthly_sales[[month_name]]
  total <- sum(sales_data)
  average <- mean(sales_data)
  print(paste(month_name, "- Total:", total, "Average:",
              round(average, 0)))
}
```

```
[1] "january - Total: 7400 Average: 1480"
[1] "february - Total: 7700 Average: 1540"
[1] "march - Total: 8100 Average: 1620"
```

Python Approach - Simple Loops

```
# ==============================================
# Demo 3: Simple Loops (Python)
# ==============================================

print("=== BASIC LOOP CONCEPT ===")
```

```
=== BASIC LOOP CONCEPT ===
```

```
# Instead of writing this manually:
print("Manual approach:")
```

```
Manual approach:
```

```
print("Processing student 1")
```

```
Processing student 1
```

```
print("Processing student 2")
```

```
Processing student 2
```

```
print("Processing student 3")
```

```
Processing student 3
```

```
# Use a loop:
print("\nLoop approach:")
```

```

Loop approach:
```

```
for i in range(1, 4):
    print(f"Processing student {i}")
```

```
Processing student 1
Processing student 2
Processing student 3
```

```
print("\n=== PRACTICAL EXAMPLE ===")
```

```

=== PRACTICAL EXAMPLE ===
```

```
# Process multiple data files
file_names = ["january_sales.csv", "february_sales.csv",
↪  "march_sales.csv"]

for filename in file_names:
    # Simulate processing each file
    print(f"Loading {filename}")
    print(f"Calculating totals for {filename}")
    print(f"Saving results for {filename}")
    print("---")
```

```
Loading january_sales.csv
Calculating totals for january_sales.csv
Saving results for january_sales.csv
---
Loading february_sales.csv
Calculating totals for february_sales.csv
Saving results for february_sales.csv
---
Loading march_sales.csv
Calculating totals for march_sales.csv
Saving results for march_sales.csv
---
```

```
print("=== LOOP WITH CALCULATIONS ===")
```

```
=== LOOP WITH CALCULATIONS ===
```

```
# Calculate statistics for multiple datasets
monthly_sales = {
    "january": [1200, 1500, 1800, 1300, 1600],
    "february": [1400, 1700, 1200, 1900, 1500],
    "march": [1600, 1300, 2000, 1400, 1800]
}

for month_name, sales_data in monthly_sales.items():
    total = sum(sales_data)
    average = sum(sales_data) / len(sales_data)
    print(f"{month_name} - Total: {total}, Average: {average:.0f}")
```

```
january - Total: 7400, Average: 1480
february - Total: 7700, Average: 1540
march - Total: 8100, Average: 1620
```

Loops allow you to repeat the same operation across many items without duplicating code. They are especially useful for processing multiple files, datasets, or groups, and they help reduce errors by centralizing the logic in one place. When you notice yourself performing the same steps manually, a loop is often the simplest and most effective form of automation.

AI Integration

AI tools can help you recognize when a loop is the right solution. If you find yourself writing similar lines of code with only small differences — new filenames, new months, new variables — you can ask the AI to suggest a loop structure that captures the pattern. The AI can also help you rewrite repetitive code into a clean loop, check whether your loop handles all cases correctly, or suggest more efficient looping patterns when your datasets grow. This turns the AI into a partner that helps you scale your workflow without adding complexity.

9.10.1.4 Deciding When Automation Is Worth It

Automation is powerful, but it isn't free. Even simple automation takes time to design, test, and refine. That means the real skill isn't just knowing how to automate — it's knowing when automation actually pays off. Analysts make this judgment constantly: is it worth spending a few hours building a script, or is it faster to just do the task manually?

A helpful way to think about this is to compare the time you spend doing the task manually with the time it would take to automate it. High-frequency tasks — daily reports, weekly summaries, repeated file cleaning — often pay back the automation effort quickly. One-time or rare tasks usually don't. But frequency isn't the only factor. Some tasks are so error-prone or tedious that automation is worthwhile even if it doesn't save much time. Others are so simple that automating them would add unnecessary complexity.

The examples below walk through a simple decision framework. By estimating the time required for both manual work and automation, you can make a clear, evidence-based choice. This mindset helps you invest your time wisely and build automation only where it creates real value.

9.10.1.4.1 Simple Decision Framework

```
# ============================================
# Demo 4: When to Automate (R)
# ============================================

print("=== AUTOMATION DECISION FRAMEWORK ===")
```

```
[1] "=== AUTOMATION DECISION FRAMEWORK ==="
```

```
# Simple questions to ask yourself:
print("Ask yourself these questions:")
```

```
[1] "Ask yourself these questions:"
```

```
print("1. How often do I do this task?")
```

```
[1] "1. How often do I do this task?"
```

```
print("2. How long does it take each time?")
```

```
[1] "2. How long does it take each time?"
```

```
print("3. How long would it take to automate?")
```

```
[1] "3. How long would it take to automate?"
```

```
print("4. Am I likely to make mistakes doing it manually?")
```

```
[1] "4. Am I likely to make mistakes doing it manually?"
```

```
print("\n=== EXAMPLES ===")
```

```
[1] "\n=== EXAMPLES ==="
```

```
# Example 1: Daily report
print("Example 1: Daily report generation")
```

```
[1] "Example 1: Daily report generation"
```

```
print("- Task time: 30 minutes")
```

```
[1] "- Task time: 30 minutes"
```

```
print("- Frequency: Every day (5 times per week)")
```

```
[1] "- Frequency: Every day (5 times per week)"
```

```
print("- Weekly time: 2.5 hours")
```

```
[1] "- Weekly time: 2.5 hours"
```

```
print("- Automation time: 4 hours to set up")
```

```
[1] "- Automation time: 4 hours to set up"
```

```
print("- Decision: AUTOMATE (pays off in 2 weeks)")
```

```
[1] "- Decision: AUTOMATE (pays off in 2 weeks)"
```

```
# Example 2: One-time analysis
print("\nExample 2: One-time data cleaning")
```

```
[1] "\nExample 2: One-time data cleaning"
```

```
print("- Task time: 2 hours")
```

```
[1] "- Task time: 2 hours"
```

```
print("- Frequency: Just once")
```

```
[1] "- Frequency: Just once"
```

```
print("- Total time: 2 hours")
```

```
[1] "- Total time: 2 hours"
```

```
print("- Automation time: 6 hours to set up")
```

```
[1] "- Automation time: 6 hours to set up"
```

```
print("- Decision: DO MANUALLY (not worth automating)")
```

```
[1] "- Decision: DO MANUALLY (not worth automating)"
```

```
# Example 3: Monthly task
print("\nExample 3: Monthly summary report")
```

```
[1] "\nExample 3: Monthly summary report"
```

```
print("- Task time: 1 hour")
```

```
[1] "- Task time: 1 hour"
```

```
print("- Frequency: Once per month")
```

```
[1] "- Frequency: Once per month"
```

```
print("- Yearly time: 12 hours")
```

```
[1] "- Yearly time: 12 hours"
```

```
print("- Automation time: 8 hours to set up")
```

```
[1] "- Automation time: 8 hours to set up"
```

```
print("- Decision: MAYBE (depends on how long you'll use it)")
```

```
[1] "- Decision: MAYBE (depends on how long you'll use it)"
```

```
# ===============================================
# Demo 4: When to Automate (Python)
# ===============================================

def should_i_automate(task_time_hours, times_per_year,
 ↪  automation_hours):
    """Simple calculator to help decide if automation is worth it."""
    manual_time_per_year = task_time_hours * times_per_year
    print(f"Manual time per year: {manual_time_per_year} hours")
    print(f"Automation setup time: {automation_hours} hours")

    if automation_hours < manual_time_per_year:
        savings = manual_time_per_year - automation_hours
        print(f"AUTOMATE! You'll save {savings} hours per year")
    else:
        extra_cost = automation_hours - manual_time_per_year
        print(f"DO MANUALLY. Automation would cost {extra_cost} extra
         ↪  hours")

print("=== AUTOMATION DECISION EXAMPLES ===")
```

```
=== AUTOMATION DECISION EXAMPLES ===
```

```
print("Example 1: Daily report (30 min, 5 times/week)")
```

```
Example 1: Daily report (30 min, 5 times/week)
```

```
should_i_automate(0.5, 250, 4)
```

```
Manual time per year: 125.0 hours
Automation setup time: 4 hours
AUTOMATE! You'll save 121.0 hours per year
```

```
# 30 min = 0.5 hours, 250 times/year, 4 hours to automate

print("\nExample 2: One-time analysis (2 hours, once)")
```

```

Example 2: One-time analysis (2 hours, once)
```

```
should_i_automate(2, 1, 6) # 2 hours, 1 time, 6 hours to automate
```

```
Manual time per year: 2 hours
Automation setup time: 6 hours
DO MANUALLY. Automation would cost 4 extra hours
```

```
print("\nExample 3: Monthly report (1 hour, 12 times/year)")
```

```
Example 3: Monthly report (1 hour, 12 times/year)
```

```
should_i_automate(1, 12, 8) # 1 hour, 12 times, 8 hours to automate
```

```
Manual time per year: 12 hours
Automation setup time: 8 hours
AUTOMATE! You'll save 4 hours per year
```

Automation has an upfront cost, so it's not always the right choice. Tasks that happen frequently or take significant time are usually strong candidates for automation, while one-off tasks are often better done manually. You should also consider how error-prone the manual process is and how long you expect to repeat the task. A thoughtful decision about when to automate ensures that your time is spent where it has the greatest impact.

AI Integration

AI tools can help you evaluate whether automation is worth the effort. If you describe the task — how long it takes, how often you do it, and what steps are involved — the AI can estimate the potential time savings and suggest whether automation is a good investment. It can also help you break down the automation work into smaller steps, identify parts that are easy to automate, or point out hidden complexity you might not have considered. This makes the decision process faster, clearer, and more grounded in real numbers.

9.10.2 Practice

Use the code below for all questions. You may choose either the R version or the Python version. The questions are the same for both.

9.10.2.1 R Version

```r
# Repetition example
math_grades <- c(85, 92, 78, 88, 95)
english_grades <- c(82, 89, 91, 76, 88)
science_grades <- c(90, 85, 83, 92, 87)

math_avg <- mean(math_grades)
english_avg <- mean(english_grades)
science_avg <- mean(science_grades)

# Automated version
check_grades <- function(grades) {
```

```
  avg <- mean(grades)
  pass <- sum(grades >= 70)
  return(list(average = avg, passing = pass))
}

# If-then logic
assign_letter <- function(score) {
  if (score >= 90) return("A")
  else if (score >= 80) return("B")
  else if (score >= 70) return("C")
  else return("F")
}

# Loop example
months <- list(
  jan = c(1200, 1500, 1800),
  feb = c(1400, 1700, 1200),
  mar = c(1600, 1300, 2000)
)

for (m in names(months)) {
  total <- sum(months[[m]])
  avg <- mean(months[[m]])
}
```

9.10.2.2 Python Version

```
# Repetition example
math_grades = [85, 92, 78, 88, 95]
english_grades = [82, 89, 91, 76, 88]
science_grades = [90, 85, 83, 92, 87]

math_avg = sum(math_grades) / len(math_grades)
english_avg = sum(english_grades) / len(english_grades)
science_avg = sum(science_grades) / len(science_grades)

# Automated version
def check_grades(grades):
    avg = sum(grades) / len(grades)
    passing = sum(1 for g in grades if g >= 70)
    return avg, passing

# If-then logic
```

```
def assign_letter(score):
    if score >= 90: return "A"
    elif score >= 80: return "B"
    elif score >= 70: return "C"
    else: return "F"

# Loop example
months = {
    "jan": [1200, 1500, 1800],
    "feb": [1400, 1700, 1200],
    "mar": [1600, 1300, 2000]
}

for name, sales in months.items():
    total = sum(sales)
    avg = sum(sales) / len(sales)
```

9.10.3 Questions

1. Identify one place in the code where the same logic is repeated manually. Quote the specific lines.
2. Rewrite that repeated logic using a function. Show the function definition.
3. Run your function on at least two different grade lists and show the output.
4. Modify the assign_letter function so that scores below 60 return "F" and scores between 60–69 return "D". Show your updated code.
5. Use a loop to print the letter grade for each score in this list: c(95, 72, 61, 88) or [95, 72, 61, 88]. Show the loop and the output.
6. Identify one task in your own workflow (outside this lab) that could be automated. Describe the repeated pattern.
7. Estimate the time tradeoff: How long does the task take manually, how often do you do it, and how long would automation take?
8. Ask an AI assistant to suggest an automation strategy for the task you identified. Summarize one concrete suggestion it gave you.

Chapter 10

When Code Breaks: Debugging

10.1 Learning Outcomes

10-1: Recognize that programming errors are normal and approach them as problem-solving opportunities.

10-2: Differentiate between syntax, runtime, and logic errors and apply suitable debugging strategies for each.

10-3: Use systematic debugging workflows—observe, hypothesize, test, evaluate, and iterate—to efficiently resolve errors.

10-4: Utilize diagnostic tools (e.g., print statements, head(), str(), summary()) to examine data and code behavior.

10-5: Apply strategies like "divide and conquer" and evidence-based debugging to identify and fix complex issues.

10-6: Build confidence in debugging by documenting fixes, reflecting on lessons learned, and maintaining a personal debugging toolkit.

10.2 Introduction

Alex stared at his computer screen in frustration. His code had been working perfectly yesterday, but now it was throwing an error: `Error in mean(data$temperature): object 'data' not found`. He felt like a failure. Surely "real" programmers didn't make these kinds of mistakes?

If Alex could see into the offices of professional data scientists, he'd discover something surprising: they spend significant time debugging code. The difference isn't that experts don't make errors—it's that they've learned to debug systematically rather than panic.

This chapter normalizes errors as natural parts of programming and teaches you systematic approaches to finding and fixing problems. The key insight is both liberating and practical: **debugging is problem-solving, not punishment**.

10.3 The Reality of Programming Errors

Everyone makes errors, even highly skilled data scientists. For example, Dr. Martinez, a senior data scientist, keeps a debugging log. On a typical Tuesday, she fixed a typo, dealt with broken import scripts due to new data files, corrected analysis that used the wrong month's data, handled a function failure caused by missing values, and troubleshot a plot that broke after a package update. Five separate debugging sessions in one day illustrate that errors are a natural part of programming.

Errors are inevitable because modern analysis involves many moving parts, data often doesn't match assumptions, translating ideas into computer instructions is tricky, and software and requirements constantly change. Rather than seeing errors as a sign of failure, it helps to reframe your mindset: instead of thinking, "I'm terrible—my code doesn't work," approach each error as an "interesting puzzle" to solve. Each problem you encounter is a learning opportunity that strengthens your programming skills and improves your understanding of the tools and data you work with.

10.4 Understanding Error Types

Errors in programming come in different types, and each requires a different approach to fix. Syntax errors occur before the code runs and usually involve typos, missing punctuation, or incorrect grammar in your code. The way to debug these is to carefully check the code for mistakes, such as a missing parenthesis in mean(data$gpa(. Runtime errors happen while the code is executing, often because a file, variable, or data element doesn't exist. Debugging these errors involves verifying that all inputs and resources are available, like checking that a file exists before running read.csv("missing.csv"). Logic errors only appear after the code has run; the program executes without crashing, but the results are incorrect. These require testing your code with known cases and validating your assumptions, such as noticing a wrong temperature conversion.

Error Type	When It Occurs	Debugging Strategy	Example
Syntax	Before code runs	Check grammar, typos, punctuation	mean(data$gpa (missing)
Runtime	During execution	Verify data, files, variables exist	read.csv("missing.csv")
Logic	After code runs	Test with known cases, check assumptions	Wrong temperature conversion

10.4.1 Quick Error Identification

When debugging, it helps to quickly identify the type of error you're facing. Start by asking: does the code run at all? If it doesn't, you're likely dealing with a syntax error, so check for typos, missing punctuation, or incorrect grammar. If the code runs but produces no output or crashes during execution, this indicates a runtime error—verify that all data, files, and variables exist. If the code runs and produces output but the results are incorrect, you're facing a logic error, so examine your assumptions and test with known cases. If the output is correct, then congratulations—you've successfully executed your code.

10.4.2 Reading Error Messages

Error messages are like clues that tell you what went wrong—they aren't punishments. Learning to decode them systematically makes debugging much faster.

Take this example:

```
Error in mean(survey_data$satisfaction_score):
argument is not numeric or logical: returning NA
```

This message has three key parts. First, the **location** tells you where the error occurred: mean(survey_data$satisfaction_score). Second, the **problem** explains what went wrong: the argument isn't numeric, so mean() can't calculate it. Third, the **action** shows what R did instead: it returned NA as a placeholder.

By breaking an error message into location, problem, and action, you can quickly understand the issue and know what to fix.

10.4.3 Common Error Patterns

When coding, certain errors appear frequently. Recognizing these patterns helps you fix problems quickly. For example, the message object 'x' not found means a variable doesn't exist—usually due to a typo or a missing assignment. Could not find function "func" indicates that a required library hasn't been loaded, so calling library() for the appropriate package will fix it. Subscript out of bounds happens when you try to access a row or column that doesn't exist, which can be resolved by checking your data's dimensions. Finally, messages about missing observations in cov/cor occur when calculations encounter missing values; adding na.rm = TRUE or using use = "complete.obs" tells R how to handle them. Understanding these patterns turns error messages from obstacles into guides for quick debugging.

Error Message	Translation	Quick Fix
`object 'x' not found`	Variable doesn't exist	Check spelling, create variable
`could not find function "func"`	Function/library not loaded	Load required library
`subscript out of bounds`	Accessing non-existent row/column	Check data dimensions
`missing observations in cov/cor`	Missing values in calculation	Add `na.rm = TRUE` or `use = "complete.obs"`

10.5 Systematic Debugging Workflow

Instead of randomly trying fixes when errors occur, a systematic debugging workflow helps you investigate and solve problems efficiently. Start by **observing** exactly what is happening—look carefully at error messages and unexpected outputs. Next, **hypothesize** what might be causing the problem, such as a missing variable or a misused function. Then, **test** one specific fix at a time rather than changing multiple things at once. After that, **evaluate** whether the fix worked and what you learned from it. If the problem persists, **iterate** by refining your hypothesis and repeating the process. This methodical approach turns debugging into a structured investigation, making errors less frustrating and more educational.

10.5.1 The Divide and Conquer Strategy

When complex code fails, test each piece separately:

```
# Instead of debugging this complex pipeline all at once:
result <- raw_data %>%
  filter(age > 18) %>%
  group_by(department) %>%
  summarize(avg_salary = mean(salary)) %>%
  arrange(desc(avg_salary))

# Test each step individually:
step1 <- raw_data %>% filter(age > 18)
print(nrow(step1))  # Did filtering work?

step2 <- step1 %>% group_by(department)
print(group_keys(step2))  # Are groups correct?

# Continue testing each step...
```

10.5.2 The Power of Print Statements

Add diagnostic prints to see what's actually happening:

```
analyze_survey <- function(data) {
  print(paste("Input:", nrow(data), "rows"))

  filtered_data <- data[data$age > 18, ]
  print(paste("After filtering:", nrow(filtered_data), "rows"))

  if (nrow(filtered_data) == 0) {
    print("WARNING: No data left after filtering!")
    return(NULL)
  }

  result <- mean(filtered_data$satisfaction)
  print(paste("Result:", result))
  return(result)
}
```

10.6 Smart Debugging vs. Random Guessing

Smart debugging is about being systematic rather than guessing blindly. Consider two approaches: Emma spends two hours randomly changing plot types, modifying colors, copying code from the internet, and making multiple changes at once, but doesn't solve the problem. James, on the other hand, solves the same issue in twenty minutes by following a clear process: he inspects the data with print(head(data)), checks the function syntax in the documentation, creates a minimal test case, compares it to the broken plot, and quickly identifies missing values as the root cause. The contrast shows that a methodical approach saves time, reduces frustration, and reliably uncovers the true source of errors.

10.6.1 Evidence-Based Debugging

Evidence-based debugging focuses on gathering information instead of guessing. Start by examining your data using functions like head(), str(), and summary() to understand its structure and contents. Test your code with simple, known inputs to see if outputs match expectations. Change or check only one thing at a time to isolate the cause of the problem, and always verify assumptions instead of taking them for granted. This approach turns debugging into a systematic investigation rather than a trial-and-error process.

10.7 Quick Reference: Common Errors and Fixes

Problem	Likely Cause	Quick Fix
`object 'x' not found`	Typo or variable not created	Check spelling, run creation code

Problem	Likely Cause	Quick Fix
`could not find function`	Library not loaded	`library(package_name)`
`cannot open connection`	File doesn't exist	Check file path and name
`subscript out of bounds`	Wrong row/column number	Check `nrow()`, `ncol()`, `names()`
`non-numeric argument`	Text in math function	Check data types with `str()`
`missing observations`	NA values in calculation	Add `na.rm = TRUE`
Empty plot	Wrong variable names	Check `names(data)` for exact spelling
`unexpected symbol`	Missing comma or parenthesis	Check syntax carefully

10.7.1 Debugging Toolkit Checklist

A good debugging toolkit helps you work efficiently and systematically. Before you start, make sure to read the error message carefully, identify exactly where the problem occurs, and form a specific hypothesis about its cause. Use investigation tools like print() statements to check intermediate results, and functions such as head(), str(), and summary() to examine your data. Test with simple examples where you know the expected results, and make one change at a time, verifying its effect. Seek help only after you've tried systematic debugging, can create a minimal reproducible example, and can clearly explain what you expected versus what actually happened.

10.8 Building Debugging Confidence

Building confidence in debugging starts with adopting a growth mindset. Instead of thinking that errors mean you're bad at programming, see each error as an opportunity to learn something valuable. Approach debugging as a journey: encounter an error, apply a systematic process to solve it, and reflect on what you've learned. Each successful fix builds your skills and prepares you to tackle more complex problems. Celebrating small victories helps reinforce this progress. Keep a "debugging victories" log noting what error you solved, the root cause, what you learned, and how it will help you next time. Over time, this practice turns debugging from a frustrating task into a confidence-building skill.

10.9 Conclusion

Debugging transforms from frustration into valuable problem-solving skill as you develop systematic approaches. The debugging skills you've learned—systematic investigation, evidence gathering, hypothesis testing—will serve you well beyond programming.

In the next chapter, we'll explore how AI can assist with programming and debugging while maintaining your own problem-solving skills. The systematic approaches you've learned here will help you evaluate and verify AI-generated solutions.

Remember: every expert programmer has spent countless hours debugging. The difference isn't that experts don't encounter errors—it's that they approach errors systematically and without panic.

Debugging is problem-solving, not punishment. Each error you solve makes you a more capable analyst and resilient problem-solver. What once seemed like obstacles become opportunities for deeper understanding and skill development.

10.10 Review Questions

1. Why is it important to normalize errors as a natural part of programming?
2. Describe the key difference between syntax errors, runtime errors, and logic errors. Give an example of each.
3. What questions can help you quickly identify what type of error you are facing?
4. Explain how reading error messages systematically can speed up debugging. What are the three parts of an error message in R?
5. What does the error message object 'x' not found usually indicate, and how can it be fixed?
6. How can the message could not find function "func" be resolved?
7. What does the error subscript out of bounds mean, and how would you check for it?
8. Why is it recommended to follow a systematic debugging workflow rather than randomly changing code?
9. Explain the "divide and conquer" strategy for debugging complex code.
10. How can print statements assist in debugging? Provide an example of a diagnostic print.
11. Compare "smart debugging" and "random guessing" with a brief example of each approach.
12. What is evidence-based debugging, and which R functions are particularly helpful for examining data during this process?

13. List at least five items from a "debugging toolkit" that help systematically identify and solve errors.
14. How can keeping a "debugging victories" log build confidence and improve programming skills over time?

10.11 Ch 10 Lab Debugging

Every programmer — beginner or expert — spends a significant amount of time debugging. Code breaks for all kinds of reasons: typos, missing parentheses, unexpected data, or simply misunderstanding how a function works. Errors aren't a sign that something is wrong with you as a learner; they're a normal and unavoidable part of writing code. In fact, debugging is one of the most valuable skills you can develop as an analyst because it teaches you how to think clearly, test ideas, and solve problems systematically.

In this lab, you'll learn how to approach errors with confidence instead of frustration. You'll practice reading error messages, identifying common patterns, and breaking problems into smaller pieces you can test and verify. Rather than guessing or rewriting code blindly, you'll learn a structured way to diagnose issues and confirm your fixes. This mindset will save you time, reduce stress, and make your code more reliable.

Throughout the lab, you'll also use Positron's debugging features — error highlighting, inline help, and AI-powered explanations — to understand not just what went wrong, but why.

10.11.1 Demonstration

10.11.1.1 Everyone Gets Errors

One of the most important truths in programming is also one of the least talked about: everyone gets errors. Beginners get them. Experts get them. Entire engineering teams get them. Errors aren't a sign that you're doing something wrong — they're a sign that your code is running, checking your instructions, and giving you feedback about what it doesn't understand.

In this demonstration, you'll intentionally trigger some of the most common beginner mistakes: typos, missing parentheses, wrong data types, and variables that don't exist yet. These aren't exotic or rare problems — they're the everyday errors that every programmer encounters, often multiple times a day. The difference between frustration and confidence is learning how to read these messages and use them as clues.

By walking through these examples in both R and Python, you'll see how predictable many errors actually are. You'll also see how small the fixes usually are — a missing bracket, a misspelled function name, or a variable defined in the wrong place. Once you understand the pattern, debugging becomes less about guessing and more about noticing what the computer is telling you.

This is the mindset shift of debugging: errors aren't roadblocks — they're signposts. They point you directly to what needs attention, and with practice, you'll learn to interpret them quickly and calmly.

10.11.1.2 The Reality of Programming Errors

R Approach - Common Beginner Errors

```
# ===============================================
# Demo 1: Errors Are Normal (R)
# Let's intentionally make some common mistakes
# ===============================================

print("=== THE REALITY: EVERYONE MAKES ERRORS ===")
```

```
[1] "=== THE REALITY: EVERYONE MAKES ERRORS ==="
```

```
print("Even experienced programmers see errors every day!")
```

```
[1] "Even experienced programmers see errors every day!"
```

```
print("The difference is they know how to fix them quickly.")
```

```
[1] "The difference is they know how to fix them quickly."
```

```
# ERROR 1: Typo in function name
print("\n--- Error 1: Typo in function name ---")
```

```
[1] "\n--- Error 1: Typo in function name ---"
```

```
# This will cause an error:
# meen(c(1, 2, 3, 4, 5)) # Should be "mean"

# The correct version:
mean(c(1, 2, 3, 4, 5))
```

```
[1] 3
```

```
# ERROR 2: Missing parenthesis
print("\n--- Error 2: Missing parenthesis ---")
```

```
[1] "\n--- Error 2: Missing parenthesis ---"
```

```
# This will cause an error:
# print("Hello world" # Missing closing parenthesis

# The correct version:
```

```
print("Hello world")
```

```
[1] "Hello world"
```

```
# ERROR 3: Wrong data type
print("\n--- Error 3: Wrong data type ---")
```

```
[1] "\n--- Error 3: Wrong data type ---"
```

```
# This will cause an error:
# mean("hello") # Can't calculate mean of text

# The correct version:
mean(c(1, 2, 3, 4, 5))
```

```
[1] 3
```

```
# ERROR 4: Object not found
print("\n--- Error 4: Object not found ---")
```

```
[1] "\n--- Error 4: Object not found ---"
```

```
# This will cause an error:
# print(my_variable) # Variable doesn't exist yet

# The correct version:
my_variable <- "Now it exists!"
print(my_variable)
```

```
[1] "Now it exists!"
```

```
print("\n=== KEY INSIGHT ===")
```

```
[1] "\n=== KEY INSIGHT ==="
```

```
print("Errors are feedback, not failure!")
```

```
[1] "Errors are feedback, not failure!"
```

```
print("They tell you exactly what needs to be fixed.")
```

```
[1] "They tell you exactly what needs to be fixed."
```

Python Approach - Common Beginner Errors

```
# ============================================
# Demo 1: Errors Are Normal (Python)
```

```
# Let's intentionally make some common mistakes
# ==============================================

print("=== THE REALITY: EVERYONE MAKES ERRORS ===")
```

```
=== THE REALITY: EVERYONE MAKES ERRORS ===
```

```
print("Even experienced programmers see errors every day!")
```

```
Even experienced programmers see errors every day!
```

```
print("The difference is they know how to fix them quickly.")
```

```
The difference is they know how to fix them quickly.
```

```
# ERROR 1: Typo in function name
print("\n--- Error 1: Typo in function name ---")
```

```

--- Error 1: Typo in function name ---
```

```
# This will cause an error:
# statistics.meen([1, 2, 3, 4, 5]) # Should be "mean"

# The correct version:
import statistics
print(statistics.mean([1, 2, 3, 4, 5]))
```

```
3
```

```
# ERROR 2: Missing parenthesis
print("\n--- Error 2: Missing parenthesis ---")
```

```

--- Error 2: Missing parenthesis ---
```

```
# This will cause an error:
# print("Hello world" # Missing closing parenthesis

# The correct version:
print("Hello world")
```

```
Hello world
```

```
# ERROR 3: Wrong data type
print("\n--- Error 3: Wrong data type ---")
```

```
--- Error 3: Wrong data type ---
```

```
# This will cause an error:
# statistics.mean("hello") # Can't calculate mean of text

# The correct version:
print(statistics.mean([1, 2, 3, 4, 5]))
```

```
3
```

```
# ERROR 4: Variable not defined
print("\n--- Error 4: Variable not defined ---")
```

```

--- Error 4: Variable not defined ---
```

```
# This will cause an error:
# print(my_variable) # Variable doesn't exist yet

# The correct version:
my_variable = "Now it exists!"
print(my_variable)
```

```
Now it exists!
```

```
print("\n=== KEY INSIGHT ===")
```

```

=== KEY INSIGHT ===
```

```
print("Errors are feedback, not failure!")
```

```
Errors are feedback, not failure!
```

```
print("They tell you exactly what needs to be fixed.")
```

```
They tell you exactly what needs to be fixed.
```

Errors are a normal and expected part of programming, not a sign that you're doing something wrong. Most issues come from small, fixable mistakes like typos, missing parentheses, or undefined variables. Error messages are designed to help you — they point you to the line that failed and often describe exactly what the computer couldn't understand. Once you learn to read these messages and recognize common patterns, debugging becomes far less intimidating. Each error you fix strengthens your understanding and builds confidence in your ability to troubleshoot your own code.

AI Integration

AI tools can help you make sense of errors more quickly by translating technical messages into plain language and pointing you toward the most likely cause. When something breaks, you can ask the AI to explain what the error means, why it happened, and which line of code to inspect first. Instead of guessing or rewriting large sections of your script, the AI can guide you toward small, targeted checks — verifying object names, confirming data types, or isolating a single expression. This turns debugging into a structured, supported process and helps you build the habits that experienced programmers rely on every day.

10.11.1.3 Reading Error Messages

Error messages can feel intimidating at first, but they're one of the most helpful tools you have as a programmer. Every message contains clues about what went wrong, where it happened, and what the computer expected instead. Once you learn how to read these clues systematically, debugging becomes far faster and far less frustrating.

Most error messages follow predictable patterns. They tell you the type of problem (like a missing object or a wrong data type), point to the line where it occurred, and describe what the computer couldn't understand. Even though the wording can look technical, the underlying meaning is usually straightforward once you know what to look for.

In this demonstration, you'll walk through some of the most common error messages in both R and Python. For each one, you'll see the original code, the exact message the computer produces, and a plain-language translation of what it means. These examples show how small mistakes — a misspelled function name, a missing parenthesis, or an undefined variable — lead to clear, interpretable messages that guide you toward the fix.

The goal isn't to memorize every error you might encounter. Instead, it's to build a habit of reading messages carefully, identifying the key pieces of information, and using them to narrow down the problem. Once you understand how to decode error messages, debugging becomes a logical process rather than a guessing game.

R Approach - Decoding Error Messages

```
# ============================================
# Demo 2: Reading Error Messages (R)
# ============================================

print("=== HOW TO READ ERROR MESSAGES ===")
```

```
[1] "=== HOW TO READ ERROR MESSAGES ==="
```

```
print("Error messages have a pattern - let's learn to decode them!")
```

```
[1] "Error messages have a pattern - let's learn to decode them!"
```

```
# Example 1: Function not found
print("\n--- Example 1: Function not found ---")
```

```
[1] "\n--- Example 1: Function not found ---"
```

```
print("If you run: meen(c(1,2,3))")
```

```
[1] "If you run: meen(c(1,2,3))"
```

```
print("Error message: 'Error: could not find function \"meen\"'")
```

```
[1] "Error message: 'Error: could not find function \"meen\"'"
```

```
print("Translation: R doesn't know what 'meen' is")
```

```
[1] "Translation: R doesn't know what 'meen' is"
```

```
print("Fix: Check spelling - probably meant 'mean'")
```

```
[1] "Fix: Check spelling - probably meant 'mean'"
```

```
# Example 2: Object not found
print("\n--- Example 2: Object not found ---")
```

```
[1] "\n--- Example 2: Object not found ---"
```

```
print("If you run: print(student_data)")
```

```
[1] "If you run: print(student_data)"
```

```
print("Error message: 'Error: object 'student_data' not found'")
```

```
[1] "Error message: 'Error: object 'student_data' not found'"
```

```
print("Translation: You haven't created 'student_data' yet")
```

```
[1] "Translation: You haven't created 'student_data' yet"
```

```
print("Fix: Create the variable first, or check spelling")
```

```
[1] "Fix: Create the variable first, or check spelling"
```

```
# Example 3: Wrong number of arguments
print("\n--- Example 3: Wrong arguments ---")
```

```
[1] "\n--- Example 3: Wrong arguments ---"
```

```
print("If you run: mean()")
```

```
[1] "If you run: mean()"
```

```
print("Error message: 'Error in mean.default() :")
```

```
[1] "Error message: 'Error in mean.default() :"
```

```
print("argument \"x\" is missing'")
```

```
[1] "argument \"x\" is missing'"
```

```
print("Translation: mean() needs data to work with")
```

```
[1] "Translation: mean() needs data to work with"
```

```
print("Fix: Provide data: mean(c(1,2,3))")
```

```
[1] "Fix: Provide data: mean(c(1,2,3))"
```

```
# Example 4: Syntax error
print("\n--- Example 4: Syntax error ---")
```

```
[1] "\n--- Example 4: Syntax error ---"
```

```
print("If you run: print('hello'")
```

```
[1] "If you run: print('hello'"
```

```
print("Error message: 'Error: unexpected end of input'")
```

```
[1] "Error message: 'Error: unexpected end of input'"
```

```
print("Translation: R expected more code (missing closing quote)")
```

```
[1] "Translation: R expected more code (missing closing quote)"
```

```
print("Fix: Add the missing quote: print('hello')")
```

```
[1] "Fix: Add the missing quote: print('hello')"
```

```
print("\n=== ERROR MESSAGE ANATOMY ===")
```

```
[1] "\n=== ERROR MESSAGE ANATOMY ==="
```

```
print("1. 'Error' or 'Warning' - tells you the severity")
```

```
[1] "1. 'Error' or 'Warning' - tells you the severity"
```

```
print("2. Location - where the problem occurred")
```

```
[1] "2. Location - where the problem occurred"
```

```
print("3. Description - what went wrong")
```

```
[1] "3. Description - what went wrong"
```

```
print("4. Sometimes a suggestion for fixing it")
```

```
[1] "4. Sometimes a suggestion for fixing it"
```

Python Approach - Decoding Error Messages

```
# ==============================================
# Demo 2: Reading Error Messages (Python)
# ==============================================

print("=== HOW TO READ ERROR MESSAGES ===")
```

```
=== HOW TO READ ERROR MESSAGES ===
```

```
print("Error messages have a pattern - let's learn to decode them!")
```

```
Error messages have a pattern - let's learn to decode them!
```

```
# Example 1: Name not defined
print("\n--- Example 1: Name not defined ---")
```

```

--- Example 1: Name not defined ---
```

```
print("If you run: print(student_data)")
```

```
If you run: print(student_data)
```

```
print("Error message: 'NameError: name 'student_data' is not defined'")
```

```
Error message: 'NameError: name 'student_data' is not defined'
```

```
print("Translation: Python doesn't know what 'student_data' is")
```

```
Translation: Python doesn't know what 'student_data' is
```

```
print("Fix: Create the variable first, or check spelling")
```

```
Fix: Create the variable first, or check spelling
```

```
# Example 2: Type error
print("\n--- Example 2: Type error ---")
```

```
--- Example 2: Type error ---
```

```
print("If you run: len(5)")
```

```
If you run: len(5)
```

```
print("Error message: 'TypeError: object of type 'int' has no len()'")
```

```
Error message: 'TypeError: object of type 'int' has no len()'
```

```
print("Translation: You can't get the length of a number")
```

```
Translation: You can't get the length of a number
```

```
print("Fix: Use len() on lists or strings: len([1,2,3])")
```

```
Fix: Use len() on lists or strings: len([1,2,3])
```

```
# Example 3: Syntax error
print("\n--- Example 3: Syntax error ---")
```

```
--- Example 3: Syntax error ---
```

```
print("If you run: print('hello'")
```

```
If you run: print('hello'
```

```
print("Error message: 'SyntaxError: unterminated string literal'")
```

```
Error message: 'SyntaxError: unterminated string literal'
```

```
print("Translation: You started a string but didn't finish it")
```

```
Translation: You started a string but didn't finish it
```

```
print("Fix: Add the missing quote: print('hello')")
```

```
Fix: Add the missing quote: print('hello')
```

```
# Example 4: Index error
print("\n--- Example 4: Index error ---")
```

```
--- Example 4: Index error ---
```

```
print("If you run: my_list = [1,2,3]; print(my_list[5])")
```

```
If you run: my_list = [1,2,3]; print(my_list[5])
```

```
print("Error message: 'IndexError: list index out of range'")
```

```
Error message: 'IndexError: list index out of range'
```

```
print("Translation: You asked for item 5, but the list only has 3
↪  items")
```

```
Translation: You asked for item 5, but the list only has 3 items
```

```
print("Fix: Use a valid index: my_list[0], my_list[1], or my_list[2]")
```

```
Fix: Use a valid index: my_list[0], my_list[1], or my_list[2]
```

```
print("\n=== ERROR MESSAGE ANATOMY ===")
```

```

=== ERROR MESSAGE ANATOMY ===
```

```
print("1. Error type (NameError, TypeError, etc.) - category of
↪  problem")
```

```
1. Error type (NameError, TypeError, etc.) - category of problem
```

```
print("2. Description - what specifically went wrong")
```

```
2. Description - what specifically went wrong
```

```
print("3. Line number - where the error occurred")
```

```
3. Line number - where the error occurred
```

```
print("4. Code snippet - shows the problematic line")
```

```
4. Code snippet - shows the problematic line
```

Error messages follow predictable patterns, and learning to read them systematically is one of the fastest ways to improve your debugging skills. They tell you what type of problem occurred, where it happened, and what the computer expected instead. Once you recognize common error types — missing objects, wrong data types, syntax issues, out-of-range indexes — you can diagnose problems much more quickly. The goal isn't to memorize every message, but to understand how to extract the important clues so you can fix issues efficiently and keep your analysis moving.

AI Integration

AI tools can help you make sense of error messages when they feel confusing or overly technical. If you paste an error into the AI assistant, it can translate the message into plain language, highlight the part that matters most, and point you toward the likely cause. This is especially helpful when the message includes a long traceback or unfamiliar terminology. The AI can also suggest small diagnostic steps — checking a variable name, printing a value, or running a single line on its own — that help you confirm your understanding. Instead of treating error messages as something you have to decode alone, you can use the AI as a guide that helps you interpret the clues quickly and confidently.

10.11.1.4 Common Error Patterns and Fixes

Most beginner errors aren't mysterious — they fall into a handful of predictable patterns that show up again and again. Once you learn to recognize these patterns, debugging becomes much faster because you know exactly where to look first. Spelling mistakes, missing parentheses, undefined variables, and data-type mismatches account for a large share of the issues new programmers encounter in both R and Python.

In this demonstration, you'll walk through the most common categories of beginner errors and see how they appear in each language. For every pattern, you'll look at an example of code that breaks, the message the computer produces, and the simple fix that resolves it. The goal isn't to memorize every possible mistake — it's to train your eye to notice the clues that point to these familiar patterns.

Once you start recognizing these categories automatically, debugging becomes less about trial and error and more about pattern matching. With practice, you'll be able to diagnose many issues within seconds because you've seen the pattern before.

R Approach - Error Pattern Recognition

```
# ============================================
# Demo 3: Common Error Patterns (R)
# ============================================

print("=== COMMON ERROR PATTERNS AND FIXES ===")
```

```
[1] "=== COMMON ERROR PATTERNS AND FIXES ==="
```

```
# PATTERN 1: Spelling and Capitalization
print("\n--- Pattern 1: Spelling/Capitalization ---")
```

```
[1] "\n--- Pattern 1: Spelling/Capitalization ---"
```

```
print("Problem: R is case-sensitive and spelling-sensitive")
```

```
[1] "Problem: R is case-sensitive and spelling-sensitive"
```

```r
# Wrong:
# Mean(c(1,2,3)) # Should be lowercase 'mean'
# lenght(c(1,2,3)) # Should be 'length'

# Right:
mean(c(1,2,3))
```

```
[1] 2
```

```r
length(c(1,2,3))
```

```
[1] 3
```

```r
print("Fix: Check spelling and capitalization carefully")
```

```
[1] "Fix: Check spelling and capitalization carefully"
```

```r
# PATTERN 2: Missing or Extra Parentheses
print("\n--- Pattern 2: Parentheses Problems ---")
```

```
[1] "\n--- Pattern 2: Parentheses Problems ---"
```

```r
print("Problem: Every opening parenthesis needs a closing one")
```

```
[1] "Problem: Every opening parenthesis needs a closing one"
```

```r
# Wrong:
# mean(c(1,2,3) # Missing closing parenthesis
# mean((c(1,2,3))) # Extra parentheses (works but unnecessary)

# Right:
mean(c(1,2,3))
```

```
[1] 2
```

```r
print("Fix: Count your parentheses - they should match")
```

```
[1] "Fix: Count your parentheses - they should match"
```

```r
# PATTERN 3: Using Variables Before Creating Them
print("\n--- Pattern 3: Variable Order ---")
```

```
[1] "\n--- Pattern 3: Variable Order ---"
```

```r
print("Problem: You must create variables before using them")
```

```
[1] "Problem: You must create variables before using them"
```

```
# Wrong order:
# print(my_result) # my_result doesn't exist yet
# my_result <- 42

# Right order:
my_result <- 42
print(my_result)
```

```
[1] 42
```

```
print("Fix: Create variables before using them")
```

```
[1] "Fix: Create variables before using them"
```

```
# PATTERN 4: Wrong Data Types
print("\n--- Pattern 4: Data Type Mismatches ---")
```

```
[1] "\n--- Pattern 4: Data Type Mismatches ---"
```

```
print("Problem: Functions expect certain types of data")
```

```
[1] "Problem: Functions expect certain types of data"
```

```
# Wrong:
# mean("hello") # Can't calculate mean of text
# length(42) # length() is for vectors, not single numbers

# Right:
mean(c(1,2,3)) # Numbers for mathematical functions
```

```
[1] 2
```

```
length(c(1,2,3)) # Vectors for length()
```

```
[1] 3
```

```
print("Fix: Match data types to function expectations")
```

```
[1] "Fix: Match data types to function expectations"
```

```
print("\n=== QUICK DEBUGGING CHECKLIST ===")
```

```
[1] "\n=== QUICK DEBUGGING CHECKLIST ==="
```

```
print("1. Check spelling and capitalization")
```

```
[1] "1. Check spelling and capitalization"
```

```
print("2. Count parentheses and quotes")
```

```
[1] "2. Count parentheses and quotes"
```

```
print("3. Make sure variables exist before using them")
```

```
[1] "3. Make sure variables exist before using them"
```

```
print("4. Check that data types match function requirements")
```

```
[1] "4. Check that data types match function requirements"
```

Python Approach - Error Pattern Recognition

```
# ============================================
# Demo 3: Common Error Patterns (Python)
# ============================================

print("=== COMMON ERROR PATTERNS AND FIXES ===")
```

```
=== COMMON ERROR PATTERNS AND FIXES ===
```

```
# PATTERN 1: Indentation Errors
print("\n--- Pattern 1: Indentation ---")
```

```

--- Pattern 1: Indentation ---
```

```
print("Problem: Python uses indentation to group code")
```

```
Problem: Python uses indentation to group code
```

```
# Wrong:
# if True:
# print("This should be indented")

# Right:
if True:
    print("This is properly indented")
```

```
This is properly indented
```

```
print("Fix: Use consistent indentation (4 spaces is standard)")
```

```
Fix: Use consistent indentation (4 spaces is standard)
```

```
# PATTERN 2: Name Errors
print("\n--- Pattern 2: Name Errors ---")
```

```

--- Pattern 2: Name Errors ---
```

```
print("Problem: Using variables before defining them")
```

```
Problem: Using variables before defining them
```

```
# Wrong order:
# print(my_result) # my_result doesn't exist yet
# my_result = 42

# Right order:
my_result = 42
print(my_result)
```

```
42
```

```
print("Fix: Define variables before using them")
```

```
Fix: Define variables before using them
```

```
# PATTERN 3: Type Errors
print("\n--- Pattern 3: Type Errors ---")
```

```

--- Pattern 3: Type Errors ---
```

```
print("Problem: Using wrong data types with functions")
```

```
Problem: Using wrong data types with functions
```

```
# Wrong:
# len(42) # Can't get length of a number
# "hello" + 5 # Can't add string and number

# Right:
len("hello") # Length of string
```

```
5
```

```
"hello" + str(5) # Convert number to string first
```

```
'hello5'
```

```
print("Fix: Match data types to function expectations")
```

```
Fix: Match data types to function expectations
```

```
# PATTERN 4: Index Errors
print("\n--- Pattern 4: Index Errors ---")
```

```

--- Pattern 4: Index Errors ---
```

```
print("Problem: Trying to access items that don't exist")
```

```
Problem: Trying to access items that don't exist
```

```
my_list = [1, 2, 3]
# Wrong:
# print(my_list[5]) # List only has 3 items (indices 0, 1, 2)

# Right:
print(my_list[0]) # First item
```

```
1
```

```
print(my_list[-1]) # Last item
```

```
3
```

```
print("Fix: Remember Python uses 0-based indexing")
```

```
Fix: Remember Python uses 0-based indexing
```

```
print("\n=== QUICK DEBUGGING CHECKLIST ===")
```

```

=== QUICK DEBUGGING CHECKLIST ===
```

```
print("1. Check indentation consistency")
```

```
1. Check indentation consistency
```

```
print("2. Make sure variables are defined before use")
```

```
2. Make sure variables are defined before use
```

```
print("3. Check data types match function requirements")
```

```
3. Check data types match function requirements
```

```
print("4. Verify list/string indices are valid")
```

```
4. Verify list/string indices are valid
```

```
print("5. Count parentheses and quotes")
```

```
5. Count parentheses and quotes
```

Most beginner errors fall into a small set of predictable patterns, and learning to recognize them dramatically speeds up debugging. Spelling mistakes, mismatched parentheses, undefined variables, and data-type mismatches account for a large share of the issues you'll encounter in R and Python. Each language has its own common pitfalls — like indentation in Python or case sensitivity in R — but the underlying idea is the same: once you know what these patterns look like, you can diagnose and fix problems much more quickly. A simple checklist can catch most errors, and with practice, these patterns become second nature.

AI Integration

AI tools can help you spot error patterns long before you recognize them on your own. If you paste an error message or a broken code snippet into the AI assistant, it can identify which category the problem belongs to — a spelling mistake, a missing parenthesis, a type mismatch, or an indexing issue. This is especially helpful when you're not sure where to start looking. The AI can also point out subtle issues you might overlook, such as inconsistent indentation in Python or using a variable before defining it. Over time, this guidance trains your eye to notice these patterns automatically, making you faster and more confident at debugging.

10.11.1.5 Systematic Debugging

When code breaks, the natural reaction is often to start changing things at random—adding parentheses, renaming variables, copying examples from the internet, or commenting out large chunks of code just to "see what happens." This trial-and-error approach sometimes works, but it's slow, frustrating, and makes it hard to understand what actually fixed the problem.

A more effective approach is to treat debugging like an investigation. Instead of guessing, you read the error message carefully, identify where the problem occurred, and form a specific hypothesis about what might be wrong. Then you run small, targeted tests—like adding print statements or checking whether a variable exists—to confirm or reject that hypothesis. If you're wrong, you move on to the next most likely explanation.

10.11.1.5.1 The Debugging Workflow

```
# ==========================================
# Demo 4: Systematic Debugging (R)
```

```r
# ============================================

print("=== THE SYSTEMATIC DEBUGGING APPROACH ===")
```

```
[1] "=== THE SYSTEMATIC DEBUGGING APPROACH ==="
```

```r
print("Don't guess randomly - be a detective!")
```

```
[1] "Don't guess randomly - be a detective!"
```

```r
# STEP 1: Read the error message carefully
print("\n--- Step 1: Read the Error Message ---")
```

```
[1] "\n--- Step 1: Read the Error Message ---"
```

```r
print("Example error: 'Error in mean(student_ages)")
```

```
[1] "Example error: 'Error in mean(student_ages)"
```

```r
print(": object 'student_ages' not found'")
```

```
[1] ": object 'student_ages' not found'"
```

```r
print("What it tells us:")
```

```
[1] "What it tells us:"
```

```r
print("- The problem is in the mean() function")
```

```
[1] "- The problem is in the mean() function"
```

```r
print("- Specifically with 'student_ages'")
```

```
[1] "- Specifically with 'student_ages'"
```

```r
print("- The object doesn't exist")
```

```
[1] "- The object doesn't exist"
```

```r
# STEP 2: Locate the problem
print("\n--- Step 2: Find the Exact Location ---")
```

```
[1] "\n--- Step 2: Find the Exact Location ---"
```

```r
print("Look at the line mentioned in the error")
```

```
[1] "Look at the line mentioned in the error"
```

```
print("Check: Is 'student_ages' spelled correctly?")
```

```
[1] "Check: Is 'student_ages' spelled correctly?"
```

```
print("Check: Did I create 'student_ages' earlier?")
```

```
[1] "Check: Did I create 'student_ages' earlier?"
```

```
# STEP 3: Use print statements to investigate
print("\n--- Step 3: Use Print Statements ---")
```

```
[1] "\n--- Step 3: Use Print Statements ---"
```

```
print("Add print statements to see what's happening:")
```

```
[1] "Add print statements to see what's happening:"
```

```
# Debugging example:
print("Debugging example:")
```

```
[1] "Debugging example:"
```

```
print("Before the problem line, add:")
```

```
[1] "Before the problem line, add:"
```

```
print("print('About to calculate mean')")
```

```
[1] "print('About to calculate mean')"
```

```
print("print(exists('student_ages'))") # Check if variable exists
```

```
[1] "print(exists('student_ages'))"
```

```
# STEP 4: Test the fix
print("\n--- Step 4: Test Your Fix ---")
```

```
[1] "\n--- Step 4: Test Your Fix ---"
```

```
student_ages <- c(20, 22, 19, 21, 23) # Create the missing variable
print("Created student_ages:")
```

```
[1] "Created student_ages:"
```

```
print(student_ages)
```

```
[1] 20 22 19 21 23
```

```
print("Now mean() should work:")
```

```
[1] "Now mean() should work:"
```

```
print(mean(student_ages))
```

```
[1] 21
```

```
# STEP 5: Clean up debugging code
print("\n--- Step 5: Clean Up ---")
```

```
[1] "\n--- Step 5: Clean Up ---"
```

```
print("Remove the print statements you added for debugging")
```

```
[1] "Remove the print statements you added for debugging"
```

```
print("Keep only the working code")
```

```
[1] "Keep only the working code"
```

```
print("\n=== THE DEBUGGING MINDSET ===")
```

```
[1] "\n=== THE DEBUGGING MINDSET ==="
```

```
print("1. Stay calm - errors are normal")
```

```
[1] "1. Stay calm - errors are normal"
```

```
print("2. Read the error message carefully")
```

```
[1] "2. Read the error message carefully"
```

```
print("3. Form a hypothesis about what's wrong")
```

```
[1] "3. Form a hypothesis about what's wrong"
```

```
print("4. Test your hypothesis")
```

```
[1] "4. Test your hypothesis"
```

```
print("5. If wrong, try the next most likely cause")
```

```
[1] "5. If wrong, try the next most likely cause"
```

```
# ============================================
# Demo 4: Systematic Debugging (Python)
# ============================================
```

```
print("=== THE SYSTEMATIC DEBUGGING APPROACH ===")
```

```
=== THE SYSTEMATIC DEBUGGING APPROACH ===
```

```
print("Don't guess randomly - be a detective!")
```

```
Don't guess randomly - be a detective!
```

```
# STEP 1: Read the error message carefully
print("\n--- Step 1: Read the Error Message ---")
```

```

--- Step 1: Read the Error Message ---
```

```
print("Example error: 'NameError: name 'student_ages' is not defined'")
```

```
Example error: 'NameError: name 'student_ages' is not defined'
```

```
print("What it tells us:")
```

```
What it tells us:
```

```
print("- It's a NameError (variable problem)")
```

```
- It's a NameError (variable problem)
```

```
print("- The variable 'student_ages' doesn't exist")
```

```
- The variable 'student_ages' doesn't exist
```

```
print("- We tried to use it before defining it")
```

```
- We tried to use it before defining it
```

```
# STEP 2: Locate the problem
print("\n--- Step 2: Find the Exact Location ---")
```

```

--- Step 2: Find the Exact Location ---
```

```
print("Look at the line number in the error")
```

```
Look at the line number in the error
```

```
print("Check: Is 'student_ages' spelled correctly?")
```

```
Check: Is 'student_ages' spelled correctly?
```

```
print("Check: Did I define 'student_ages' earlier?")
```

```
Check: Did I define 'student_ages' earlier?
```

```
# STEP 3: Use print statements to investigate
print("\n--- Step 3: Use Print Statements ---")
```

```

--- Step 3: Use Print Statements ---
```

```
print("Add print statements to see what's happening:")
```

```
Add print statements to see what's happening:
```

```
# Debugging example:
print("Debugging example:")
```

```
Debugging example:
```

```
print("Before the problem line, add:")
```

```
Before the problem line, add:
```

```
print("print('About to calculate mean')")
```

```
print('About to calculate mean')
```

```
print("print('student_ages' in locals()) # Check if variable exists")
```

```
print('student_ages' in locals()) # Check if variable exists
```

```
# STEP 4: Test the fix
print("\n--- Step 4: Test Your Fix ---")
```

```

--- Step 4: Test Your Fix ---
```

```
student_ages = [20, 22, 19, 21, 23] # Create the missing variable
print("Created student_ages:")
```

```
Created student_ages:
```

```
print(student_ages)
```

```
[20, 22, 19, 21, 23]
```

```
print("Now statistics.mean() should work:")
```

Now statistics.mean() should work:

```
import statistics
print(statistics.mean(student_ages))
```

```
21
```

```
# STEP 5: Clean up debugging code
print("\n--- Step 5: Clean Up ---")
```

```

--- Step 5: Clean Up ---
```

```
print("Remove the print statements you added for debugging")
```

```
Remove the print statements you added for debugging
```

```
print("Keep only the working code")
```

```
Keep only the working code
```

```
print("\n=== THE DEBUGGING MINDSET ===")
```

```

=== THE DEBUGGING MINDSET ===
```

```
print("1. Stay calm - errors are normal")
```

```
1. Stay calm - errors are normal
```

```
print("2. Read the error message carefully")
```

```
2. Read the error message carefully
```

```
print("3. Form a hypothesis about what's wrong")
```

```
3. Form a hypothesis about what's wrong
```

```
print("4. Test your hypothesis")
```

```
4. Test your hypothesis
```

```
print("5. If wrong, try the next most likely cause")
```

```
5. If wrong, try the next most likely cause
```

Systematic debugging is far more effective than randomly changing code and hoping for the best. Error messages give you valuable clues about what went wrong and where to look. By forming a hypothesis, running small tests, and checking your assumptions, you can isolate the problem quickly and fix it with confidence. Print statements and simple checks help you see what your code is doing, and testing one fix at a time ensures you understand the cause of the issue. Once everything works, you clean up the temporary debugging code and keep only the final solution. With practice, this structured approach becomes second nature and makes debugging a predictable, manageable part of your workflow.

AI Integration

AI tools can support systematic debugging by helping you narrow down the problem instead of guessing. When you encounter an error, you can paste the message or the broken line of code into the AI assistant and ask what it means, what the likely causes are, or what to check first. The AI can walk you through the same steps you're learning in this lab: interpreting the message, inspecting variables, testing small hypotheses, and confirming whether your fix makes sense. It can also suggest targeted print statements or quick checks that reveal what your code is actually doing. Used this way, the AI becomes a debugging partner that reinforces good habits and helps you stay focused on evidence rather than trial-and-error changes.

10.11.2 Practice

You may complete this assignment in either R or Python. The questions refer to the same broken script. Use the version for the language you are working in.

10.11.2.1 R version:

```
student_ages <- c(20, 21, "twenty-two", 23)
average_age <- mean(student_age)
print("Average age is: " , average_age)
```

10.11.2.2 Python version:

```
student_ages = [20, 21, "twenty-two", 23]
import statistics
average_age = statistics.mean(student_age)
print("Average age is: ", average_age)
```

10.11.3 Questions

1. Run the script in your chosen language. Copy the first error message exactly as it appears.
2. Which line of the script caused the first error?
3. What variable name is incorrect in the script?

4. Fix the variable name error. Write the corrected line of code.
5. Run the script again. What is the next error message you receive?
6. What is the data type problem in the student_ages list or vector?
7. Fix the data type problem by correcting the list or vector. Write the corrected line of code.
8. Run the script again. What error do you see in the print statement?
9. Fix the print statement so it runs correctly. Write the corrected line of code.
10. After all fixes, run the script. What is the final output?

Chapter 11

AI as a Programming Assistant

11.1 Learning Outcomes

11-1: Understand the difference between using AI as a solution generator versus a learning accelerator.

11-2: Identify the strengths and limitations of AI programming assistants and how they impact analysis.

11-3: Develop effective prompting strategies to obtain explanations, guidance, and learning from AI tools.

11-4: Apply systematic verification and testing to ensure AI-generated code works correctly on real data.

11-5: Maintain critical thinking and oversight when collaborating with AI, ensuring decisions and understanding remain human-driven.

11-6: Integrate AI responsibly into academic and professional contexts, balancing productivity with transparency and learning objectives.

11.2 Introduction

Maya discovered ChatGPT during her second week of learning R. Suddenly, instead of struggling through documentation and Stack Overflow posts, she could ask questions in plain English and get working code instantly. "This is amazing!" she thought. "I don't need to learn programming anymore—AI can do it all for me."

Three weeks later, Maya faced a problem. Her AI-generated code worked perfectly on the sample data, but failed mysteriously on her real dataset. She couldn't debug it because she didn't understand what the code was actually doing. She realized she'd been using AI as a crutch rather than a learning tool.

This chapter teaches responsible AI use in programming. The key insight is both empowering and cautionary: **AI accelerates learning when used critically**.

11.3 What AI Can and Cannot Do

AI programming assistants have become remarkably capable, but understanding their strengths and limitations is crucial for using them effectively. Think of AI as a knowledgeable but imperfect assistant—one that can provide valuable help but requires your oversight.

AI excels at generating code based on clear descriptions, helping with syntax when you know what you want to accomplish, and explaining complex code in understandable terms. It can assist with debugging by identifying common error patterns, translate code between programming languages, and add helpful documentation to existing code.

However, AI has significant limitations. It lacks awareness of your specific context—it doesn't know your data, your project goals, or the constraints you're working within. AI may not understand the best practices specific to your field, cannot assess whether your data is appropriate for a particular analysis, and struggles with truly novel problems that require creative thinking.

The landscape of AI programming tools is diverse. Chat-based tools like ChatGPT are excellent for explanations and learning but can't execute code. Code-integrated tools like GitHub Copilot provide real-time assistance but may suggest inappropriate solutions. Specialized tools can be very helpful within their scope but are limited outside their focus area.

11.4 Learning to Ask Better Questions

The quality of help you get from AI depends heavily on how you ask for it. There's an important distinction between prompting for solutions and prompting for learning.

When you ask AI to "write R code to analyze my survey data," you're asking for a solution. This might give you working code, but it doesn't help you understand the underlying concepts. In contrast, when you ask AI to "explain what type of analysis would be appropriate for survey data with age, income, and satisfaction variables, and show me the R code with explanations of each step," you're prompting for learning.

Effective prompting provides AI with context. Explain what you're working on and what you're trying to accomplish. Specify which programming language you're using and your skill level. Provide examples of your data structure or desired output. Be clear about what kind of help you need—explanations, debugging help, or alternative approaches.

For example, instead of asking "How do I make a plot in R?" you might ask: "I'm analyzing customer satisfaction survey data for a class project. I'm using R and I'm a beginner. My data has columns for customer_id, age, income, and satisfaction_score (rated 1-5). I want to create a scatter plot showing the relationship between income and satisfaction, and I'd like you to explain the ggplot2 syntax as you show me the code."

11.5 Working Safely with AI Code

AI can produce impressive-looking code that contains subtle errors or uses outdated approaches. The first step in working with AI-generated code is to read and understand it completely. If you can't explain what each line does and why it's there, you're not ready to use the code.

Always test AI-generated code systematically. Start with simple, controlled examples where you know what the expected output should be. Create small test datasets with known characteristics and verify that the code produces the results you expect. Only after the code passes these tests should you apply it to your real data.

AI-generated code often has predictable issues. It may use outdated functions or packages, be overly complex when simpler solutions would work better, or lack proper error handling. For example, AI might suggest using an older package like `plyr` for data manipulation when the modern `dplyr` package would be more appropriate.

Before using any AI-generated code on your real data, create simple test cases. Make a small dataset with known characteristics and verify that the code produces expected results. This approach helps you catch problems early and builds confidence in the code's correctness.

11.6 The Learning Partnership Approach

Maya's journey illustrates the crucial difference between using AI to accelerate learning and using it to avoid learning altogether. In her first few weeks, she treated AI as a magic solution generator, copying and pasting whatever code AI provided. This worked initially, but when she encountered problems that didn't fit standard patterns, she was stuck.

The turning point came when Maya shifted her approach. Instead of asking "Give me code to analyze my data," she started asking "What's the best approach for this type of analysis problem?" She began requesting explanations of the reasoning behind different approaches and asking follow-up questions when she didn't understand something.

This shift transformed AI from a replacement for learning into a learning accelerator. Maya could explore more sophisticated techniques because AI helped her understand the syntax and implementation details. She could experiment with different approaches because AI could explain the trade-offs. Most importantly, she developed the ability to evaluate and improve AI suggestions based on her growing understanding.

The key is to maintain your role as the thinking, decision-making human in the partnership. AI should help you implement your ideas and understand new concepts, not make analytical decisions for you. When you find yourself unable to explain how your code works, or when you panic if AI-generated code doesn't work, these are warning signs that you're outsourcing too much of your thinking to AI.

11.7 Academic and Professional Context

Understanding appropriate AI use in different contexts is crucial for your success. In academic settings, the key principle is transparency and alignment with learning objectives. Using AI to explain concepts you're studying is generally acceptable—it's like having access to a knowledgeable tutor. Getting help with syntax and debugging is typically fine, as these are implementation details rather than core learning objectives.

However, many academic contexts require disclosure when AI has contributed significantly to your work. Some uses of AI are generally prohibited, such as submitting AI-generated work as your own without disclosure, using AI to complete take-home exams, or having AI write entire assignments.

In professional settings, AI use should enhance your productivity while meeting your organization's standards and policies. The key considerations are transparency with your team, adherence to organizational policies, and ensuring that AI supports rather than replaces your professional expertise.

When disclosure is required, good disclosure includes what tool you used, for what purpose, the extent of the assistance, and how you verified the results. For example: "I used ChatGPT-4 to help debug an error in my data visualization code. It generated initial ggplot2 syntax, which I then modified and tested with my specific data."

11.8 Building Your AI Workflow

Developing a productive relationship with AI programming tools is a gradual process. Start by using AI primarily as a tutor—ask it to explain concepts you're studying and request step-by-step breakdowns of complex code. This builds your foundational understanding while familiarizing you with how AI tools work.

As you become more comfortable, begin using AI as a coding partner. Collaborate with AI on problem-solving approaches, use it for syntax help when you know what you want to accomplish, and ask for debugging assistance when you encounter errors. At this stage, you're still making the key analytical decisions, but AI is helping with implementation details.

Eventually, you can use AI as a specialized assistant for specific tasks like documentation, exploring new techniques, or optimizing code you've already written. At this advanced stage, you have sufficient expertise to evaluate AI suggestions critically and integrate them effectively into your work.

Throughout this progression, maintain a systematic approach. Before asking for help, understand your problem and what kind of assistance you need. When AI provides suggestions, understand the reasoning behind them. Always test AI-generated code with your own data and adapt suggestions to fit your specific needs.

11.9 The Critical Thinking Balance

As AI tools become more sophisticated, maintaining your critical thinking skills becomes increasingly important. Before using any AI-generated code, ask yourself whether the approach makes sense for your specific problem. Can you explain the logic behind the solution? How will you verify that it's working correctly?

The goal isn't to avoid AI or to become dependent on it, but to develop a productive partnership that enhances your learning and capabilities. This requires understanding the capabilities and limitations of different AI tools, learning effective prompting techniques, and developing skills for verifying AI-generated content.

Remember that AI is rapidly evolving. The specific tools and capabilities will change, but the fundamental principles of responsible use—critical evaluation, systematic verification, and learning-focused application—will remain constant.

11.10 Conclusion

AI programming assistants represent a powerful new tool in your analytical toolkit. The key insight that AI accelerates learning when used critically will serve you throughout your career. By maintaining your curiosity, developing verification habits, and using AI to enhance rather than replace your thinking, you can harness these tools to become a more effective analyst.

In the next chapter, we'll explore how to build reproducible data analyses—a skill that becomes even more important when AI is part of your workflow. The critical thinking skills you've learned here will help ensure that AI-assisted analyses meet the same standards of rigor and reproducibility as traditional approaches.

The future of data analysis will likely involve close collaboration between human analysts and AI tools. Those who learn to navigate this partnership thoughtfully will have significant advantages in their academic and professional work.

11.11 Review Questions

1. What is the difference between using AI as a solution generator versus a learning accelerator?
2. List two strengths and two limitations of AI programming assistants.
3. Why is it important to understand AI-generated code before using it on your real data?

4. How can effective prompting improve the quality of AI's help? Give a short example.
5. Describe Maya's key turning point in using AI responsibly.
6. What steps should you take to verify AI-generated code before applying it to real datasets?
7. In academic settings, what are some generally acceptable uses of AI programming assistants?
8. What are some uses of AI that are typically prohibited in academic contexts?
9. What should good AI disclosure include when it's required?
10. Describe the three stages of developing a productive relationship with AI programming tools.
11. What questions should you ask yourself before using AI-generated code to maintain critical thinking?
12. How can AI tools enhance rather than replace your analytical capabilities?

11.12 Ch 11 Lab AI as a Programming Assistant

AI programming assistants are becoming a normal part of how people write, read, and reason about code. Whether you're working in R, Python, or another language entirely, AI tools can help you explore unfamiliar functions, understand error messages, generate examples, and think through problems step by step. But they're not magic, and they're not a substitute for your own understanding. The real skill is learning how to work with AI in a way that strengthens your thinking rather than replacing it.

In this lab, you'll learn how to treat AI as a partner in the programming process — one that can explain concepts, suggest approaches, and help you debug, while still requiring you to evaluate, test, and refine the code yourself. You'll practice asking clear, specific questions, checking AI generated code for accuracy, and using the assistant to deepen your understanding instead of shortcutting it. You'll also learn when AI is helpful, when it isn't, and how to navigate academic and professional expectations around responsible use.

By the end of this lab, you'll have a practical workflow for combining your own reasoning with AI support, giving you the confidence to explore new ideas, tackle unfamiliar problems, and learn more efficiently.

11.12.1 Demonstration

AI programming assistants are becoming a normal part of how people write and reason about code. They are fast, helpful, and surprisingly good at recognizing patterns in common programming tasks. But they are not general problem solvers, and they are not substitutes for your own understanding. In this lab section, you will explore what AI does well, where it struggles, and how to recognize the difference while you work.

11.12.1.1 What AI Does Well

AI is at its best when the task is clear, concrete, and based on familiar programming patterns. For example, when a student asks, "What does this R code do?" and provides:

```
sample <- c(1, 2, 3, 4, 5)
mean(sample)
```

the AI can immediately explain that the code creates a numeric vector and calculates its average. This kind of explanation is exactly the sort of pattern recognition task AI excels at.

AI is also reliable when fixing small mistakes. If you type `meen(c(1,2,3))` and ask why it fails, the AI will point out that the function name is misspelled and should be `mean()`. These quick corrections are one of the most useful ways to use an AI assistant during early debugging.

Another strength is suggesting alternative approaches. If you ask, "Show me three ways to calculate an average in R," the AI can demonstrate the base R `mean()` function, the manual `sum()/length()` method, or a `dplyr::summarise()` pipeline. These examples help you see multiple ways to solve the same problem.

Finally, AI is good at translating code between languages. If you ask it to convert `mean(c(1,2,3,4,5))` from R to Python, it can show you how to use `statistics.mean([1,2,3,4,5])`. This is especially helpful when you are learning a second language or switching between R and Python in the same project.

11.12.1.2 Hands On Example

Ask the AI: "Explain this R code line by line:"

```
x <- rnorm(10)
mean(x)
```

Then ask:"Show me two other ways to compute the mean."

Compare the explanations. Notice how consistent and confident AI is when the task is simple and well defined.

11.12.1.3 What AI Struggles With

AI begins to struggle as soon as the task requires understanding your specific context. It does not know your dataset, your research question, or your goals unless you explicitly tell it. If you ask a vague question, the AI will guess — and its guess may not match what you intended.

This becomes especially clear in domain specific or advanced analysis. If you ask about a specialized statistical method, the AI may give a generic explanation that does not fit your situation or may even suggest an approach that is inappropriate for your field.

AI also has difficulty detecting logical errors. It can fix syntax, but it often misses deeper issues such as incorrect assumptions, flawed analysis logic, or misinterpretations of results. A piece of code may run without errors while still producing the wrong answer, and AI will not necessarily catch that.

Another limitation is that AI knowledge has a cutoff. It may not know the newest packages, updated functions, or recent changes in syntax. If you rely on AI for cutting edge tools, you may receive outdated or incomplete information.

Finally, AI will try to be helpful even when your question is unclear. If you ask something vague, it will fill in the gaps with its best guess. Sometimes that guess is reasonable; other times it leads you in the wrong direction.

11.12.1.4 Hands On Example

Ask the AI: "What is the best statistical test for my data?" Do not provide any context. Then ask again, but this time include:

• the type of data • the number of groups • whether the data is paired or independent • your research question

Compare the two answers. The first one will be vague or incorrect. The second will be far more accurate. This exercise shows how much AI depends on the context you provide.

AI is excellent at explaining code, fixing small errors, and helping you explore unfamiliar functions. It is fast, consistent, and reliable when the task is well defined. But it does not know your data, your goals, or the context behind your analysis unless you provide it. It can miss logical errors, misunderstand domain specific methods, and sometimes produce answers that sound confident but are not correct. The more you understand these strengths and limitations, the more effectively you can use AI. Treat it as a tool that supports your thinking, not a replacement for it. When you verify its suggestions, provide clear context, and stay in control of the reasoning, AI becomes a powerful partner that helps you learn faster and write better code.

11.12.1.5 Learning to Ask Better Questions

AI assistants don't respond to what you meant — they respond to what you said. A vague prompt like "my code doesn't work" forces the AI to guess, and guessing almost always leads to generic or unhelpful answers. When you give the assistant context, show your code, and explain what you're trying to accomplish, the quality of the response improves dramatically. Asking good questions is a skill, and it directly shapes the kind of help you receive.

In this section, you'll explore the difference between weak and strong questions and practice rewriting vague prompts into clear, specific ones. You'll learn simple patterns for telling the AI what you're trying to do, what language you're using, what you've already tried, and what result you want. The goal isn't to trick the AI into giving better answers — it's to communicate your problem clearly enough that the assistant can actually help you think through it.

11.12.1.5.1 Weak Questions and Why They Fail

Students often begin with questions like "Help me with R," "My code doesn't work," or "Fix this." These questions give the AI nothing to work with. There is no code, no error message, no goal, and no context. The assistant has to guess what you're doing, and its guess may not match your actual problem. When the AI doesn't know what you're trying to accomplish, it can only offer generic advice.

11.12.1.5.2 Strong Questions and Why They Work

A strong question gives the AI something concrete to respond to. For example, asking "How do I calculate the mean of a numeric vector in R?" or "I'm getting the error 'object not found' — what does it mean?" gives the assistant a clear task. When you ask, "Show me how to create a bar chart in R using ggplot2," the AI knows exactly what you want. Even a transformation request like "Convert this R code to dplyr: subset(data, age > 25)" is specific enough for the assistant to produce a correct and useful answer.

These questions work because they include details: the task, the language, the error message, or the code you're working with. They tell the AI what you want to accomplish instead of asking it to guess.

11.12.1.6 The CLEAR Pattern for Better Questions

A helpful way to structure your questions is to use the CLEAR pattern:

Context — what you're trying to do **Language** — R or Python **Error** — the exact message **Attempt** — what you've already tried **Result** — what you want to happen

For example, instead of saying "Help with data," you might say:

"I'm analyzing student survey data in R. I want to calculate the average age by major. My data frame has columns for name, age, and major. How do I group by major and calculate means?"

This gives the AI everything it needs to provide a correct and relevant answer.

11.12.1.7 Hands On Example

Ask the AI the following vague prompt: "My code doesn't work." Look at the response — it will be generic, broad, and not very helpful.

Now try again with a clear version: "I'm trying to filter rows in pandas where age > 25. Here is my code: df[df['age'] > 25] I'm getting the error TypeError: '>' not supported between instances of str and int. How do I fix this?"

Compare the two answers. The second one will be dramatically more specific and actionable because the AI has something real to work with.

11.12.1.8 Hands On Example

Try asking the AI: "Give me code to read a CSV file." You'll get a short answer, but not much understanding.

Now ask: "Show me how to read a CSV file in Python and explain what each parameter does."

This time, the AI will walk you through the function, the arguments, and how they work. This is the difference between using AI as a shortcut and using it as a learning tool.

Asking better questions is one of the most important skills you can develop when working with an AI assistant. Clear, specific prompts give the AI enough information to understand what you're trying to do, what language you're using, and where you're stuck. When you include context, show your code, and share the exact error message, the AI can respond with explanations and solutions that actually fit your situation. Vague requests force the AI to guess, which usually leads to generic or unhelpful answers. The more intentional you are in how you communicate, the more useful the AI becomes. Treat each question as a chance to clarify your own thinking — what you want, what you've tried, and what result you're aiming for. When you do that, the AI becomes a far more effective partner in your learning and problem solving process.

11.12.1.9 Working Safely with AI Code

AI can generate code quickly, but speed isn't the same as safety. Even when the code looks clean and confident, it may be based on assumptions about your files, your data, or your goals that aren't correct. That's why AI generated code should never be treated as something you can copy, paste, and run without thinking. Your role is to evaluate it the same way you would evaluate code from a colleague: read it carefully, test it on small examples, and make sure you understand what every line is doing before you trust it with real data.

In this section, you'll learn practical habits for reviewing AI suggestions—checking for risky operations, verifying logic with simple test data, and breaking code into smaller pieces you can inspect. You'll also see how to use your own domain knowledge to catch mistakes the AI can't anticipate, such as incorrect assumptions about your variables, missing edge cases, or methods that don't fit your analysis. The goal is to build a workflow where AI helps you move faster, but you remain firmly in control of the decisions and the results. By practicing these safety steps now, you'll develop the instincts that experienced analysts rely on: read first, test small, verify results, and only then apply the code to your real work.

11.12.1.10 Reading AI Generated Code Before Running It

Before running any AI-generated code, take a moment to read through it line by line. Ask yourself:

- Do I understand what each line does?
- Are the variable names what I expect?
- Does the logic match what I asked for?
- Are there any operations that could be risky (like deleting files or overwriting data)?

```
# Example: AI-generated code to read and filter data
# Always read this carefully before running!

data <- read.csv("student_survey.csv")
filtered_data <- data[data$age > 18, ]
write.csv(filtered_data, "adult_students.csv")
```

Questions to ask: - Does the file path exist? - Is the column name "age" correct? - Do I want to overwrite "adult_students.csv" if it exists?

A common situation is a student asking, "AI gave me this code to filter my dataset. Should I just run it?" Suppose the assistant suggests:

```
data <- read.csv("myfile.csv")
result <- data[data$age > 25, ]
write.csv(result, "output.csv")
```

Before running anything, pause and ask yourself whether you actually have a file named myfile.csv, whether your dataset contains an age column, and whether you want to overwrite output.csv. These questions may seem simple, but skipping them is one of the fastest ways to accidentally delete files, overwrite results, or run code that doesn't apply to your data at all. Reading the code first prevents a surprising number of mistakes.

11.12.1.11 Hands On Example

Paste the code above into the editor. Before running it, ask the AI: "Explain what each line of this code does and what risks I should check for." Notice how the explanation changes your understanding of the code's impact.

11.12.1.12 Testing Code on Small, Safe Examples

Before using AI generated code on your real dataset, test it on a tiny example you create yourself. For instance, if the AI suggests filtering rows where age > 25, you might create a small data frame:

```
name    age
Alice   22
Bob     30
Charlie 19
```

If the filter is correct, only Bob should remain. If the result doesn't match your expectations, the logic is wrong—even if the code runs without errors. Testing on small examples gives you a controlled environment where mistakes are easy to spot.

11.12.1.13 Hands On Example

Ask the AI: "Create a tiny R data frame with three people and an age column so I can test filtering logic." Then run the filter yourself and confirm the output matches what you expect.

11.12.1.14 Understanding Code One Piece at a Time

Instead of running everything at once, break the code into smaller pieces. Load the file first and inspect the data. Run the filter separately and print the result. Save the output only after you're sure it's correct. If any step surprises you, stop and investigate. This incremental approach makes it much easier to catch errors early.

11.12.1.15 Verifying Results With Your Own Reasoning

Even correct looking code can produce incorrect results. AI cannot validate your domain knowledge—only you can. Ask yourself whether the numbers are reasonable, whether the patterns match what you know about the data, and whether there are outliers or missing values the AI didn't consider. Think about whether the method itself makes sense for your field. A line of code that runs without errors is not the same as a line of code that answers your question correctly.

11.12.1.16 Hands On Example

Ask the AI to calculate a summary statistic—such as the mean of a group—and then compute the same value manually on a small dataset. If the numbers don't match, investigate why. This exercise helps you see how easily logic errors can slip through.

11.12.1.17 Knowing When to Slow Down

Some AI generated code deserves extra caution. Code that deletes or overwrites files, installs unfamiliar packages, performs irreversible operations, or handles sensitive data should always be reviewed carefully. If the assistant produces complex code you don't understand, that's a sign to slow down, ask for an explanation, and test each part before running anything.

Working with AI generated code is safest when you stay in control of the process. AI can write code quickly, but it doesn't know your files, your data, or your goals unless you tell it—and even then, it can make incorrect assumptions. Reading the code before you run it, testing it on small examples, and checking whether the results make sense are essential habits. These steps protect your data, help you catch mistakes early, and ensure you understand what the code is actually doing.

The goal isn't to distrust AI, but to use it responsibly. When you combine AI's speed with your own judgment—verifying logic, applying domain knowledge, and keeping backups—you create a workflow that is both efficient and safe. With practice, these habits become second nature, allowing you to benefit from AI assistance without giving up control of your analysis.

11.12.1.18 Building an Effective AI Workflow

Using AI well isn't about asking one good question — it's about having a repeatable way of working with the assistant from start to finish. If you treat each interaction as a shortcut, you may get code that runs, but you won't necessarily understand it or be able to adapt it later. A more effective approach is to treat AI as part of a workflow: define the problem, ask structured questions, test and validate the code, and then document what you learned so you can reuse it.

In this section, you'll practice a "learning partnership" model for working with AI. You'll begin by clearly defining your goal and the data you have. You'll move into focused questions about concepts and implementation. You'll test AI generated code on small, safe examples and verify that the results make sense. Finally, you'll document the solution and the reasoning behind it so it becomes part of your long term toolkit.

11.12.1.19 Defining Your Problem Clearly

Before you ask the AI anything, pause and write down what you're trying to do. For example, imagine you're working in R and want to compare average test scores between two groups. A clear problem definition might look like this:

"I want to compare average test scores between two groups. My data is a CSV with columns student_id, group, and test_score. I tried using mean() on the whole column, but I need group level means. I need to know how to calculate mean test scores by group in R."

This short description gives the AI enough context to help you effectively.

11.12.1.20 Hands On Example

Type the following into the AI chat: "I have a CSV file with columns student_id, group, and test_score. I want to compare the average test score for each group. I tried mean(data$test_score) but that gives me only one number. How do I calculate group means in R?"

Ask the AI to show you the code. Then ask it to explain why this approach works.

11.12.1.21 Asking Structured, Progressive Questions

Once you've defined your problem, move through a sequence of questions that build on each other. Start with a conceptual question such as, "What's a good way to compare average test scores between groups in R?" After you understand the idea, ask for implementation: "Show me how to do this using dplyr with my columns group and test_score." Once you have code, ask for verification: "Is this code correct for calculating mean test scores by group?" Finally, ask for learning: "Explain how this code works, line by line."

You can follow the same pattern in Python. For example, if you're analyzing sales data, you might begin with, "What's the best way to analyze monthly sales trends by product category in pandas?" Then move to, "Show me pandas code to group by category and month and sum sales," and follow up with, "How can I check that these grouped results are correct?"

11.12.1.22 Hands On Example

Ask the AI: "What's the best way to group sales data by category and month in pandas?"

Then follow up with: "Here is my sample data. Show me the exact code."

```python
import pandas as pd

df = pd.DataFrame({
    "date": ["2024-01-01", "2024-01-01", "2024-02-01", "2024-02-01"],
    "product": ["A", "B", "A", "B"],
    "category": ["Electronics", "Books", "Electronics", "Books"],
    "sales": [100, 50, 120, 60]
})
```

After the AI gives you code, ask: "Explain each line and show me how to manually verify one of the results."

11.12.1.23 Implementing and Testing on Small, Safe Examples

Once you have AI generated code, don't run it on your full dataset yet. Start with a tiny example you create yourself. In R, you might build a small data frame:

```
sample <- data.frame(
  student_id = 1:6,
  group = c("A", "A", "A", "B", "B", "B"),
  test_score = c(85, 92, 78, 88, 95, 82)
)
```

Then run the AI's code:

```
library(dplyr)
sample %>% group_by(group) %>% summarise(mean_score = mean(test_score))
```

Now manually compute the averages: Group A: (85 + 92 + 78) / 3 Group B: (88 + 95 + 82) / 3

If the numbers match, the logic is correct. If not, you've caught a problem before it touched your real data.

11.12.1.24 Hands On Example

Ask the AI:"Using the sample data below, calculate the mean test score for each group manually."

Then compare your manual results to the AI's code output. If they differ, ask the AI to help you debug the discrepancy.

11.12.1.25 Validating With Your Own Reasoning

Even when the code runs and the numbers look tidy, you still need to ask whether the method makes sense for your question. Think about whether there are missing values, outliers, or multiple groups the AI didn't consider. Ask yourself whether someone in your field would agree that this is an appropriate approach. AI can propose methods, but it cannot decide whether they are suitable for your specific context.

11.12.1.26 Documenting What You Learned

Once you have something that works and makes sense, take time to document it. Add comments explaining what the code does and why you chose this approach. Save the example, along with a short note about when and why you would use it. For instance, you might write:

"This code calculates mean test scores by group using dplyr::summarise(). I chose this approach because it is readable and works well with grouped data. The group_by(group) step ensures that the mean is calculated separately for each group."

This turns a one time AI interaction into a reusable pattern.

11.12.1.27 Hands On Example

Ask the AI: "Help me write a commented R script that loads a CSV, groups by a column, and calculates a summary statistic. Include explanations so I can reuse this later."

Save the script as a template for future assignments.

11.12.1.28 Why This Workflow Matters

An effective AI workflow is systematic, not accidental. You begin by clarifying what you're trying to do, then use AI to explore approaches, generate code, and explain the reasoning behind it. At each step, you stay actively involved: testing on sample data, checking results against your expectations, and adjusting the code as needed. This keeps you in the role of decision maker rather than passive recipient.

When you use AI as a learning partner instead of a replacement for understanding, each interaction strengthens your skills. A structured workflow—problem definition, targeted questions, careful testing, and thoughtful documentation—helps you get reliable results today and makes you more capable of solving similar problems on your own in the future.

11.12.2 Practice

1. Ask the AI to explain the following R code line by line. Paste the explanation into your notes and describe one thing you learned from it:

```
sample <- c(1, 2, 3, 4, 5)
mean(sample)
```

2. Type the incorrect code `meen(c(1,2,3))` and ask the AI to fix it. Record the corrected version and explain why the original failed.
3. Ask the AI to show you three different ways to compute an average in R. Run each method on a small vector you create yourself and compare the results.
4. Ask the AI to convert the R code `mean(c(1,2,3,4,5))` into Python. Run the Python version and confirm that it produces the same value.
5. Ask the AI the vague question "What is the best statistical test for my data?" Then ask again with full context about your dataset. Compare the two answers and describe the difference.
6. Write a weak question such as "My code doesn't work" and ask it. Then rewrite it using the CLEAR pattern and ask again. Summarize how the quality of the

answer changed.

7. Create a tiny R data frame with three rows and an age column. Ask the AI to filter rows where age > 25. Run the code and verify manually whether the output is correct.

8. Ask the AI to explain what each line of the following code does and identify any risks before running it:

```
data <- read.csv("myfile.csv")
result <- data[data$age > 25, ]
write.csv(result, "output.csv")
```

9. Ask the AI to calculate group means using the sample data below. Then compute the same means manually and compare the results.

```
student_id: 1,2,3,4,5,6
group: A,A,A,B,B,B
test_score: 85,92,78,88,95,82
```

10. Ask the AI to help you write a commented R or Python script that loads a dataset, performs a grouped summary, and prints the results. Save the script and describe when you would reuse it.

Chapter 12

Building Reproducible Data Analyses

12.1 Learning Outcomes

12-1: Explain the importance of reproducibility in academic, professional, and collaborative data analysis contexts.

12-2: Describe the complete data analysis workflow (cleaning, exploration, formal analysis, communication) and the role of documentation at each phase.

12-3: Compare scripts, notebooks, and reports, and select the most appropriate format for reproducible analyses.

12-4: Identify common reproducibility failures (e.g., version confusion, environment issues, manual steps) and implement strategies to prevent them.

12-5: Apply practices such as version control, automation, and structured workflows to build reproducible habits and ensure analyses can be rerun by others.

12.2 Introduction

Dr. Chen received an urgent email from her department chair. A journal reviewer had questioned the results from a paper she'd published six months ago and wanted to see the analysis code. Dr. Chen confidently opened her project folder, expecting to find everything neatly organized. Instead, she found a maze of files with names like "analysis_final.R," "analysis_final_v2.R," and "analysis_REALLY_final.R." Her data files were scattered across multiple folders, and she couldn't remember which version of the code had produced the published results.

After three days of detective work, Dr. Chen managed to reconstruct her analysis, but the experience taught her a valuable lesson about reproducibility. She realized that creating an analysis that works once is only half the job—the other half is ensuring that it can be understood and rerun by others, including her future self.

This chapter ties together all the concepts you've learned into practical workflows for building reproducible data analyses. We'll explore the journey from raw data to final results, understand why reproducibility matters beyond academic requirements, and learn to create analyses that stand the test of time.

The key insight is both practical and professional: **a good analysis can be rerun by someone else**.

12.3 The Complete Analysis Journey

Most programming courses focus on individual techniques—how to clean data, create plots, or run statistical tests. But real data analysis is about connecting these techniques into coherent workflows that transform raw data into meaningful insights. Understanding this complete journey is essential for creating reproducible work.

The analysis journey typically begins with raw, messy data that needs to be understood and cleaned. This might involve loading data from multiple sources, dealing with missing values, standardizing formats, and identifying potential quality issues. The cleaning phase often takes longer than expected and requires careful documentation of decisions made along the way.

Once the data is clean, the exploration phase begins. This involves understanding the structure and patterns in your data through summary statistics, visualizations, and preliminary analyses. Exploration is inherently iterative—you discover something interesting, which leads to new questions, which require different analyses. This iterative nature makes reproducibility challenging because it's tempting to skip documenting the dead ends and false starts.

The formal analysis phase applies specific statistical methods or modeling approaches to answer your research questions. This might involve hypothesis testing, regression analysis, machine learning, or other techniques depending on your goals. The key is to document not just what you did, but why you chose particular approaches and how you validated your results.

Finally, the communication phase transforms your technical results into insights that others can understand and act upon. This might involve creating reports, presentations, or interactive dashboards. The communication products should be connected to your analysis code so that updates to the data or methods automatically flow through to the final outputs.

Throughout this journey, reproducibility requires that each step be documented, automated where possible, and organized in a way that others can follow. This doesn't mean documenting every false start, but it does mean creating a clear path from raw data to final results that someone else could follow.

12.4 Choosing Your Analysis Format

One of the first decisions in any analysis project is how to organize your work. Should you write scripts, create notebooks, or build reports? Each approach has strengths and is suited to different types of analytical work. Understanding these differences helps you choose the right format and avoid common pitfalls.

Scripts are the most straightforward approach—text files containing a sequence of commands that execute from top to bottom. Scripts work well when you have a clear, defined analytical task that you want to automate or repeat regularly. They're excellent for data processing pipelines, routine reports, and production analyses where efficiency and reliability are paramount. The linear nature of scripts makes them easy to understand and debug, and they integrate well with version control systems.

However, scripts can be limiting for exploratory work where you don't know exactly what you're looking for. They don't naturally accommodate the iterative nature of data exploration, and they separate code from results, making it harder to communicate your findings to others.

Notebooks represent a different philosophy, organizing work into cells that can contain code, text, or visualizations. You can run these cells individually and see results immediately, making notebooks excellent for exploration and experimentation. The ability to combine code, results, and explanations in a single document makes notebooks powerful tools for communication and collaboration.

The interactive nature of notebooks supports the natural workflow of data analysis—you run some code, examine the results, document your observations, and then decide what to do next. This makes notebooks particularly valuable for learning, teaching, and sharing analytical insights with both technical and non-technical audiences.

But notebooks have their own challenges. Because you can run cells in any order, it's possible to create notebooks that don't run cleanly from top to bottom. This can make them less reproducible than scripts. Notebooks can also become unwieldy for large, complex analyses, and they're more difficult to manage with traditional version control systems.

Reports represent the most sophisticated approach, combining the computational power of scripts with the communication capabilities of traditional documents. Reports can include code, results, visualizations, and narrative text, all integrated into a polished final product. The code is embedded in the document, but the final output looks like a professional report or academic paper.

Reports are ideal when you need to communicate findings to non-technical audiences, ensure your results stay synchronized with your analysis, or create documentation that will be referenced over time. Because the code is embedded in the document, you can be confident that your results accurately reflect your analysis, and you can easily update the entire report when your data or methods change.

The choice between these formats isn't about which is "better"—it's about matching your approach to your goals and context. Many analysts use all three approaches for different aspects of their work: scripts for data cleaning and automated processes, notebooks for exploration and experimentation, and reports for final documentation and communication.

12.5 Creating End-to-End Workflows

The real test of reproducibility is whether someone else can start with your raw data and recreate your final results. This requires thinking beyond individual analyses to complete workflows that connect all the pieces of your analytical process.

An effective workflow begins with clear organization. Create a project structure that makes sense to others, not just to you. This typically involves separate folders for raw data, processed data, analysis code, output files, and documentation. Use consistent naming conventions that make it easy to understand what each file contains and how files relate to each other.

The workflow should handle data processing systematically. Instead of manually cleaning data each time you run an analysis, create scripts that automate the cleaning process. This ensures consistency and makes it easy to apply the same cleaning steps to new data. Document any assumptions you make during cleaning and provide ways to verify that the cleaning worked correctly.

Version control becomes crucial for reproducible workflows. Even if you're working alone, tracking changes to your code and data helps you understand how your analysis evolved over time. When working with others, version control is essential for coordinating changes and avoiding conflicts. Modern version control systems like Git can seem intimidating at first, but they're worth learning for any serious analytical work.

Environment management is another key component. Your analysis might depend on specific versions of software packages, and these dependencies should be documented and, where possible, automated. This might involve creating requirements files that specify exact package versions, using virtual environments to isolate project dependencies, or using containerization technologies for complete environment reproducibility.

The workflow should include validation steps that verify your results make sense. This might involve comparing results to known benchmarks, checking that totals add up correctly, or running sensitivity analyses to ensure your conclusions are robust. These validation steps should be automated so they run every time you update your analysis.

Finally, the workflow should produce clear, well-documented outputs. This includes not just your final results, but also intermediate outputs that help others understand your process. Create summary statistics, diagnostic plots, and other outputs that make it easy to verify that each step of your analysis worked correctly.

12.6 Why Reproducibility Matters Beyond Academia

While reproducibility is often discussed in academic contexts, it's equally important for practical data analysis work in business, government, and other settings. Understanding why reproducibility matters in these contexts helps motivate the extra effort required to create truly reproducible analyses.

In collaborative environments, reproducibility enables effective teamwork. When your colleagues can understand and build on your work, projects move faster and produce better results. Team members can review each other's analyses, catch errors before they become problems, and combine different analytical approaches more effectively. Without reproducibility, each team member works in isolation, leading to duplicated effort and inconsistent results.

Reproducibility also enables quality assurance and error detection. When analyses can be easily rerun and verified, it's much easier to catch mistakes and ensure accuracy. This is particularly important in high-stakes environments where analytical errors can have serious consequences. Reproducible analyses can be audited, validated, and improved over time.

From a business perspective, reproducibility supports scalability and efficiency. Analyses that can be easily updated with new data or applied to new situations provide ongoing value rather than one-time insights. This is particularly valuable for routine reporting, monitoring systems, and decision-support tools that need to be updated regularly.

Reproducibility also supports knowledge transfer and institutional memory. When analysts leave organizations or move to different projects, their work can continue to provide value if it's properly documented and reproducible. This reduces the risk of losing important analytical capabilities when personnel change.

In regulated industries, reproducibility may be a legal or compliance requirement. Organizations need to be able to demonstrate how their analytical results were produced, particularly when those results inform important decisions or public policies. Reproducible analyses provide the documentation and audit trail necessary to meet these requirements.

Finally, reproducibility supports continuous improvement. When analyses are well-documented and easy to modify, they can be refined and enhanced over time. New data sources can be incorporated, better methods can be applied, and insights can be deepened through iterative improvement.

12.7 Common Reproducibility Failures

Understanding how reproducibility breaks down helps you avoid common pitfalls and build more robust analytical workflows. Many reproducibility failures stem from seemingly minor decisions that accumulate over time to create major problems.

One of the most common failures is the "works on my machine" problem. Your analysis runs perfectly on your computer but fails when someone else tries to run it. This often happens because of differences in software versions, file paths, or system configurations. The solution involves documenting and, where possible, controlling the computational environment your analysis depends on.

Data versioning problems represent another common failure mode. Your analysis works with the data you have today, but fails when applied to updated data with slightly different formats or contents. This happens when analyses make implicit assumptions about data structure that aren't documented or validated. Robust analyses include checks for data quality and format, and they handle common variations gracefully.

File path and organization issues can make analyses impossible to reproduce. Hard-coded file paths that work on your computer but not others, scattered files with unclear relationships, and inconsistent naming conventions all contribute to reproducibility failures. The solution involves using relative paths, clear organization schemes, and consistent naming conventions.

Undocumented manual steps represent a particularly insidious reproducibility failure. Your analysis might depend on manual data cleaning, parameter selection, or other steps that you perform but don't document. When someone else tries to reproduce your work, these undocumented steps create insurmountable barriers. The solution involves automating manual steps where possible and clearly documenting steps that must remain manual.

Version confusion is another common problem. You have multiple versions of your analysis code, but you can't remember which version produced your final results. This often happens during the iterative development process when you create multiple versions without clear version control. The solution involves systematic version control and clear documentation of which version corresponds to which results.

Finally, dependency problems occur when your analysis relies on external resources that change or become unavailable over time. This might include websites that go offline, databases that change structure, or software packages that are updated in incompatible ways. While you can't prevent all external changes, you can document dependencies clearly and, where possible, create local copies of critical external resources.

12.8 Documentation as Analysis Infrastructure

Good documentation isn't an afterthought—it's an integral part of creating reproducible analyses. Think of documentation as infrastructure that supports your analytical work, making it more valuable and longer-lasting.

Effective documentation operates at multiple levels. At the project level, documentation explains the overall goals, data sources, and analytical approach. This high-level documentation helps others understand the context and purpose of your work. It should explain what problem you're trying to solve, what data you're using, and what methods you're applying.

At the code level, documentation explains the logic and reasoning behind your analytical choices. This includes comments that explain complex operations, decisions about data cleaning and processing, and justifications for statistical methods. The goal isn't to explain every line of code, but to explain the thinking behind your approach.

At the results level, documentation interprets findings and explains their significance. This includes not just what you found, but what it means, what limitations exist, and what questions remain unanswered. Results documentation helps others understand not just your findings, but their context and implications.

Documentation should be integrated into your analytical workflow, not added as a separate step. This might involve using literate programming approaches that combine code and explanation, creating automated reports that update when your analysis changes, or maintaining analysis logs that track decisions and changes over time.

The key is to document for your future self and for others who might need to understand or build on your work. Ask yourself: if you returned to this analysis in six months, would you be able to understand what you did and why? If a colleague needed to verify or extend your work, would they have sufficient information to do so effectively?

Good documentation also includes information about what didn't work. While you don't need to document every false start, it's valuable to note major approaches you tried and why you abandoned them. This prevents others from repeating the same unsuccessful experiments and helps them understand why you chose your final approach.

12.9 Building Reproducible Habits

Creating reproducible analyses isn't just about following a checklist—it's about developing habits and workflows that make reproducibility natural and automatic. These habits become more important as your analyses become more complex and as you work more frequently with others.

Start every project with organization. Before you write any code, set up a clear folder structure and decide how you'll organize your work. Create separate folders for different types of files and use consistent naming conventions. This upfront investment pays dividends throughout the project and makes it much easier to maintain organization as the project grows.

Document decisions as you make them, not after the fact. When you decide to exclude certain data points, choose a particular statistical method, or handle missing values in a specific way, document the reasoning immediately. These decisions seem obvious when you make them, but they become mysterious when you return to the analysis later.

Automate repetitive tasks rather than doing them manually. If you find yourself doing the same data cleaning steps repeatedly, write a script to automate them. If you're creating the same types of plots for different variables, write a function to generate them systematically. Automation not only saves time but also ensures consistency and makes your process more transparent.

Test your analyses with different data to ensure they're robust. This might involve running your analysis on a subset of your data, applying it to historical data where you know the expected results, or testing it with simulated data that has known properties. Testing helps you catch errors and ensures that your analysis will work correctly in different situations.

Use version control even for solo projects. Version control helps you track changes over time, experiment with different approaches without fear of losing working code, and maintain a clear record of how your analysis evolved. Modern version control systems also make it easier to collaborate with others when projects grow beyond individual work.

Finally, regularly review and refine your reproducibility practices. What worked well in your last project? What caused problems? How could you improve your organization, documentation, or workflow for next time? Reproducibility is a skill that improves with practice and reflection.

12.10 Conclusion

Building reproducible data analyses represents the culmination of all the programming skills you've learned throughout this course. It requires combining technical skills with organizational thinking, individual expertise with collaborative awareness, and immediate problem-solving with long-term planning.

The habits and workflows you develop now will serve you throughout your career, whether you continue in academia or move into industry roles. The ability to create analyses that others can understand, verify, and build upon is increasingly valuable in our data-driven world.

As you continue developing your analytical skills, remember that reproducibility isn't a burden—it's an investment in the value and impact of your work. Analyses that can be understood and rerun by others have longer lifespans, greater influence, and more opportunities for improvement and extension.

The key insight that a good analysis can be rerun by someone else will guide you toward creating work that meets the highest standards of scientific rigor and professional quality. By building reproducibility into your analytical practice from the beginning, you're not just learning to program—you're learning to contribute meaningfully to the collective enterprise of understanding data and solving problems.

The journey from writing code that works to creating analyses that others can understand and build upon represents a fundamental shift in how you think about programming and data analysis. It's the difference between solving problems for yourself and contributing to the broader community of analysts and researchers working to understand our complex world.

12.11 Review Questions

1. Why is reproducibility important in both academic and professional data analysis contexts?
2. Describe the typical phases of a complete data analysis journey. Why is documenting each phase crucial for reproducibility?
3. Compare scripts, notebooks, and reports as formats for analysis. What are the advantages and limitations of each?
4. List at least three common reproducibility failures and explain how to prevent them.
5. What role does version control play in reproducible workflows, even for solo projects?
6. How can automation contribute to reproducibility, and what are some examples of tasks to automate?
7. Why is documentation considered "analysis infrastructure," and what should it include at the project, code, and results levels?
8. What habits can analysts develop to make reproducibility a natural part of their workflow?

12.12 Ch 12 Lab Making Your Work Understandable

This lab teaches you a set of simple, repeatable habits that make your analysis clear, organized, and easy to understand—both for collaborators and for your future self. You'll practice lightweight organization, clear commenting, consistent naming, and quick documentation techniques that take only a few extra minutes but prevent confusion, reduce rework, and make your analyses far easier to revisit and reuse. By the end, you'll be able to structure your files so others can follow your workflow, write comments that explain your reasoning, choose meaningful names for files and variables, create brief documentation that helps others run and interpret your work, and build everyday habits that make your analyses more transparent, maintainable, and trustworthy.

12.12.1 Demonstration

One of the most important people who will need to understand your analysis is your future self. Weeks or months from now, you won't remember the details that feel obvious today. Strong organization and documentation habits protect you from confusion, lost time, and avoidable mistakes.

Consider this common scenario: three months after completing an analysis, you rediscover a small project folder containing four files—analysis.R, data.csv, results.txt, and plot.png. When you open analysis.R, you find only a few lines of code:

```
data <- read.csv("data.csv")
x <- data$column1
y <- data$column2
result <- mean(x)
print(result)
```

With no context, your future self is left trying to reconstruct the entire purpose of the work. Questions immediately pile up: What was this analysis trying to answer? Where did data.csv come from? What do column1 and column2 represent? Why were you calculating the mean? What does the printed result actually mean? And perhaps most importantly—can you trust any of this without knowing how it was produced?

This is the "mystery analysis" problem. Without clear organization and documentation, even simple work becomes opaque, fragile, and difficult to reuse. Good habits prevent this from happening in the first place.

12.12.1.1 The Solution: Clear Documentation

The antidote to the "mystery analysis" problem is simple: write down what you're doing and why you're doing it. Clear documentation turns a pile of files and disconnected code into a coherent analysis that your future self—or anyone else—can understand without guesswork. Good documentation doesn't need to be long or formal. A few lines at the top of your script, meaningful variable names, and short comments that explain your reasoning are enough to transform an opaque analysis into one that is transparent and trustworthy.

Below is an example of the same simple analysis rewritten with clear purpose, context, and structure. Notice how the script now tells a story: what the analysis is for, where the data came from, what decisions were made, and what the results mean.

R Version - Improved Analysis:

```r
# Student Survey Analysis
# Purpose: Find average study hours for biology majors
# Data: Fall 2024 student survey (n=50)
# Date: 2026-02-18
# Author: [Your name]

# Load student survey data
survey_data <- data.frame(
  student_id = 1:5,
  major = c("Biology", "Math", "Biology", "Psychology", "Biology"),
  study_hours = c(15, 20, 12, 18, 25)
)

# Focus on biology majors only
biology_students <- survey_data[survey_data$major == "Biology", ]

# Calculate average study hours for biology majors
average_study_hours <- mean(biology_students$study_hours)

# Display result with context
print(paste("Average study hours for biology majors:",
 ↪  average_study_hours))
```

```
[1] "Average study hours for biology majors: 17.3333333333333"
```

```r
print(paste("Based on", nrow(biology_students), "biology students"))
```

```
[1] "Based on 3 biology students"
```

Python Version - Same Principles:

```python
# Student Survey Analysis
# Purpose: Find average study hours for biology majors
# Data: Fall 2024 student survey (n=50)
# Date: 2026-02-18
# Author: [Your name]

import pandas as pd

# Create sample data (in real analysis, this would be loaded from file)
survey_data = pd.DataFrame({
    'student_id': [1, 2, 3, 4, 5],
    'major': ['Biology', 'Math', 'Biology', 'Psychology', 'Biology'],
    'study_hours': [15, 20, 12, 18, 25]
})
```

```
print("Data loaded: Student survey with", len(survey_data),
    "responses")
```

```
Data loaded: Student survey with 5 responses
```

```
# Focus on biology majors only
biology_students = survey_data[survey_data['major'] == 'Biology']
print("Biology majors found:", len(biology_students))
```

```
Biology majors found: 3
```

```
# Calculate average study hours for biology majors
average_hours = biology_students['study_hours'].mean()

# Display result with clear context
print(f"Average study hours for biology majors: {average_hours:.1f}
    hours")
```

```
Average study hours for biology majors: 17.3 hours
```

```
print(f"Based on {len(biology_students)} biology students")
```

```
Based on 3 biology students
```

12.12.1.2 Simple File Organization

A clear, predictable project structure makes your work dramatically easier to navigate, understand, and return to later. When files are scattered across your computer or mixed with unrelated documents, even a small analysis becomes hard to follow. Without structure, it's difficult to know which script is the most recent, where the data came from, or what each file is supposed to represent.

A common problem is the "everything on the desktop" approach: a few scripts, a couple of data files, a plot, and several unrelated documents all sitting in the same place. Nothing indicates which files belong together or what the project is about. This makes it easy to lose track of versions, overwrite important work, or forget how the pieces fit.

A simple, organized folder structure solves these issues. By placing all project files in one clearly named directory—and separating data, scripts, and outputs—you create a workspace that is easy to understand at a glance. A short README file adds just enough context for someone else (or your future self) to know what the project contains and how to use it.

A typical small analysis might look like this:

```
student-survey-analysis/
  data/
    student_survey.csv
  analysis.R
  results.txt
  plot.png
  README.txt
```

This structure keeps everything for the project in one place, uses descriptive names, and separates raw data from code and outputs. Anyone opening the folder can immediately understand what the project is and where to find things.

12.12.1.3 Good File Naming Practices

Clear file names are just as important as clear folder structure. Descriptive names help you understand what a file contains without opening it. Including dates, using underscores instead of spaces, and being consistent with your naming style all contribute to clarity.

Examples of effective naming patterns include:

- student_survey_fall2024.csv
- biology_major_analysis.R
- study_hours_by_major.png

These names communicate purpose and content directly, reducing ambiguity and preventing confusion later.

R Example: Creating an Organized Structure

```r
# Create project folders
dir.create("student-survey-analysis")
dir.create("student-survey-analysis/data")

# Save data in the appropriate location
write.csv(survey_data,
↪ "student-survey-analysis/data/student_survey.csv")
```

Python Example: Creating an Organized Structure

```python
import os
import pandas as pd

# Create project folders (run once)
project_folders = [
    "student-survey-analysis",
```

```
    "student-survey-analysis/data",
    "student-survey-analysis/output"
]

for folder in project_folders:
    os.makedirs(folder, exist_ok=True)
```

12.12.2 File Naming Guidelines

- Use descriptive names that indicate purpose or content
- Include dates when they help distinguish versions
- Use underscores instead of spaces
- Keep your naming style consistent across the project

12.12.2.1 Writing Helpful Comments

Good comments explain the reasoning behind your code, not the mechanics of what each line does. A reader can already see the operations in the code itself; what they cannot see is your intent. Comments are most useful when they clarify your purpose, describe what the data represents, or explain how a particular step contributes to the overall analysis. When comments simply restate the code, they add no value and quickly become clutter.

A common example of unhelpful commenting is adding notes that repeat the function names or describe obvious syntax. These comments do nothing to help a future reader understand the analysis. What's missing is the context: the research question, the meaning of the data, and the logic behind each analytical decision.

To illustrate the difference, the following examples show how comments become meaningful when they focus on purpose and interpretation rather than literal code behavior.

12.12.2.2 Bad Comments (Don't do this!)

```
# Bad comments that just repeat the code:
data <- read.csv('data.csv') # Read CSV file
x <- mean(data$age) # Calculate mean of age
print(x) # Print x
```

12.12.2.3 Good Comments (Do this!)

R Example - Helpful Comments:

```r
# Student Survey Analysis - Biology Major Study Habits
# Research question: Do biology majors study more than other majors?
# Data: Fall 2024 student survey, n=100 students
# Date: 2026-02-18

# Load survey data collected from intro biology classes
survey_data <- data.frame(
  student_id = 1:6,
  major = c("Biology", "Math", "Biology", "Psychology", "Biology",
   ↪  "Math"),
  study_hours = c(15, 20, 12, 18, 25, 22),
  gpa = c(3.2, 3.8, 2.9, 3.5, 3.9, 3.6)
)

# Focus analysis on biology majors only
# We want to compare their study habits to the overall average
biology_students <- survey_data[survey_data$major == "Biology", ]

# Calculate average study hours for biology majors
# This will be compared to the overall class average
bio_avg_hours <- mean(biology_students$study_hours)

# Calculate overall class average for comparison
overall_avg_hours <- mean(survey_data$study_hours)

# Display results with context
print(paste("Biology majors average:", bio_avg_hours, "hours per
 ↪  week"))
```

```
[1] "Biology majors average: 17.3333333333333 hours per week"
```

```r
print(paste("Overall class average:", overall_avg_hours, "hours per
 ↪  week"))
```

```
[1] "Overall class average: 18.6666666666667 hours per week"
```

```r
# Interpret the finding
if (bio_avg_hours > overall_avg_hours) {
  print("Biology majors study more than average")
} else {
  print("Biology majors study about the same as average")
}
```

```
[1] "Biology majors study about the same as average"
```

Python Example - Comment Best Practices:

```
# Student Performance Analysis
# Goal: Understand relationship between study time and academic success
# Data source: End-of-semester student survey (Fall 2024)
# Analysis date: 2026-02-18

import pandas as pd

# Create sample dataset (in real analysis, would load from file)
# Each row represents one student's survey response
student_data = pd.DataFrame({
    'student_id': range(1, 7),
    'major': ['Biology', 'Math', 'Biology', 'Psychology', 'Biology',
     ↪  'Math'],
    'study_hours_per_week': [15, 20, 12, 18, 25, 22],
    'current_gpa': [3.2, 3.8, 2.9, 3.5, 3.9, 3.6]
})

# Research Question 1: Do biology majors have different study habits?
# Filter to biology majors to analyze their specific patterns
biology_majors = student_data[student_data['major'] == 'Biology']

# Calculate key statistics for comparison
bio_avg_study = biology_majors['study_hours_per_week'].mean()
bio_avg_gpa = biology_majors['current_gpa'].mean()

# Calculate overall averages for context
overall_avg_study = student_data['study_hours_per_week'].mean()
overall_avg_gpa = student_data['current_gpa'].mean()

# Simple interpretation of findings
# This helps readers understand what the numbers mean
if bio_avg_study > overall_avg_study:
    print("Finding: Biology majors study more than average")
else:
    print("Finding: Biology majors study about the same as other
     ↪  majors")
```

```
Finding: Biology majors study about the same as other majors
```

12.12.2.4 Comment Guidelines

Effective comments typically address:

- why a step is being taken
- what the data represents or where it came from
- the assumptions or reasoning behind an analytical choice
- how to interpret the results that follow

Comments should not be used to:

- restate what the code already makes obvious
- describe simple syntax or operations
- narrate each line of code mechanically

Good comments make your analysis readable, explainable, and reusable. They turn code into a clear narrative that others—and your future self—can understand without guesswork.

12.12.2.5 Creating Simple Documentation

Even a small analysis becomes far more useful when it comes with a short, clear description of what it does and how to run it. You do not need a long report or a polished website—often a single README file is enough. The goal is simple: give a future reader (including your future self) enough context to understand the purpose of the project, where the data came from, how to execute the code, and what the main results were. Good documentation turns an isolated script into a reusable, trustworthy analysis.

A helpful README usually answers the same core questions: What is this analysis about? What research questions does it address? What data does it use, and where did that data come from? Which files are included, and what does each one do? How should someone run the code, and where will they find the outputs? Finally, who can they contact if something is unclear? When you cover these points in plain language, you remove guesswork and make it much easier for others to build on your work.

12.12.2.6 Basic README Template

Below is an example of a minimal but effective README.txt for an R-based analysis:

```
Student Survey Analysis - Fall 2024
===================================

What this analysis does:
- Examines study habits of different majors
- Compares biology majors to other students
- Looks at relationship between study time and GPA

Data source:
- Student survey from BIOL 101 classes
- Collected November 2024
```

```
- 100 student responses
- Self-reported study hours and GPA

Files in this project:
- student_survey.csv: Raw survey data
- analysis.R: Main analysis script
- results.txt: Summary of findings
- study_hours_plot.png: Visualization of results

How to use:
1. Open analysis.R in RStudio
2. Make sure student_survey.csv is in the data/ folder
3. Run the entire script
4. Results will appear in console and save to results.txt

Questions or problems:
Contact [your name] at [your email]

Last updated: 2026-02-18
```

This README is short, but it clearly explains the purpose, data source, file roles, and steps to run the analysis.

12.12.2.7 Python Documentation Example

For a Python-based workflow, the same principles apply. Here is an example README.md:

```
# Student Performance Analysis

## Purpose

This analysis examines the relationship between study habits and
 ↪  academic performance among college students.

## Research Questions

1. Do biology majors study more hours than other majors?
2. Is there a relationship between study time and GPA?
3. What factors predict academic success?

## Data

- **Source**: End-of-semester student survey
- **Collection date**: Fall 2024
```

```
- **Sample size**: 100 students
- **Variables**: major, study_hours_per_week, current_gpa,
↪  year_in_school

## Files

- `student_survey.csv` - Raw survey data
- `analysis.py` - Main analysis script
- `results/` - Output folder with results and plots
- `README.md` - This documentation file

## How to Run

1. Make sure you have pandas installed: `pip install pandas`
2. Place `student_survey.csv` in the same folder as `analysis.py`
3. Run: `python analysis.py`
4. Check the `results/` folder for output

## Key Findings

- Biology majors study an average of 18.5 hours per week
- Overall class average is 17.2 hours per week
- Moderate positive correlation between study time and GPA (r = 0.45)

## Contact

[Your name] - [your email]

Last updated: February 18, 2026
```

12.12.2.8 Documentation Best Practices

This version adds research questions and key findings, which is especially useful when you want readers to understand not just how to run the code, but what the analysis concluded.

- Keep it simple: Use plain language and avoid unnecessary jargon.
- Lead with essentials: Start with purpose, research questions, and data source.
- Explain how to run it: Provide clear, step-by-step instructions to execute the analysis.
- Summarize results: Include a brief statement of key findings when possible.
- Make contact easy: Add a name and email so questions can be directed to the right person.

In practice, you are documenting five things: what the analysis does, where the data came from, how to run the code, what the results mean, and who to contact. If your README answers those questions clearly, your analysis is well documented.

12.12.3 Practice

12.12.3.1 Fix the Mystery Analysis

You are given unclear code with vague variable names and no explanation. Rewrite it so someone else could understand it.

R Version

```
d <- read.csv('data.csv')
x <- d[d$col1 == 'A', ]
y <- mean(x$col2)
print(y)
```

Python Version

```
df = pd.read_csv('file.csv')
x = df[df['cat'] == 'B']
result = x['num'].sum()
print(result)
```

Think about:

- What the dataset might represent
- What the columns might mean
- Why someone might filter the data
- What the result represents
- How comments and variable names could clarify the purpose

12.12.3.2 Questions

1. What is one change you would make to the mystery code to make it clearer?
2. Why would using descriptive variable names improve the rewritten code?
3. What context would you add to help a future reader understand the result?

12.12.3.3 Organize a Messy Project

A student has these files scattered everywhere:

- data.csv
- analysis.R
- analysis2.R

- final.R
- plot.png
- results.txt
- backup.csv

The project is about:

- Coffee shop sales
- Weekend vs. weekday comparisons
- Seasonal patterns
- Data from Jan–Dec 2024

Design a clear folder structure and rename files.

12.12.3.4 Questions

4. What folder structure would you create for this project, and why?
5. Choose one file you would rename and explain why your new name is clearer.
6. How does your organization help someone understand the project more quickly?

12.12.3.5 Write a Simple README

Scenario:

- Student exercise habits
- Relationship between exercise and stress
- 200 responses, Spring 2024

Key findings:

- Students exercising 3+ times/week report lower stress
- Walking is most popular (45%)
- Exercise habits vary by academic year

Write a README that includes:

- Purpose
- Data source
- Key findings
- How to run the analysis
- Contact information

12.12.3.6 Questions

7. What key information did you include in your README to explain the purpose of the analysis?
8. How did you describe the data source in your README?

9. What instructions did you give for running the analysis?
10. Across all three practices, what is one habit you used that will help your future self understand your work later?

Chapter 13

Translating from R to Python

13.1 Learning Outcomes

13-1: Explain the "translation mindset" and how programming concepts transfer between languages, distinguishing conceptual knowledge from syntax.

13-2: Apply the Iceberg Principle to identify which analytical skills and problem-solving strategies transfer directly when learning a second language.

13-3: Translate data analysis workflows from R to Python using a concept-first approach, maintaining logical structure while adapting syntax.

13-4: Compare and contrast R and Python for data manipulation, visualization, and statistical analysis, and select the appropriate language based on task and context.

13-5: Implement practical strategies for efficient language translation, including hands-on practice, leveraging existing knowledge, and using documentation and translation guides.

13.2 Introduction

Jessica had been using R for psychology research for two years when she landed a summer internship at a tech company. On her first day, her supervisor handed her a Python script and said, “We’ll need you to adapt your statistical analysis skills to our Python workflow.” Jessica’s heart sank—she’d finally gotten comfortable with R.

Three weeks later, Jessica realized something remarkable: she wasn’t learning programming from scratch. She was translating concepts she already understood into different syntax. The hard part—understanding data analysis, systematic problem-solving, and logical workflows—she already knew. Python was just a different way of expressing the same ideas.

This chapter reveals what Jessica discovered: learning a second programming language is fundamentally different from learning your first. You’re not starting over; you’re building bridges between what you know and how another language expresses those concepts.

13.3 The Translation Mindset

13.3.1 What You Already Know

When you learned your first programming language, you actually learned two things simultaneously: programming concepts and specific syntax. The concepts are universal—the syntax is just the surface layer.

You understand what it means to calculate an average, filter data based on conditions, or create visualizations. These analytical concepts exist independently of any programming language. R taught you to think `mean(data$column)`, but the underlying concept—“find the central tendency of this set of numbers”—remains the same in any language.

13.3.2 The Iceberg Principle

Programming knowledge resembles an iceberg. The syntax you see represents maybe 20% of what you know. The other 80%—your understanding of data structures, logical thinking, problem decomposition, and analytical workflow—transfers directly to any language.

When Marcus switched from R to Python for his economics thesis, he progressed quickly. "I thought I'd be googling basic syntax for weeks," he said. "But I already knew how to think about the problems. I just needed to learn how Python spelled the solutions."

13.3.3 Concept-First Translation

The key to successful language translation is thinking concept-first, syntax-second. Instead of memorizing Python equivalents for every R function, start with the analytical goal and then find the Python way to achieve it.

Don't think "How do I write `filter()` in Python?" Instead, think "I want to keep only rows that meet certain conditions" and then discover that Python uses Boolean indexing or the `.query()` method.

13.4 What Transfers Directly

13.4.1 Your Analytical Thinking

The most valuable skill you've developed isn't knowing that `summary()` gives descriptive statistics in R. It's knowing when you need descriptive statistics, what they tell you about your data, and how they fit into your analytical workflow. This knowledge transfers completely.

13.4.2 Data Concepts and Workflow Logic

You understand what a data frame is—a rectangular structure with rows as observations and columns as variables. This concept is identical whether you're working with R's `data.frame` or Python's `DataFrame`.

Your understanding of the typical data analysis workflow—import, clean, explore, model, communicate—is completely transferable. You know to examine data structure first, check for missing values, create visualizations to understand distributions, then proceed with sophisticated analyses. This logical progression remains constant across languages.

13.4.3 Problem-Solving Strategies

You've learned to break complex problems into manageable pieces, test code incrementally, and systematically debug when things go wrong. These meta-skills are perhaps the most valuable and apply universally.

13.5 What Looks Different But Means the Same

13.5.1 The Grammar of Data Manipulation

R and Python have different grammatical structures for expressing identical data manipulation concepts. R's tidyverse uses pipe-based grammar that reads like English, while Python's pandas uses method chaining.

Filtering data and calculating group means:

R with dplyr:

```
results <- data %>%
  filter(age > 18) %>%
  group_by(treatment) %>%
  summarize(mean_score = mean(score))
```

Python with pandas:

```
results = (data
    .query('age > 18')
    .groupby('treatment')
    .agg({'score': 'mean'}))
```

The syntax differs, but the logical flow is identical: start with data, keep only adults, group by treatment, calculate mean scores. Once you recognize this pattern, translation becomes intuitive.

13.5.2 Different Paths to the Same Destination

Languages provide multiple ways to accomplish the same task, reflecting different design philosophies rather than superiority.

Creating visualizations:

R's ggplot2 uses grammar of graphics:

```
ggplot(data, aes(x = height, y = weight)) +
  geom_point() +
  geom_smooth(method = "lm")
```

Python offers multiple approaches:

```
# Using seaborn (most similar to ggplot2)
sns.scatterplot(data=data, x='height', y='weight')
sns.regplot(data=data, x='height', y='weight', scatter=False)
```

The end result—a scatter plot with fitted line—is identical. Your understanding of effective visualization principles transfers completely.

13.6 Common Translation Patterns

13.6.1 Setup and Import Phase

Every analysis starts with loading libraries and importing data. The pattern is identical; only commands differ:

R setup:

```
library(tidyverse)
data <- read.csv("filename.csv")
```

Python setup:

```
import pandas as pd
import matplotlib.pyplot as plt
data = pd.read_csv("filename.csv")
```

13.6.2 Data Exploration Phase

Initial exploration follows similar patterns. You want to understand structure, check missing values, and examine distributions:

Task	R Command	Python Command
Data dimensions	`dim(data)`	`data.shape`
Summary statistics	`summary(data)`	`data.describe()`
Data structure	`str(data)`	`data.info()`
First few rows	`head(data)`	`data.head()`

13.6.3 Core Data Operations

Operation	R Syntax	Python Syntax
Select columns	`select(data, col1, col2)`	`data[['col1', 'col2']]`
Filter rows	`filter(data, age > 21)`	`data[data['age'] > 21]`
Create new column	`mutate(data, new = old * 2)`	`data['new'] = data['old'] * 2`
Group and summarize	`group_by(treatment) %>% summarize(mean = mean(score))`	`data.groupby`

13.7 Practical Translation Strategies

13.7.1 Start with What You Know

When approaching a new analysis in Python, begin by outlining your approach using concepts you already understand:

1. What data do I need to load?
2. What cleaning steps are required?
3. What visualizations will help me understand the data?
4. What statistical tests or models do I need?
5. How will I present the results?

Then translate each step into Python syntax, focusing on one operation at a time.

13.7.2 Use Your R Knowledge as a Bridge

When you encounter a new Python concept, relate it back to something you know in R. For example, when learning about Python's `.apply()` method, connect it to R's `apply()` family of functions. Both allow you to apply a function across rows or columns of data.

13.7.3 Leverage Documentation and Resources

Both languages have excellent documentation. When you know what you want to accomplish but not the specific syntax, search for "Python equivalent of R [function name]" or consult translation guides that map R functions to Python methods.

13.8 When to Use Which Language

13.8.1 R's Strengths

R excels in statistical analysis, academic research, and exploratory data analysis. Its extensive statistical packages and publication-ready graphics make it ideal for research environments. If your work involves complex statistical modeling or you're working in academia, R often provides more specialized tools.

13.8.2 Python's Strengths

Python excels in production environments, machine learning, and integration with larger software systems. Its general-purpose nature makes it valuable when data analysis is part of a broader application. If you're working in industry or need to deploy models in production systems, Python often provides better integration options.

13.8.3 The Practical Reality

Many data professionals use both languages, choosing the best tool for each specific task. Your R knowledge makes learning Python much easier, and knowing both languages makes you more versatile and valuable in the job market.

13.9 Conclusion

Key success factors for translating from R to Python begin with focusing on concepts over syntax. Instead of memorizing Python commands, concentrate on understanding how the language expresses analytical ideas you already know. By keeping the focus on the underlying concepts, you ensure that your analytical thinking transfers smoothly between languages and that you don't get bogged down in superficial differences.

Another important factor is consistent practice through translation exercises. Take analyses you have already completed in R and recreate them in Python. This hands-on approach reinforces the mapping between concepts and syntax, helping you internalize the patterns and workflows in the new language.

It is equally important to embrace the differences between the languages. Python is not R, and each language has its own idioms, conventions, and best practices. Trying to make Python behave exactly like R can create confusion and slow learning. Instead, appreciate the unique strengths of each language and use them appropriately.

Finally, build your skills gradually. Begin with simple operations and focus on mastering them before moving on to more complex analyses. As your Python vocabulary grows, you can progressively tackle larger tasks, ensuring that your proficiency develops steadily and sustainably.

13.10 Review Questions

1. What is the "translation mindset" and why is it important when learning a second programming language?
2. Explain the Iceberg Principle in the context of learning a new language. Which skills transfer directly, and which require new syntax learning?
3. How does the concept-first approach differ from a syntax-first approach when translating R code to Python? Give an example.
4. Compare R's dplyr pipe-based data manipulation with Python's pandas method chaining. How do the logical workflows remain the same despite syntax differences?
5. List at least three core data operations (e.g., selecting columns, filtering rows, grouping/summarizing) and their R and Python equivalents.

6. What practical strategies can help you translate analyses from R to Python efficiently?
7. Describe scenarios where R might be preferable to Python, and vice versa, in professional or academic work.
8. Why is consistent practice and hands-on translation important for mastering a second programming language?

Chapter 14

Evaluating Code Quality and Responsibility

14.1 Learning Outcomes

14-1: Explain the importance of code clarity, maintainability, and readability in professional data analysis, distinguishing them from cleverness or purely performance-focused programming.

14-2: Apply best practices for writing trustworthy and maintainable code, including documentation, version control, and collaborative code review.

14-3: Evaluate trade-offs between code clarity and performance, using algorithmic thinking, data structures, and libraries to optimize efficiently without sacrificing readability.

14-4: Recognize ethical responsibilities in data analysis, including algorithmic fairness, transparency, data privacy, and the responsible use of AI-generated code.

14-5: Develop professional judgment and iterative improvement skills, learning from feedback, examples of quality code, and experience to produce reliable, collaborative, and ethically sound analyses.

14.2 Introduction

Two months into her first data analyst position, Rachel received a code review that changed how she thought about programming forever. Her supervisor, Dr. Kim, had left detailed comments on her analysis script: "This code produces the correct results, but I can't understand how it works. Can you revise it so that someone else could maintain it if needed?"

Rachel was confused. The code worked perfectly. It was even quite clever—she'd used some advanced techniques she'd found online to make it run faster. Why did it matter if it was hard to understand?

Six months later, Rachel understood. She was asked to update that same analysis with new data, and she couldn't figure out how her own code worked. The clever optimizations that had seemed so impressive now looked like cryptic puzzles. She spent more time deciphering her old code than it would have taken to write clear, simple code from scratch.

This experience taught Rachel a fundamental truth about professional programming: code quality isn't about demonstrating cleverness or achieving maximum performance. It's about creating trustworthy, maintainable solutions that serve both current needs and future requirements. In the world of data analysis, where decisions based on your code can affect real people and organizations, quality becomes a matter of professional responsibility.

14.3 What Makes Code "Good" for Data Analysis

14.3.1 The Trust Factor

Good code in data analysis serves a different purpose than good code in other domains. When you're building a video game, users care about performance and features. When you're analyzing data that will inform business decisions, policy changes, or scientific conclusions, the primary concern is trustworthiness.

Dr. Martinez, a senior researcher at a public health institute, puts it this way: "When I review code for a study that might influence vaccination policy, I'm not looking for the most elegant algorithm. I'm looking for code that I can verify is doing exactly what it claims to do. Lives might depend on getting this right."

This shift in priorities—from cleverness to clarity, from optimization to verification—defines what makes code good in analytical contexts. Your code needs to be a clear record of your analytical reasoning, not just a tool that produces results.

14.3.2 Maintenance Reality

Most analytical code has a longer lifespan than its authors expect. That quarterly report you're writing might need to be updated monthly. The research analysis you're doing for your thesis might need to be replicated by other researchers. The data pipeline you're building for a class project might become the foundation for a larger system.

Tom learned this lesson when he returned to his undergraduate research project two years later as a graduate student. His advisor wanted to extend the analysis with new data, but Tom's old code was incomprehensible. "I remember thinking I was so smart for writing such compact code," Tom reflected. "But compact and clever aren't the same as good. I had to rewrite everything from scratch."

14.3.3 Clarity as a Professional Skill

Writing clear code is a professional skill that extends far beyond programming. It demonstrates your ability to think systematically, communicate complex ideas effectively, and consider the needs of others who might work with your analysis. These are exactly the skills that employers and collaborators value most.

Clear code also makes you more effective. When you can easily understand and modify your own work, you can iterate faster, catch errors more quickly, and build more sophisticated analyses. Clarity isn't just considerate—it's strategic.

14.4 Clarity Versus Performance

14.4.1 The False Dilemma

Beginning programmers often assume they must choose between code that's easy to understand and code that runs efficiently. This perceived trade-off leads to premature optimization—making code more complex in pursuit of performance gains that may not be necessary or meaningful.

In most data analysis contexts, the performance difference between clear code and optimized code is negligible compared to other factors. Loading data from files, making network requests, or waiting for user input typically takes much longer than any computational optimizations you might implement.

14.4.2 When Performance Actually Matters

There are legitimate cases where performance considerations become important. If you're processing datasets with millions of rows, running simulations with thousands of iterations, or building real-time systems, efficiency matters. But even in these cases, the best approach is usually to start with clear, correct code and then optimize specific bottlenecks if needed.

Dr. Chen, who analyzes genomic datasets with billions of data points, describes her approach: "I always write the clearest version first. Then I profile the code to see where it's slow. Usually, 90% of the runtime comes from 10% of the code. I optimize that 10% and leave the rest readable."

14.4.3 The Readability-Performance Balance

When you do need to optimize performance, document your reasoning clearly. Explain why optimization was necessary, what alternatives you considered, and how the optimized version works. This documentation helps future maintainers (including yourself) understand both the technical implementation and the business justification.

Consider this example of documented optimization:

```
# Original clear version (kept for reference):
# results = [complex_calculation(item) for item in large_dataset]

# Optimized version for performance (processes 10M+ records):
# Using numpy vectorization reduces runtime from 45 minutes to 3 minutes
# Trade-off: less readable but necessary for production timeline
results = np.vectorize(complex_calculation)(np.array(large_dataset))
```

The comment preserves both the clear version and the reasoning behind the optimization, making the code maintainable despite its complexity.

14.5 Efficiency at a Conceptual Level

14.5.1 Algorithmic Thinking

True efficiency in data analysis often comes from choosing the right approach rather than optimizing the implementation details. Understanding when to use different data structures, algorithms, or analytical techniques can provide much larger performance gains than micro-optimizations.

For example, if you need to look up values repeatedly in a large dataset, using a dictionary or hash table instead of searching through a list can reduce your runtime from hours to seconds. This is algorithmic efficiency—choosing the right tool for the job rather than making the wrong tool work faster.

14.5.2 Data Structure Decisions

The way you organize your data can have enormous impacts on both performance and code clarity. Understanding when to use lists versus dictionaries, when to reshape data from wide to long format, or when to use specialized data structures like sets can make your code both faster and more intuitive.

Maria discovered this when analyzing survey responses. Her initial approach stored all responses in a single large list and searched through it repeatedly. After learning about pandas DataFrames and their built-in grouping operations, she rewrote her analysis to be both faster and more readable. “I wasn’t just optimizing the code,” she said. “I was optimizing my thinking about the problem.”

14.5.3 The Power of Libraries

One of the most effective ways to achieve both clarity and performance is to leverage well-designed libraries. Libraries like pandas, NumPy, or the tidyverse have been optimized by experts and tested by millions of users. Using these tools appropriately often provides better performance than custom implementations while keeping your code readable and maintainable.

This doesn’t mean blindly using libraries for everything, but rather understanding when established tools can solve your problems more effectively than custom code. The best programmers are often those who know which problems have already been solved well by others.

14.6 Ethical Considerations in Programming

14.6.1 The Responsibility of Code

Code is not neutral. Every analytical decision you make—how you handle missing data, which variables you include in models, how you define categories or groups—embeds assumptions and values that can affect real people. Recognizing this responsibility is crucial for ethical programming.

Dr. Rodriguez, who analyzes hiring data for a large corporation, explains the weight of these decisions: "When I write code to analyze resume screening, I'm not just processing data. I'm potentially affecting whether thousands of people get job opportunities. Every line of code needs to be defensible from both a technical and ethical standpoint."

14.6.2 Algorithmic Bias and Fairness

Bias can enter analytical code in subtle ways. Historical data often reflects past discrimination, and algorithms trained on this data can perpetuate or amplify these biases. Even seemingly neutral technical decisions—like how you handle missing data or outliers—can have disparate impacts on different groups.

Consider a student loan approval algorithm that uses zip code as a predictor. This might seem like a reasonable proxy for economic stability, but it can also perpetuate residential segregation patterns and discriminate against applicants from historically disadvantaged communities. The code might be technically correct but ethically problematic.

14.6.3 Transparency and Explainability

Ethical code in data analysis should be explainable to stakeholders who will be affected by its results. This means not just documenting what your code does, but explaining why you made specific analytical choices and what limitations or assumptions are built into your approach.

When Sarah built a model to predict student success for her university's admissions office, she included extensive documentation explaining which factors the model considered, which it ignored, and what the predictions meant in practical terms. "The admissions committee needed to understand not just the results, but the reasoning behind them," she said. "They're the ones who have to defend these decisions to students and families."

14.6.4 Data Privacy and Security

Responsible programming includes protecting the privacy and security of the data you work with. This means understanding what data you have access to, how it should be handled, and what your obligations are to the people whose information you're analyzing.

Even in academic contexts, data privacy matters. Research data often contains sensitive information about participants, and your code should reflect appropriate safeguards. This might mean anonymizing data early in your analysis pipeline, avoiding unnecessary data collection, or ensuring that intermediate results don't inadvertently reveal private information.

14.6.5 Environmental and Social Impact

The computational resources required for data analysis have real environmental costs. While individual analyses rarely have significant environmental impact, developing awareness of resource usage and efficiency can contribute to more sustainable computing practices.

More broadly, consider the social implications of your analytical work. Are you solving problems that matter? Are your methods accessible to others who might benefit from them? Are you contributing to knowledge in ways that serve the broader community rather than just narrow interests?

14.7 AI-Generated Code and Attribution

14.7.1 The New Landscape of Code Creation

AI tools like GitHub Copilot, ChatGPT, and other code generation systems have fundamentally changed how many programmers work. These tools can generate sophisticated code snippets, complete functions, and even entire analytical workflows based on natural language descriptions.

This capability raises new questions about code quality, attribution, and responsibility. When AI generates code for you, who is responsible for ensuring it works correctly?

How do you verify that AI-generated code is doing what you think it's doing? What are your obligations to disclose when AI has contributed to your work?

14.7.2 Verification and Understanding

The most critical principle for using AI-generated code is that you remain responsible for understanding and verifying everything that runs under your name. AI tools can produce code that looks sophisticated but contains subtle errors, uses inappropriate methods, or makes incorrect assumptions about your data.

Jake learned this lesson when he used an AI tool to generate code for a statistical analysis. The generated code looked professional and ran without errors, but it was using the wrong statistical test for his data type. "The AI gave me exactly what I asked for," Jake reflected, "but I didn't ask for the right thing. I had to learn enough statistics to know whether the code was appropriate for my problem."

14.7.3 Attribution and Academic Integrity

In academic contexts, using AI-generated code raises questions about attribution and intellectual honesty. Different institutions and instructors have different policies about AI assistance, ranging from complete prohibition to full acceptance with proper disclosure.

The key principle is transparency. If AI tools contribute significantly to your code, document that contribution clearly. This might mean adding comments that indicate which sections were AI-generated, describing your process for verifying AI-generated code, or including a statement about AI assistance in your methodology.

14.7.4 Learning Versus Outsourcing

There's an important distinction between using AI as a learning tool and using it to outsource your thinking. AI can be valuable for understanding syntax, exploring different approaches to problems, or getting unstuck when you're facing technical challenges. But if you're using AI to generate code you don't understand for problems you haven't thought through carefully, you're missing the educational value of programming.

The goal should be to use AI tools to enhance your capabilities rather than replace your analytical thinking. This means engaging critically with AI-generated suggestions, understanding the reasoning behind different approaches, and developing the judgment to know when AI recommendations are appropriate for your specific context.

14.8 Transparency and Collaboration

14.8.1 Code as Communication

In collaborative environments, your code serves as a form of communication with your teammates, supervisors, and future self. This communication function is just as important as the computational function. Code that produces correct results but can't be understood or modified by others creates bottlenecks and risks for any collaborative project.

Dr. Park, who leads a research team analyzing climate data, emphasizes this communication aspect: "When team members write code that only they can understand, it creates single points of failure. If someone leaves the team or gets sick, we can't maintain their analyses. Clear, well-documented code is a form of knowledge sharing that makes the whole team more resilient."

14.8.2 Documentation as Professional Practice

Good documentation goes beyond commenting individual lines of code. It includes explaining the overall purpose of your analysis, describing your data sources and any preprocessing steps, documenting your analytical choices and their justifications, and providing examples of how to use or modify your code.

This documentation serves multiple audiences: colleagues who need to understand your work, supervisors who need to verify your methods, and future researchers who might want to replicate or extend your analysis. Writing good documentation is a professional skill that demonstrates your ability to think about your work from others' perspectives.

14.8.3 Version Control and Collaboration Tools

Version control systems like Git provide a structured way to track changes in your code over time, collaborate with others, and maintain backup copies of your work. While the technical details of version control can seem intimidating initially, the conceptual benefits are straightforward: you can experiment with changes without fear of breaking working code, collaborate with others without conflicts, and maintain a complete history of your analytical decisions.

Even if you're working alone, version control provides valuable benefits. You can try different approaches to a problem and easily revert to previous versions if new approaches don't work. You can maintain separate versions of your analysis for different purposes. And you have a complete backup of your work that's not dependent on any single computer or storage device.

14.8.4 Collaborative Code Review

Code review—having others examine your code before it's used for important decisions—is a standard practice in professional software development that's increasingly common in data analysis contexts. Code review serves multiple purposes: it catches errors that the original author missed, ensures that code meets team standards for clarity and documentation, and provides opportunities for knowledge sharing and learning.

Effective code review focuses on clarity, correctness, and maintainability rather than personal preferences or stylistic choices. The goal is to improve the quality and reliability of analytical work, not to demonstrate superiority or enforce arbitrary standards.

14.9 Building Professional Judgment

14.9.1 The Development of Taste

Professional judgment in programming develops gradually through experience, feedback, and reflection. Like developing taste in any domain, it requires exposure to both good and bad examples, understanding of the criteria that distinguish quality work, and practice applying those criteria to your own work.

This judgment includes knowing when to prioritize different aspects of code quality. In a research context, reproducibility and transparency might be most important. In a business context, maintainability and performance might take precedence. In an educational context, clarity and learning value might be the primary concerns.

14.9.2 Learning from Others

One of the best ways to develop professional judgment is to read and analyze code written by experienced practitioners. Open-source projects, published research code, and examples from respected sources provide models of how experienced programmers approach different types of problems.

Pay attention not just to what the code does, but how it's organized, documented, and structured. Notice how experienced programmers handle error cases, organize complex logic, and communicate their reasoning through code and comments.

14.9.3 The Iterative Nature of Quality

Code quality is not a binary characteristic—code is not simply good or bad. Instead, quality exists on a spectrum and can be improved iteratively. The goal is not to write perfect code immediately, but to develop the ability to recognize areas for improvement and the skills to make those improvements systematically.

This iterative approach applies to both individual projects and your development as a programmer. Each project provides opportunities to practice quality principles, learn from mistakes, and refine your approach. Over time, writing clear, responsible code becomes a natural part of your programming process rather than an additional burden.

14.10 The Professional Context

14.10.1 From Student to Professional

The transition from academic programming to professional programming involves a shift in priorities and responsibilities. Academic code often prioritizes getting results for a specific assignment or research question. Professional code must consider long-term maintenance, collaboration with others, and integration with larger systems.

This doesn't mean that academic code should ignore quality principles, but rather that the specific quality criteria might differ. Academic code should prioritize reproducibility and transparency to support scientific integrity. Professional code should prioritize maintainability and reliability to support business operations.

14.10.2 Industry Standards and Expectations

Different industries and organizations have different standards for code quality, but certain principles are universal. Code should be readable by others, documented appropriately for its context, and tested sufficiently to ensure reliability. Understanding these expectations and developing the skills to meet them is crucial for career success.

Many organizations have specific coding standards, review processes, and quality assurance procedures. Learning to work within these frameworks while maintaining your own professional standards is an important skill for any data analyst or programmer.

14.10.3 Continuous Learning and Adaptation

The field of data analysis evolves rapidly, with new tools, techniques, and best practices emerging regularly. Maintaining professional competence requires ongoing learning and adaptation. This includes staying current with technical developments but also evolving your understanding of ethical responsibilities and professional standards.

The principles of code quality—clarity, reliability, maintainability, and ethical responsibility—remain constant even as specific tools and techniques change. Focusing on these fundamental principles provides a stable foundation for navigating technological change throughout your career.

14.11 Conclusion

Code quality is about respect—for your future self, your colleagues, those affected by your work, and the professional community you join. This respect shows through clear, well-documented code, thorough testing, ethical decision-making, and transparency.

Tools alone aren't enough; professional success requires judgment, discipline, and ethical awareness. Code quality isn't about cleverness or perfection—it's about creating trustworthy, maintainable solutions that serve current and future needs.

The journey from code that works to code that works well is ongoing. Each project is an opportunity to practice, learn, and refine your approach. Trust is earned through consistent competence, integrity, and consideration for others, qualities essential in data analysis with real-world impact.

14.12 Review Questions

1. Why is code clarity often more important than cleverness or performance in professional data analysis?
2. Explain how the maintenance reality of analytical code impacts the way you should write and document your scripts.
3. What is the false dilemma between clarity and performance, and when does performance optimization truly matter?
4. How can algorithmic thinking and appropriate data structure choices improve both code efficiency and readability?
5. Discuss the ethical responsibilities of data analysts when writing code. Include examples of algorithmic bias, transparency, and data privacy.
6. What principles should guide the use of AI-generated code in data analysis? How should analysts verify and document such code?
7. How does code serve as a form of communication in collaborative projects? Why is this important?
8. Describe the role of version control and code review in maintaining code quality.
9. What strategies can help develop professional judgment in programming, and why is iterative improvement important?
10. How do the priorities of academic programming differ from professional programming in terms of code quality?